Glouc

GLOUCESTERSHIRE COUNTY LIBRARY

Headquarters: SHIRE HALL, GLOUCESTER GL1 2HY

Tel. Gloucester 21444

This book should be re
stamped below, but ma
anoth   der, by giving
star

D0591311

CL.16   PD/L—3

1 154133 001 29

C 10

THE
ATHENIAN EMPIRE
AND
THE BRITISH

THOMAS CALLANDER

formerly Professor of Greek,
Queen's University, Kingston

WEIDENFELD AND NICOLSON
20 NEW BOND STREET LONDON W I

© 1961 by Thomas Callander

GLOUCESTERSHIRE
CLASS 942
COPY 001
COUNTY LIBRARY

G20029698
49382
942

R

PRINTED IN GREAT BRITAIN BY
THE LEAGRAVE PRESS LTD., LUTON AND LONDON

17/6963

THE ATHENIAN EMPIRE AND THE BRITISH

CONTENTS

		Page
	PROLOGUE	1
1	'This Blessed and Splendid Dominion'	23
2	Imperial Christianity	33
3	Sir Edward Grey and his Critics	50
	1 The Liberals, 1914	50
	2 The Historian and the Four Principles of Policy	61
4	The Fundamental Issue	79
5	'The Second Cardinal Tragedy'	95
6	Moribund Empire	111
7	Sophists and Warmongers	131
8	The Moral Issue: From Sarajevo to Suez	154

At the stroke of the midnight hour, when the world sleeps, India will wake to life and freedom. We end today a period of ill fortune and India discovers herself again.

Nehru in the Constituent Assembly, New Delhi, at 11 p.m. on August 14, 1947.

Prologue

THE ATHENIAN EMPIRE AND THE BRITISH

THE DEFECTIVE MORAL code of the ministers of our age has produced the wreckage deplored by all except the war-profiteers. Forty years ago, before the destroyers developed their plan for world domination through overwhelming killing-power to the point of grasping at absolute space power, England's noted thinker, Bernard Bosanquet, amongst others, had exposed the radical vice of such a plan by stating his own international ideal.[1] Like most critics of the war-breeding mentality then prevailing in ruling circles, he countered the drift to catastrophe by exposing the materialistic basis of current power politics. But instead of proclaiming, with pacificists generally, the over-riding claims of New Testament ethics, he reasserted the principles of a sound foreign policy as they were laid down by the greatest of the pre-Christian philosophers.

Starting with the postulate that all wars are fought for gain and that the rampant vice of his day was the sophistic doctrine—justice is the interest of the stronger—Plato, as Bosanquet pointed out, riddled that thesis by his dialectic, and laid down for all time the first principles of genuine political philosophy. Faced with the catastrophe which ruined his world—the Hellenic world—towards the end of the fifth century B.C., and realising that, as in every war, the primary responsibility rested on the rulers whom he had watched, after the death of Pericles, abusing their power to serve false purposes, Plato for the first time saw a way out of the impasse. His remedy for the appalling disaster which had overtaken Athens and Greece was—education. With the boast of Pericles in his mind —Athens the school of Greece—he could imagine no other cure for the evils of the first adequately recorded World War than a thorough overhaul of current political morality.

Nearly four and twenty centuries have passed since he penned his *Republic*, a work, wrote Emerson, fit for the education of the race. All that we are concerned with here is the treatment of the same ethical principles that must govern statesmen in the era of

[1] See page 173.

1

international conflict in which we live. Presuming that statesmen are called upon, before everything else, to promote the well-being of their peoples and, since *the good is that which all things strive after*, the whole duty of the ruler must be to ensure the good of the citizens. Such is the function of the ruler, and such is the compelling reason why he must understand the true nature of the good for man.

If this be conceded, it follows that, in practice, the task of the statesman is to determine amongst a multitude of competing or conflicting ends, purposes or objectives, which, if realised, will satisfy his fellow citizens. And it is at precisely this point that Plato offered the guidance which, because it has been ignored or rejected or reversed by the ministers of our age, to our infinite, abysmal loss, proved its immeasurable worth. In the choice of ends to be achieved by policy, Plato plumped for those that satisfy the higher appetites and desires as against the lower. If not the whole of the *Republic* then at least Book Nine should be pondered and digested by any politician who aspires to make the world he lives in, especially that of inter-state relations, better instead of worse. And this is the conviction that made Plato the most original and most constructive of the idealists; the thinker who, after four and twenty centuries of confusion and carnage centred in Europe, was used by Bosanquet and the School of Green to sharpen their protest against the materialism which sixty years ago was gathering its forces to encompass European destruction.

The perennial conflict between idealism and its numerous perversions—realism, materialism, hedonism, utilitarianism, atheism, immoralism and other heresies—will be discussed below in connection with the Greek sophists and their modern counterparts; but something must be done before we resign ourselves to the bald assertion that modern statesmanship has crashed, through its defiance of the simple truth expounded in the *Republic*—that the supreme aim of the statesman should be not the promotion of wealth in the community but of virtue.

In a hundred ways this dogma governs the teaching of Plato and his school. What can be more arresting than the famous declaration of Socrates as he rebuked his enemies for seeking wealth, reputation and honour, to the neglect of wisdom and truth and the perfecting of their souls; *for virtue does not come from money but from money comes virtue and all other good things to men, both as individuals and as a community*. No maxim could be more hackneyed, none has

2

been more insistently preached by Churchmen, moralists, social reformers; and yet in practice the message, which is in essence that of the Gospel, has been transmuted into a casuistry used to justify what it condemns. Plato, seizing upon the cardinal virtue of justice, exhibited its creative power in the sketch of his ideal state. The hive of industry resting on mutual service, each attending to his own affairs, functions happily when the ruling class, the guardians, are inspired by a disciplined study of social and political science to cultivate those interests which are bound up, not with the senses and appetites, but with the life of reflection and speculation whose rewards are wisdom and goodness.

What Plato witnessed four centuries before Christ was the antithesis of his ideal. It was the most brilliant world homo sapiens had ever known; but it was a world in eclipse. Thucydides wrote an account of the catastrophe, to serve as a warning for all time, and Plato drew the moral. The men of his day, like the politicians of Western Europe, rang in the false, rang out the true. In obedience to the sophistry to which Thrasymachus ministered—justice is the interest of the stronger—even Pericles converted the Alliance which had repelled the Persian into an Empire, exacting tribute without consent, instituting for Athens, 'the eye of Greece', the equivalent of bread and circuses at Rome, to serve the bodily needs of his countrymen. In the simplest possible terms, Plato diagnosed the immoral character of the whole conception. Pericles, for all the talk about his idealism, was a realist—a humane ruler by nature if ever there was, but a realist, and *au fond* a rigid materialist.

Instead of alleging that the statesmen of Greece, beguiled by false gods, had, so to speak, fallen down before Moloch and Mammon, as modern spiritual leaders asserted when their crisis arrived, the Athenian philosopher traced the downfall of Hellas to internal corruption which could be remedied by nothing short of a thoroughgoing intellectual and moral reform carried out in a community organised for the achievement of *virtue*. Virtue or moral exercise again implied, in actual experience, the pursuit of a comprehensive end, including all manner of good things, by groups or classes trained to perform special services, on the familiar principle of division of labour. This combined effort to realise specific ends further implies competing purposes, a hierarchy of ends and needs to be realised, each with its own values; in the fixing of which lies much of the task of the enlightened statesman or philosopher.

3

The community contemplated, not being simply 'a city of pigs', but composite, must provide satisfaction not merely for bodily wants but also for mental and spiritual needs; and it is in the healthy gratifications of both demands that the good life exists. If the desired balance is not realised, disaster is inevitable and it was because the rulers of Greek city states had destroyed this balance that the glory of Greece had gone for ever. For Plato that meant the triumph of the wicked in a world condemned to an everlasting conflict of right with wrong; only in the divine nature is goodness to be found pure and undefiled. 'It is impossible', says Socrates, in the *Theaetetus*, 'that evil should be extirpated, for of necessity something must always exist to oppose the good; nor can evil have a footing among the gods, but by necessity it haunts mortal nature and this world. For which reason we must strive to flee from this to the other world with all speed. And to flee is to become like God as far as is possible; and to be made like to God is to become righteous and holy not without wisdom!' Momentous words in that or any age!

In this and other similar pronouncements we have one leading strand of Plato's thinking—the tempered, not ascetic zeal, which drew its force from his passion for science and goodness. This led him to exalt the noble over the ignoble, the true over the false, wisdom over ignorance, the higher over the lower, in the clash of impulses which sway human conduct both individual and collective. His vigorous campaign against sensuality went so far at times as to suggest that the body is the root of all evil, in the sense that if carnal evil were abolished there would be no hunger or thirst or the like. Generally, however, his aim is rather that of the Victorians who urged a life of plain living and high thinking as a means of social uplift and a powerful reinforcement of the civilising agencies making for peace inside each nation and beyond. Recognising that the all-embracing goodness, like its parent the Godhead, could not be defined, there being no entity to which it could be subsumed and no differentia, but that the concept was regulative and ultimate, assuming now the aspect of justice, now of the true, now of the beautiful, he built up his lofty philosophy of idealism and imposed it as a perennial source of inspiration for kindred spirits everywhere. A glance at a few paragraphs in the Ninth Book of the *Republic* will show the bearings of his teachings on the grand issue of the twentieth century as well as on that of Classical Greece, whose desperate wickedness he strove to remedy.

Faced with the boundless licence and expansion of a corrupt imperialist democracy, he found the explanation in the degeneracy of the statesmen who had sought power and wealth and inferior pleasures for the citizens instead of a sober disciplined life which makes men better and therefore happy. Bosanquet has already been quoted as employing this doctrine of the high, *and therefore* the more real, satisfactions which attend the service of the soul rather than those that flow from bodily pleasures.

> If, then, to be filled with what befits nature is pleasure, then that which is more really filled with real things would cause us more really and truly to enjoy a true pleasure, while that which partakes of the less truly existent would be less truly and surely filled and would partake of a less trustworthy and less true pleasure.

Then follows the argument:

> Those, therefore, who have no experience of virtue and wisdom but are ever devoted to feasting and that sort of thing are swept downward, it seems, and back again to the centre, and so sway and roam to and fro throughout their lives, but they have never transcended all this and turned their eyes to the true upper region nor been wafted there, nor ever been really filled with real things, nor ever tasted stable and pure pleasure, but with eyes ever bent upon the earth and heads bowed down over their tables they feast like cattle, grazing and copulating, ever greedy for more of these delights: and, in their greed kicking and butting one another with horns and hooves of iron they slay one another in sateless avidity, because they are vainly striving to satisfy with things that are not real the unreal and incontinent part of their souls.

In this paragraph the keyword *greed* is used to express the Greek *pleonexia*, the vice from which every war originates, as Plato contended. Such was the principle—greed of wealth, riches, power; the cause of all wars—and here is its application. The delights commanded by wealth are specified very briefly and are not only condemned in themselves as insubstantial, as are all the bodily pleasures, but being insatiable, owing to their sieve-like emptiness, chronic kenosis, excite unlimited greed and violence. The principle is clear. The Hellenic republics at the peak of their prosperity and power committed suicide for the same reason that modern Europe plunged from the golden age to chaos—the ruling class was corrupt. In both cases power and prosperity bred hybris.

The parallel has endless facets. Firstly there was boundless greed; secondly, insatiable blood-lust; thirdly, shameless ignorance and falsehood, and fourthly measureless sensuality.

Chief among the analogous features of the two catastrophes are the following. The Thirty Years' War celebrated by Thucydides, just as the Forty Years' War of the twentieth century, had as its mainspring *greed*, *pleonexia*, although the stakes were relatively trifling. 'The truest explanation,' wrote the Father of Scientific History, 'although least discussed, I believe was the growing greatness of the Athenians and the fear thereby inspired in the Lacedaemonians; this forced them to go to war.' Thus cautiously is the Spartan side of the quarrel set forth. It was the aggressiveness of Athens that drove the Spartan Confederacy to accept the challenge of the Periclean Empire. So judged Thucydides, and not without reason. The poison of 'greatness' had afflicted his city after the miracles of Marathon and Salamis, when Aristides, Themistocles, Militades, and Pericles converted the Hellenic Alliance into an Athenian Empire, based on the *phoros*, tribute employed to create an invincible navy, which dominated the Aegean until 'the greater part of Hellas was already (by 445 B.C.) subject to them'.

The grievances in 432 B.C. when Sparta, incited by Corinth and Aegina, presented Pericles with her demands, were (1) the attacks on Corinthian interests in Northern Greece (Potidaea), (2) the enslavement of the Aeginetans, (3) the decree by which Megara was excluded from the markets of the Athenian Empire, and (4) the violation of the independence of the Hellenes. The rescinding of the Megarian decree—the thing they especially insisted upon, saying, 'there will be no war if it is rescinded'—was no small matter, for, as Pericles argued: 'It means enslavement just the same, when either the greatest or the least claim is imposed by equals upon their neighbours not by an appeal to justice but by dictation.' It is hard to believe that the speaker, the arch-imperialist, was blind to the absurdity of his position. Did he not realise that the *enslavement* which he repudiated on behalf of Athens was the identical enslavement, only far milder in degree, which he riveted round the necks of a mass of Hellenes, his equals? How could he dwell, as he did, with more than unction, on the part played by Athens in the brilliant battles for Hellenic freedom while clamping the fetters on a mass of Hellenes, without conscious hypocrisy? Had scores of Greek cities fought under the leadership of Athens

6

and Sparta in order to install an Athenian overlord instead of a Persian? The resemblance to a modern jingo premier is indeed ludicrous. The Funeral Oration is little else in fact than a splendid eulogy of Athens the liberator, designed to drown the lingering suspicions of the thoughtful citizens who remembered how the Confederacy of Delos had been liquidated and its voluntary association converted to a dependency—the status of slavery which earned Athens the title of *the tyrant city*. As to this—the real offence for which Athens was destined within thirty years to be punished—Pericles was silent. 'The military operations by which our various acquisitions were made,' said he, 'I will not recall, for I have no desire to speak at length among those who know.' But such an evasion is no answer to the perennial query—in what way do successful military operations *justify* any acquisitions whatever?

Nothing could be more magnificent than the Panegyric recorded by Thucydides—all of it in a vain effort to cover up the fatal blunder committed twenty years earlier, when the treasury of the Delian Confederacy was transferred to Athens. That transfer sealed the fate of the voluntary union of the Ionian Greeks and heralded the full-blown sea power which took under its wing 260 cities, all of them entitled to the same freedom that Pericles claimed for Athens. Such was the Greek idea of liberty—unfettered independence both in external relations and in domestic affairs. Nowhere was this passion stronger than in Athens herself and although the lure of empire overcame all scruples of political morality even in the mind of Pericles, there were vigorous opponents of jingoism in the imperial city itself. Those who, like the doughty warrior Cimon, protested against the diversion of the confederate funds to Athenian purposes—any purpose other than defence against Persia—were swept aside by the big navy enthusiasts, trading on the *pleonexia* that bewitches the common man in every age, the ungovernable greed that led the demagogues down the slippery slope to Syracuse and Aegospotami.

The attitude of Pericles to the two supreme problems, firstly how to teach his countrymen to value the Athenian way of life so that they would gladly die rather than submit to the slightest coercion from their neighbours; and secondly how to restrain their ardour and ambition when tempted to forget the unwieldy burden and the supreme need for moderation and peace, was precisely that of Rosebery, the orator of empire.[2] He too eulogised the British Empire, exalting the 'blessed dominion', the gift of 'the Almighty', a glorious structure 'cemented with men's honest blood and with a world of tears'; and he, too, avoided 'like a rock' the real issue. Neither British Premier nor Athenian Generalissimo (First Citizen) could begin to explain why it was just for Britain or for Athens to coerce peaceful neighbours and shed *their* blood for resisting. Mass killing is (or was) inseparable from retaliation and is rarely if ever wholly one-sided: the defeated, the weaker, suffer most; but it is the honest blood of the stronger, the victors, that evokes the pity of a Pericles or a Rosebery—and a world of tears. Yet infinitely more lamentable is the slaughter of the weaker side, especially when they are in the right by the law of nature.

Such is the inexorable trap set for the imperialist who outrages, it may be Greek political morality or European civilised convictions, by robbing any community of its most treasured possession—the right to govern itself. Neither Pericles nor Rosebery dared to argue the genuine pretension on which they based their right to enslave their fellowmen. The thin pretence in either case that empire is redeemed by sacrificial devotion to national *greatness* is the paltry stock-in-trade of every successful aggressor; but it can impress no-one who bears in mind the agony of the vanquished, the hatred, the suffering, intensified in the enslaved subject by a burning sense of injustice, and the corroding thirst for revenge. Added to all this, we have the inevitable resort to deliberate falsification, in a hopeless effort to hide up the motive power in every attack—desire for material gain.

The conventional defence of successful *pleonexia*—that acts of aggression must be judged by the standard of the age—is thoroughly unsound in the case of imperialist acquisitions. The standard accepted by hundreds of Greek cities, if not all, was stated by Pericles—limiting himself to Athens—as the right to resist coercion: no true Hellene adopted a code which winked at invasions of other people's independence like the aggressions—Megara, Potidaea, Aegina, enslavement of two hundred and sixty Greek cities—charged against Athens in those pages. Even Pericles could never plead that the subject cities were consenting members of the empire. His motto was *keep them well in hand*. His plantations of impoverished citizens in remote areas were comparable with those in Ireland, bitterly resented. Power politics is no modern invention. It is part and parcel of imperialism as such.

In Europe there is no such thing as a general acceptance or condoning of national *pleonexia*, conquest, annexation or dominance. Only a small group of Big Powers, with their satellites, aspired to exclusive places in the sun and drew up codes of quasi-law for the regularising of their gains. Acquiescence in the conventions as to planting the flag, frontiers, the rights conferred by priority of conquest or occupation, monopolies, and trade restrictions, was assumed by the privileged nations without the sanction of world opinion, ancient or modern. The aggressions of Athens were not merely an outrage against Hellenic political morality; they were assailed by patriotic Athenians on the same grounds as those advanced in like cases by patriotic British pacifists.

There were always idealists who deplored the injustice of conquest and domination; but the lust for power and wealth continued to defeat their best efforts, even when all civilised men became convinced by the scientists and philosophers that enslavement of peoples was indefensible. In the controversy the realists had the enormous advantage that the lure of fabulous gains stimulated greed and envy as never before. The beggarly profits that, in the antique world, dazzled the war party and conducted their dupes to the quarries of Syracuse, were but a drop in the bucket compared with the gold of the Rand, priorities in world markets, privileges, concessions, oil wells and countless raw materials whose monopoly fomented jealousy and worse in the past hundred years.

So far as the tenacity and heroism displayed by the dupes of this insatiable *pleonexia* is concerned, the Athenian seamen and their antagonists the Spartan spearmen endured, in proportion to their numbers and resources, more gruelling punishment than their modern imitators. Pericles would have been less than human if he had not gloried in his countrymen's magnificent achievements by land and sea; but it is strange that he quite failed to see that their non-military achievements, to which he devoted the bulk of his panegyric, rested on peaceful pursuits and far outshone the victories of Marathon and Salamis. Had there been more of the generous spirit exhibited by Cimon, prompting him to respect as the yoke-fellow of Athens the Spartans who, like the Prussians at Waterloo, had struck the decisive blow for liberty, Pericles must have extended his constricted view.

It is astounding to find him contending that any external interference with Athenian affairs was enslavement—Athenians never, never shall be slaves!—while he sponsored the implacable harrying of Megara and other aggressions, every aggression being a violation of the principle for which he urged his fellow-citizens to lay down their lives.

Twenty-four centuries have passed since he spoke, and countless statesmen have recited the identical appeal then uttered—many of them familiar with the rhetoric and its nemesis. Yet no European head of state has faced the question posed by the opponents of Pericles, who denounced his embellishment of the Acropolis with funds diverted from the treasury of the Delian Confederacy as 'the finery of a courtesan', to make of freedom-loving Athens a tyrant city. The two statesmen in England who came nearest the attitude adopted by the peace party at Athens were Palmerston and Gladstone. The rest up to Churchill adhered to the tradition 'wider yet and wider'.

Whatever may be said of the appalling evils engendered in Sparta by the rigorous garrison life led by its citizens, in its external relations with other members of the Peloponnesian Confederacy and with the rest of the Greek world, the conduct of her rulers was less aggressive than that of Athens in the great crisis. The role of Archidamus was morally on a higher plane than that of Pericles. Indeed it is strange that so many historians have accepted Pericles as an idealist. He was actually a stern master, ruthless in his repression of revolt or secession among the subjects of Athens. Subjection to him meant genuine enslavement, not, in this case, even justified by the theory that some men were slaves by nature. Aristotle could excuse chattel slavery by such an argument, just as for two thousand years Christians practised slave-holding on a large scale with the sanction of the Churchmen; but the argument did not hold good in the statesmanship of Pericles. Yet, during this first 'World War' it was found plausible to argue that the militarism of Sparta, which had perforce to be trigger-ready to keep a ring of enemies at bay, was, in regard to the rest of the Greek world, less defensible than the navalism of Athens, because Sparta was harsh and reactionary, whereas Athenian navalism was progressive and democratic.

Nevertheless, it is a hard fact that the efficient cause of the responsibility for the calamitous war between the Peloponnesians and the Athenians was the literal enslavement of two hundred and sixty Greek cities, each of them by rights as free as any other. So flagrant indeed was the aggression of Pericles that it is hard to comprehend his failure to enter some plea of self-defence. All he tried to do was to warn his audience that the Peloponnesian offer was delusive; if they revoked the Megarian decrees the act of appeasement, as it would be called today, would merely whet the enemy's appetite for more.

Instead of coming to terms with Sparta by redressing a wrong done to a small member of her Confederacy, he stood pat, exposing himself to the charge of violating the Thirty Years' Truce halfway through its course, and exasperating the fear and jealousy of all Dorian states. The modern parrot-cry of 'appeasement' expresses generally the identical imperial frame of mind, does it not? Although the exact extent of Pericles' culpability is hard for a modern to estimate, it is clear that his conscience was untroubled, for he could boast that no Athenian widow had put on mourning on account of him, and, in the matter of sincerity, jingoes through the ages find it easy to blur or contradict their principles.

In fact all empires are identical in substance. They are all embodiments of a principle and no matter how they are disguised, the particular empire, through its differences, reveals itself as a special form of a universal concept based on the plenary authority enjoyed by the Roman holders of the *maius imperium* symbolised by the *fasces*, the bundle of rods for scourging and the axe for beheading alleged criminals, *mali homines*, so notorious in recent years. All imperial authority reposes on this power of life and death and, no matter how it is draped or masked by forms and ceremonies, implies killing power on the one hand and on the other subjection. When called upon to exercise this plenary authority over whole communities (*regere imperio populos*) the ruler may incline to spare the subjects (*parcere subjectis*), but the resolve to crush opposition means likewise the will to smash recalcitrants (*debellare superbos*). Circumstances alter, but the principle remains, and it is as clear in the Athenian spokesmen such as Pericles and the envoys quoted by Thucydides, as in the ultimatum of a European diplomat. In the last resort all state authority rests on this basis of unlimited force; and so long as it is exercised by fellow-citizens on one another it is generally regarded as legitimate. Only in inter-state relations does such *imperium* provoke dispute and for obvious reasons. Firstly, the imperial power is an alien authority and, secondly, there is no implied and effective *consent* on the part of the subject as in the case of a citizen who voluntarily submits to the laws of the state, and, as Socrates was at pains to remind his friends, owes most of his well-being to those laws and is really their child.

As we have seen, Socrates was fully alive to the meaning of empire. The transfer of power in which he played a leading part raised a storm at home as well as abroad which was stilled but not quelled by the ostracism of Cimon. No one in the Periclean circle could be deaf to the voices raised in protest. That one Hellenic *polis* should lord it over others was an affront to the race, whose unity amid diversity was never in question. For in popular thinking the world was divided into Hellenes and Barbarians; and the Persian menace hardened the instinctive opposition. Even Plato, who realised that the separation was irrational (*Politicus*), adopted the familiar dichotomy division. His outlook was normally Hellenic, as he himself made clear throughout. If we desire to learn what the instinctive reaction to Athenian presumption must have been even at Athens, we can do no better than examine the sentiment portrayed in the relevant passages of the *Republic*. It comes out markedly in his attitude to the conduct of war for example. He refused to dignify armed conflicts between Greeks with the name of war.

Starting from the position that the Hellenic race is friendly to itself and akin, but alien and foreign to the barbarians, he argued that when Greeks fought with barbarians, being enemies by nature they would be said to be at war and this hostility must be called warfare. Greeks, however, still were friends of Greeks, and when they behaved as enemies Greece is diseased and divided by faction and *faction* is the name to be used for that hostility. Further, they should be all Phil-hellenes, regarding Greece as their own, with their holy places held in common, and not only would they refuse to speak of factions as war but they would always conduct their quarrels with an eye to reconciliation. They would not chastise Greeks with the intention of enslaving or destroying them, but behave as correctors, not enemies, all the more since only a few from time to time are their enemies, those, namely who have caused the quarrel. Especially realistic was his rejection of the modern abomination of unlimited warfare. 'They will not,' he contended, 'being Greeks, ravage Greek territory nor burn habitations, and they will not admit that in any city all the population are their enemies, men, women and children. And on all these considerations will not be willing to lay waste the soil, since the majority are their friends, nor to destroy their houses, but will carry the conflict only to the point of compelling the guilty to do justice by the pressure of the suffering innocent.'

The idealism of Plato was no eccentricity, but rather the platform of a strong minority of his countrymen. Politically, the Panhellenic ties had proved their worth. Miraculously the scattered city states had shown that union is strength and that in a crisis the bond of racial friendship, fraternity, is a priceless possession. Philhellenism had its literature and its Bible, Homer.

This was the basis on which rested the social and artistic superstructure created by Greek genius: 'Greece and her foundations are Built beneath the tide of war, Built on the crystalline sea of thought and its eternity.' In spite of geography, the scattered communities were held together by a bond of close affinity, linguistic and spiritual, which strengthened the tie of common dangers gloriously surmounted; they were *kindred spirits* animated with mutual goodwill towards all members of the family and on this Plato relied when he proposed to abolish war in the Greek area. Being a practical statesman—contrary to vulgar notions of his thinking—he stopped at that point in his pacificism. Greeks, he alleged, while abolishing war against Greeks, should treat barbarians as Greeks then treated Greeks, implying a reform of a drastic kind, as became his whole cast of mind. But the revolutionary part of his programme was the ban on war inside the Greek sphere, and, of course, on that issue he was fundamentally antagonistic to Periclean imperialism. The clash is so resounding, in fact, that it is difficult to realise that only a generation separated the two men. On the other hand, the younger generation had the benefit of experience denied to the older. Hindsight as well as insight.

Nevertheless the enigma remains—how did a statesman of integrity, as Pericles was in an eminent degree, stultify himself by claiming full-blown independence for Athens while denying the same to scores of cities inhabited by his own kith and kin? Why was he less enlightened on this tremendous problem than his colleague whom he helped to ostracise?

It is easy to identify the flaw in the mind of Pericles. He had succumbed to the temptation, presented by the triumph over the barbarian—the opportunity to convert the hegemony naturally accorded to the largest and most energetic members of the Delian Confederacy into an *arche* or empire based on despotic authority. The sparring which opened this first 'World War' reveals the depth of resentment caused by this innovation: the refrain of *tyranny* dominates all the charges brought by Sparta's allies against Athens, and *Sparta* is saluted as Liberator. The élite of Athens, moreover, echoed the current prevailing aspersion and rejected the navalism which empire called for and bred. No statesman of the calibre of Pericles could be blind to the violent breach in the Athenian tradition and its meaning. Just as in the long procession of British monarchs and ministers who since the Tudors have sanctioned imperialistic aggressions against foreigners, each has been forced into a false position damaging to his intellectual and moral integrity, so was the impeccable First Minister of Athens forced to compromise with his fondest and firmest conviction, namely that to submit to external pressure unwarranted by justice was intolerable. No diminution of an Athenian's liberty by a neighbouring state if judged by him to be unfair could, he contended, be suffered without a struggle. Which implied that, as Athens was the naval power *par excellence* in his lifetime, her war galleys always liable to be sighted at any harbour entrance, he was virtually the licensed dictator in any conflict between his city and another, responsible only to his own law courts and Assembly. To justify this resort to the maxim of all power politics, this espousing of the doctrine *justice is the interest of the stronger*, he had, therefore, to take refuge in the hoary delusion of the superiority complex. He had willy-nilly to persuade himself and his followers that Demos possessed qualities of surpassing merit which redeemed the worst aggressions conceivable to every Hellene, to wit, an unending series of oppressions which instinctively all Hellenes, including himself, regarded as *enslavement*.

In the splendid eulogy pronounced over the first victims of his war, we have the model exposition of the imperial thesis. No attempt is made to argue the right of Athens to enslave sister city states. Nowhere does he assert that because a Hellenic city is more admirable on account of its wealth, power, energy, patriotism and culture than the rest, it is *thereby entitled* to compel other cities to obey its commands. He goes so far in that direction as to declare that Athens alone 'neither affords to the enemy cause for anger at

14

the sort of people by whom he has been beaten, nor to a subject grounds for complaining that his masters are unworthy.' The 'lofty' idealism of Pericles actually rises no higher than the sophistic conception of justice as *evil to foes and good to friends* and an enemy in the last analysis includes a Hellene who refuses to part with his freedom when the tyrant city deems it just to exact from him tribute needed to support the noble edifice reared on the defeat of the Great King and its aftermath—the ruins of the Panhellenic Alliance.

There is no need to lay stress on the exaggerations of his picture of Athenian supremacy in the arts and crafts, in literature, in social and political activities—his chief fault is his underrating of Spartan military prowess. He must have known that Spartan hoplites under Leonidas at Thermopylae and under Pausanias at Plataea surpassed in sheer disciplined valour the exploits of Marathon and Salamis and, yet, he ignores the former in his determination to paint a glowing picture of Athens as the saviour of Hellas. At all costs he had to confirm in the minds of his fellow-countrymen the conviction that Athens was both the saviour and the schoolmistress of Hellas, because she excelled all other cities in graces and gifts of mind and body and in the greatness conferred on her by the wealth and power gained by her exertions.

It is the hard fate of all champions of empire to recoil from the real challenge implicit in the charge of tyranny—the demand that the alleged superiority—no matter how admirable in itself—be shown to warrant interference with a neighbour's freedom. The presumption is, in every case of aggression—and every denial of autonomy by a stranger is an aggression—that no amount of superiority, physical, mental or moral, entitles the stronger community to coerce the weaker and no recital of natural or acquired advantages or excellences by the aggressor improves his case.

Unlike his modern imitators, Pericles wasted no time in seeking to prove that his authority to impose *his* law and *his* order on less favoured cities against their will was justified by the educative value of his rule; nor did he attempt to argue that the subject gains, through submission to alien control, a degree of happiness that will really compensate him for his loss of manhood. Pericles the imperialist set out by declaring that no Athenian should yield in any conflict with Megarians, Corinthians, Aeginetans, or any other Greeks, to *force majeure* 'for it means enslavement just the same

15

when either the greatest or the least claim is imposed by equals
upon their neighbours, not by an appeal to justice but by dictation'.
This was his answer to the ultimatum presented by Sparta: 'The
Lacedaemonians desire peace and there will be peace if you give
the Hellenes their independence.'

What the average citizen, and not Pericles alone, felt was pithily
expressed by Athenian envoys at Sparta during the pre-war crisis:

> There is nothing remarkable or inconsistent with human nature in
> what we also have done, just because we accepted an empire when
> it was offered us, and then yielding to the strongest motives—
> honour, fear and self-interest—declined to give it up. Nor, again,
> are we the first who have entered upon such a course, but it has
> ever been an established rule that the weaker is kept down by the
> stronger. And at the same time we thought we were worthy to rule,
> and used to be so regarded by you also, until you fell to calculating
> what your interests were and resorted, as you do now, to the plea of
> justice—which no one, when opportunity offered of securing some-
> thing by main strength, ever yet put before force and abstained
> from taking advantage. And they are to be commended who,
> yielding to the instinct of human nature to rule over others, have
> been more observant of justice than they might have been, con-
> sidering their power.

No better exposition in brief of the philosophy current in
Periclean circles could be desired. The additional reflection—'men,
it seems, are more resentful of injustice than of violence'—instead
of prompting the jingo party to pause, merely confirmed them in
their resolve to find the subjects in the wrong as men who considered 'the present yoke is always heavy' and forgot the ruling
people's superior worth.

This, then, is the defence which satisfied the majority of Athenians on the eve of the first recorded World War; just as it has
satisfied the British and American multitudes since 1914. The
moral leaders of the world have learned nothing from ancient
experience. Thucydides and Plato, so far as they were concerned,
wrote in vain. The former exposed, with cold detachment, the
crude fact that justice and empire are incompatible. The maxim
officially pronounced by Athens at Sparta was: that it is the instinct
of human nature to rule over others; that it is an established rule
that the weaker is kept down by the stronger; that no one when
offered an opportunity of securing something by main force was

ever restrained by a plea of justice. *Pleonexia*, that is to say, is universal and natural, and there was nothing exceptional or inconsistent in what Athens had done—they could even assert that the empire was offered to them and, being accepted, had to be maintained for the strongest motives, honour, fear and self-interest.

Very modern was the suppression of the truth about the 'offer'. What the allies had offered, and in a unique crisis involving all, was the hegemony, and the bone of contention between Pericles and the Peloponnesians was simply that he was the ringleader in the supreme crime of converting hegemony into enslavement. Seeing that Athens, moreover, was 'a democracy in name' but was, in fact, 'a government ruled by its First Citizen' the utterances of the Athenian negotiators recorded by Thucydides must be regarded as the authentic voice of Pericles.

There is no ground for supposing that Thucydides exaggerated the realism of his diplomacy: his purpose clearly was to reveal the reasoning that dictated the unyielding attitude—'the empire you hold is a tyranny, which it may seem wrong to have assumed, but which certainly it is dangerous to let go.' His patriotic fervour recalled the familiar boast of the blue water schools:

> I declare that of two divisions of the world that lie open to man's use, the land and the sea, you hold the absolute mastery over the whole of one, not only to the extent to which you now exercise it, but also to whatever fuller extent you may choose; and there is no one, either the Great King or any nation of those now on the earth, who will block your path.

Again:

> We of all the Hellenes held sway over the greatest number of Hellenes, in the greatest wars held out against our foes whether united or single, and inhabited a city that was the richest in all things and the greatest.

In spite of everything, moreover, Thucydides, to whom the war spelt exile and disaster, exonerates the prime mover from the deadly, so often slurred over, charge of misguiding his city. His final judgment indeed remained, that Pericles had 'at that time abundant grounds for his own forecast that Athens might quite easily have triumphed in this war over the Peloponnesians'.

The inference is, then, that the empire which Pericles himself described as a tyranny might have continued its victorious career, and altered the whole course of European history. It was the successors of Pericles who, by reversing his counsels of moderation, through incapacity and disunion, wrecked the enterprise and provoked the censure of the great historian. It was not for the Father of Scientific History formally to indict the statesman who appeared to earn the unswerving confidence of Athens by his firm management of the city's policy in peace and war, so congenial to the austere youth who served himself as a general and was exiled for his pains by Cleon, 'the most violent of the demagogues'. When after the collapse of the Empire, he (Thucydides) returned to Athens he may have likewise refrained from explicitly condemning the national aggressions as morally indefensible, content to dwell on the glaring blunders of the war party while faithfully recording for posterity the cold unscrupulous sentiments which entailed and deserved the final disaster. It was enough for the stern moralist who set out to write a handbook for the politician that would be 'an everlasting possession' to set down the grim truth and let the moral sink in. Safer, too, during his lifetime in a community exasperated by defeat and suffering and torn with sanguinary civil strife.

Not till the consequences of defeat were seen by all Hellenes to be monstrous did Plato push the criticism latent in the pages of Thucydides to the limit and exhibit in their naked wickedness the evils latent in the worship of vulgar greatness.

The astounding aptness of the lesson can hardly be exaggerated. Hundreds of empires have risen during the intervening centuries. At first blush there need be no affinity between the British thalassocracy and an empire which had no considerable forerunner in Europe other than Minoan Crete. The Athenian empire reached its zenith before 1400 B.C., the British around A.D. 1900. Between these two dates you have a stretch of forty centuries, covering a large fraction of the ten or twelve thousand years usually allowed for the rise of our 'civilisation'. If we accept the invention of writing as a test, recorded history embraces a much briefer space of time, and the fraction of it covering the age of Classical Greece limits itself to a very few centuries of the pre-Christian era. It seems incredible that in what seems a moment of time, in a tiny corner of Europe, occupied by less than five million landsmen and islanders, endowed with scanty natural resources, there should have been created a culture, a commerce, a social order and a policy which developed the permanent type of society known as Hellenic and renowned beyond all others as the most original and brilliant. The description by the ruler of this short-lived community as a world empire and the most powerful, in spite of its scant numbers, of all then existing nations, accordingly, helps to remind us that it is intellectual quality that counts in determining what is significant in man's achievement and so explains how the momentary phase of Hellenic supremacy is of such enormous consequence in the higher study of man's evolution.

In the study of European political history especially, and most of all in appraising the meaning of British sea power, no more illuminating contrast can be adduced than the world recorded by Thucydides. At the very core of that record is the statesmanship of Pericles and it is depicted by men of his own day, more firmly than any modern in a comparable situation has attained. It took four hundred years to produce a British statesman, so ripe as a Burke, or a Gladstone, and in all that field of foreign policy which concerns us its essence remained the same. Under Elizabeth the expansion of England began in earnest. It was a process that was destined, as Lord Acton observed, to render her annals the most sanguinary of all Christian nations and nothing can be more instructive than a searching investigation of its real pattern and principles.

Fortunately, in spite of the vast bulk and confusion of these annals, under the guidance of the supreme contemporary historian and the supreme speculative genius of the age which best illuminates the tangled web of modern imperialism, these three hundred years of aggression can be sifted as easily as the century of Athenian navalism. The exciting chronicles of the navigators, pirates, traders, crusaders, slavers and conquerors reach back to the Hellenic thalassocracies and they tell one uniform story in the West, substantially one of violence and plunder gradually evolving system and measure but manifesting one and the same spirit of aggression, a spirit compounded of innumerable elements but powered by greed, by *pleonexia*.

That last qualification is what all who profit by the institution instinctively deny, often to themselves, and is what only a confident Athenian spokesman in the heyday of his naval omnipotence would venture to avow; but it is the clear purpose of Thucydides to register this imputation, this hybris, as the authentic voice of Periclean imperialism and to stamp it with the detestable hallmark

19

of political sophistry employed by expansionists in every age. Strange to say, it was Pericles, the liberal, the democrat, who descended to the level of Thrasymachus and confounded justice with *the interest of the stronger* and offered the earliest ignoble version of the hollow pretence used ever since to justify the indefensible. No statesman ever grasped more firmly the principle that in any conflict of interests between two states, a settlement based on coercion, not by an appeal to justice, is enslavement and must be resisted to the death no matter how trifling the wrong—if Athens is to be the sufferer. Athens must at all costs stand on her 'rights' and maintain what is just, in her opinion, because she was the moral leader of the world.

In this dogma is bottled up the gigantic force that from primitive times has devastated almost every corner of the habitable globe. Being a quick-witted, literate folk, the Athenian Demos knew what they were doing and were able to give a reasoned account of it. Fully aware that their wholesale coercion of weaker neighbours was emphatically condemned by Hellenic, which was for them world opinion, they deliberately flouted that opinion.

Pericles himself had lectured them:

> The empire you hold is a tyranny which it may seem wrong to have assumed, but which certainly it is dangerous to let go.

His cue is, by fair words and promises, like any modern aggressor, to cover up the injustice, which he sponsored as though he were no ruthless oppressor whose policy in its very nature relied on violence, the killing-power inherent in all imperium. He succeeded in satisfying himself that in his hands there had been no abuse of this usurped power of life and death and was able to assure himself in his last hours that no Athenian woman had worn mourning because of him.

The mere suggestion that to an Athenian it could merely *seem* wrong to have assumed the empire which they held as a tyranny was an offence to be palliated but not excused. It was no more possible for a Pericles to deny that empire made Athens the tyrant city *par excellence* of his time, than for a Cecil Rhodes to deny that *Rule Britannia* meant that England was entitled to dominion over as much of the surface of the globe, land and sea alike, as she might covet.

Rhodes never renounced his monstrous programme of conquest and control, *pace* the admirers who credited him with saner views after the intoxication of untamed expansionism had run its course. Like his countrymen in word and deed, Rhodes, wholly abandoned to the monstrous egoism of empire, then translated into conquests, with attendant butchery of unoffending 'natives' and their enslavement as well as their dispossession, had his answer to all moral scruples and that answer—we are the best people in the world—reflected a mood which has changed very little in political circles since the death of Rhodes.

Such is the dominant mood or sentiment that counts, whether in Ancient Greece or Modern Britain, and it should be truly educative to observe the stability of this blundering obsession in two communities so widely diverse in numberless ways. It is this unity in diversity that makes the Athenian-British parallel or analogy so arresting.

On the whole question of sea power nothing could be more explicit than the language of Pericles himself, as we have already seen. 'I declare,' said the great Athenian in one of his irresistible orations, 'I declare that of two divisions of the world that lie open to man's use, the land and the sea, you have the absolute mastery over the whole of one, not only to the extent to which you now exercise it, but also to whatever extent you may choose; and there is no one, either the Great King or any nation of those now on the earth who will block your path.'

This declaration, the first literary record of the familiar claim to world power founded on absolute mastery of the seaways is, of course, the forerunner of the adored British doctrine, brought up to scientific levels by Mahan and others, of world leadership based on overwhelming fleets. Hitherto empire had relied on crushing land armies with a navy as supplementary; there had been in the Greek area numerous thalassocracies before that of Athens. But at last one of the greatest national leaders of any time exalted sea power in precisely the same way as men like Rhodes and the innumerable exponents of navalism up to Seeley, Kipling and the like, whose teachings inspired the English nation since the Tudors. The vision of World Power based on *absolute mastery of the sea* dawned upon a city state consisting of a town on the Greek mainland with long walls linking the town with a heavily fortified harbour constituting together an island stronghold with a considerable hinterland, and possessed a fatal fascination for the community described above as the happy hunting-ground of the famous Greek Sophists. For the air, thanks largely to their popularising efforts, was charged with a materialist and hedonist sentiment that tended to blur the ethical outlines of a sound social and political order and in particular evolved the heresy discussed by Socrates and Thrasymachus as the theory that justice is the interest of the stronger.

Whether Pericles and his circle would have subscribed to the heresy when confronted with Socrates and his disciples cannot be asserted, but quite undeniable is the fact that Pericles in theory and in action adopted the position of Thrasymachus and was vigorously endorsed by the Athenian people as a whole. The élite who resisted the lure of his imperialism were completely dominated by the Periclean navalism with its boast of two triremes to one and its immoral claim to privileges based on superior strength. Such is the moral or immoral foundation of all imperialism, superiority in killing power.

The singular aptness of the parallel here discussed accordingly leaps to the eye. Allowance being made for the evolution of Europe during the intervening four and twenty centuries, including the abolition of chattel slavery and the substitution of slave labour by machinery, there is no genuine difference between the ancient empire and the modern either in theory or in practice.

Chapter One

'THIS BLESSED AND SPLENDID DOMINION'

ROSEBERY

WHEN BROACHING A subject so warmly debated and so thorny as British Imperialism, it seems natural to begin by sketching the writer's background. Any imputation of egoism is offset by the advantage gained from placing one's cards on the table at the outset; and this I propose to do in a few words.

Fifty years ago the two-party system seemed to be securely entrenched, and political affinities, where pronounced, generally ran on class or family lines. Was not the creed of every Englishman, as the Gilbertian quip alleged, determined as Liberal or Conservative from infancy? If you were born a Conservative you were also automatically Unionist, Tariff Reformer and Imperialist, and so you remained.

Such was the tradition that shaped my political faith and outlook up to a recent date. The following study, therefore, embodies reflections on nearly a lifetime of British Toryism, reaching from the last decade of the nineteenth century to the Second World War; fifty or sixty years during which, apart from the last phase, the rooted convictions implanted by Conservative agencies dominated the scene for the present writer. If in the long run events have proved too enlightening and shattering to warrant persistence in these convictions, it is reassuring to feel that what has uprooted many of them is the deepest conviction of all, fostered by constant communings with Greek and German idealism as restated by the School of Green, that nothing matters but the truth; and that in criticising less fundamental convictions any man is exercising his priceless faculty of self-criticism, the only kind of political criticism that, as Bosanquet observes, is worth while.

In the nineties all Conservatives and not a few Liberals were bred in the expansionist school. It was difficult to be patient with any other, and yet, had we been more realistic, we should have known that late-Victorian expansionism was at heart exclusive as well as

23

competitive, and that in a rapidly shrinking world the bare idea was questionable. For the whole conception of Empire was, of course, hateful to subject peoples; to the bulk of Americans North and South of the Rio Grande it was an offence and it was repudiated by large and growing bodies in all lands. Even in Britain overseas possessions were regarded as obsolescent by considerable sections of progressive opinion. The first British Empire had come to an inauspicious end in the Thirteen Colonies during the epoch of the French Revolution, and ever afterwards extensions of frontiers in the Second Empire caused serious misgivings. In the late nineteenth century, however, the expansionist faith seemed to be justifying itself, and was firmly established in official and popular esteem.

As we contemplate, then, the Second British Empire, which finished its career, according to that astute onlooker the *Wall Street Journal*, at the Imperial Conference of 1926, whose decisions attained full legal status with the Statute of Westminster in 1931, we must perforce, if we seek to recapture the pervasive essence of it, find it in the literature and oratory of the period. The most eloquent platform exponent of the faith, strange to say, was a Liberal, Lord Rosebery; and we cannot do better than reproduce a brief extract from the famous Glasgow Rectorial Address of 1900, in which he let himself go. This is how he delivered himself of his imperial message to his enraptured academic audience:

> How marvellous it [The British Empire] all is! Built not by saints and angels, but the work of men's hands; cemented with men's honest blood and with a world of tears, welded by the best brains of centuries past; not without the taint and reproach incidental to all human work, but constructed on the whole with pure and splendid purpose. . . . Growing as trees grow, while others slept; fed by the faults of others as well as by the character of our fathers; reaching with the ripple of a resistless tide over tracts and islands and continents, until our little Britain woke up to find herself the foster mother of nations and the source of united empires. Do we not hail in this, less the energy and fortune of a race than the supreme direction of the Almighty? Shall we not, while we adore the blessing, acknowledge the responsibility? And while we see, far away in the rich horizons, growing generations fulfilling the promise, do we not own with resolution mingled with awe the honourable duty incumbent on ourselves? Shall we then falter or fail? The answer is not doubtful. We will rather pray that strength may be given us, adequate and abundant, to shrink from no sacrifice in

fulfilment of our mission; . . . that we may transmit their bequest to our children, aye, and please God, to their remote descendants, enriched and undefiled, this blessed and splendid dominion.

Similar, if less polished, oratory in the same strain resounded throughout Britain during the latter half of the Victorian era. Thereafter its tone was less confident. The Boer War marked a turning-point; and, as we shall see, there has never since then been an occasion when a Minister rose to equal heights of national glorification. But Rosebery was in his day only the most eloquent exponent of empire. He had ardent forerunners and fellow-workers, headed by Mr Joseph Chamberlain, Cecil Rhodes and Rudyard Kipling. Of the forerunners Tennyson and Ruskin are outstanding, and serve as a reminder that, with rare exceptions, the literary talent of the age was, in tune with the ruling class at large, ardently nationalist and imperialist. Consequently, although the Victorians have somewhat faded, their political gospel, if not so implicitly trusted as of old, has not yet lost its grip on public opinion. To reinforce, however, the impression left on our minds by Rosebery, and to stamp on our memories the intensity of the sentiments which inspired the bulk of the nation during the last quarter of the nineteenth century, let us spare a few moments for Ruskin and Rhodes. Firstly Rhodes.

There is no mistaking the creed or the code of the chief empire-builder of his time. The delicate and impecunious youth who in 1870 had sought health and wealth in South Africa had by 1890 achieved both objects. His health established, he sought wealth with redoubled energy. 'I have money to make,' he declared; 'it may be the root of all evil, but it's also the root of all power, and it's power that I want.'

The power that he wanted so passionately was the power to realise a dream, the Cape to Cairo dream. Taking Ruskin's homilies on empire-building as his guide, and seasoning his master's lesson with the Darwinian hypothesis, he applied to the political field the doctrine of 'Natural Selection and the Survival of the Fittest' in its undiluted English form. 'We happen to be the best people in the world, with the highest ideals of decency and justice and liberty and peace, and the more of the world we inhabit, the better it is for humanity.'

In so 'arguing' he was frankly following Ruskin, whose disciple he professed to be. The impetuous sage had averred that:

We English had a destiny now possible to us, the highest ever set before a nation to be accepted or refused. Will you, youths of England make your country again *a royal throne of Kings, a sceptred isle*, for all the world a source of light, a centre of peace? This is what England must do or perish. She must found colonies as fast and far as she is able, formed of the most energetic and worthiest of men; seizing any piece of fruitful land she can set her foot on and there teaching her colonists that their chief virtue is to be fidelity to their country and that their first aim is to be to advance the power of England by land and sea.

Thus Ruskin.

Delirious as this utterance may seem, Rhodes actually improves on his teacher:

We, the English-speaking people, have the power to gather the whole civilised world into one great Empire: every inch of it that is fit for white habitation. What about the whole continent of South America, the sea-board of China and Japan, the Holy Land, Mesopotamia, the Malay Archipelago? It's our duty to build up this irresistible power. When once that is done, war, man's greatest misfortune, will become impossible. However, you and I had better begin with Africa.

What Rosebery, Ruskin and Rhodes preached was nothing new. For after all they merely voiced in florid language what was in the air. From James Thomson's *Rule Britannia!* (1740) to Elgar-Benson's *Land of Hope and Glory*, from Shakespeare to Kipling, stretches an anthology of patriotic song and poetry unmatched elsewhere in the world. In support political propaganda was not confined to ruling groups and their spokesmen. The vast apparatus of publicity and indoctrination, schools and colleges, theatres and concert-halls, the Press, the Churches, reviews and the book-trade disseminated their lessons. British historiography, in fact, reflecting all this conditioning, is so saturated with imperial sentiment as to create out of our island story a veritable mythology of heroic and beneficent conquest. It is then the latest phase of this spirit of acquisitiveness operating in the foreign field that we examine in these pages. Yet, in action the spirit of naked self-interest is, of course, compounded with other emotions which must be allowed for if we are to do justice to our imperial mission. The stupendous force and persistence, however, of the urge towards competitive expansionism remains the master-key of the whole phenomenon.

26

The spectacular success of the forward policy after 1870 blinded the nation to its true meaning. The lurking dangers forcibly set forth by Rosebery and others made little impression. Few had the foresight to measure the extent of British entanglements; and just as little did the man in the street grasp the consequences of foreign rivalry. The rapid increase in population *seemed* to require more elbow-room for our surplus. If foreign peoples were jealous they should remember our teeming millions and shining virtues.

The population of which we speak had been 5,000,000 in 1600 and by 1700 had slowly climbed to 5,250,000. Then comes a striking advance. In the eighteenth century the numbers nearly doubled; so that the nineteenth century starts with 9,000,000 souls, as revealed by the census of 1801. After that the figure climbed fast, to reach 26,500,000 in the 1871–81 decade; in 1901 it reached 37,000,000 and in 1931 mounted to 44,800,000. In 1945 it touched 47,000,000.

That the population was only 9,000,000 in 1800 is truly surprising. And equally surprising is the growth since that date, especially since during the nineteenth century there was a veritable swarming (shared by Europe generally) to distant lands, which not merely filled up the United States but peopled the Dominions and consolidated the overseas territories, Canada, Australia, New Zealand and (with Dutch priority) South Africa. These possessions, situated mainly in the temperate zones of both hemispheres, together with large tracts of Asia, made up the First British Empire, and the agencies which created it were trade, emigration and war. More than two centuries of almost incessant fighting, with Portugal and Spain, Holland and France, were needed to found and protect it; and most of it survived into the Second and Third Empires, which form the subject of these chapters. It is, however, the later annexations in the final quarter of the nineteenth century that chiefly count. These accretions atoned for the heavy loss in North America, but created fresh problems, destined to strain the *Pax Britannica* as never before.

A glance at the Second British Empire after Waterloo reveals a pause of sixty years followed by a spurt of expansion, widening its bounds to an aggregate which absorbed one-fifth of the globe, or forty times the area of the German Empire. From the First Empire it inherited vast possessions. In North America alone nearly 4,000,000 square miles invited pioneers and settlers. And these lands, together with Australasia and Africa, by the end of the century provided homes for nearly 15,000,000 white British subjects.

In the North American colonies in 1900 the figure was given as 7,260,169, mostly Canadians. Africa in an area of 535,000 square miles made room for nearly 7,000,000 'colonials', mostly coloured. In Australia, 3,000,000 square miles were occupied by 5,000,000 inhabitants. Our Asiatic Empire of 1,800,000 square miles (mostly India) had an estimated population of 290,000,000, and in our Protectorates lived about 56,000,000 subjects, of whom Asia accounted for 1,200,000; Africa, with Egypt and the Soudan for 54,730,000; and Oceania for 30,000.

In an area of about 13,000,000 square miles the population was estimated at nearly 367,000,000. How much of this territory and this population, which constituted the Empire in 1900, had belonged to the First British Empire as it stood about 1760?

Out of the 13,000,000 square miles of overseas possessions forming the British Empire in 1900 not much less than 8,000,000 survived from the First Empire. Apart from the transfer of power from the East India Company to the United Kingdom in 1858, which represented a long step of consolidation, no great annexations occurred in the first three-quarters of the nineteenth century. It was not till the last quarter that the gigantic expansion began which, in twenty-five years, yielded fresh acquisitions comprising 5,000,000 square miles, territories forty times as large as Great Britain and populated by about 90,000,000 persons.

Mr J. A. Hobson and others have dwelt on the meaning of this startling growth.[1] Their findings, however, are known to few compared with the multitudes who drank in the Rosebery, Rhodes and Ruskin gospel. Their wisdom and foresight are little regarded by politicians or people. And yet, in order to understand the last half-century of catastrophe and the forces at work today, it is important to remember that there was comparative quiescence from 1815 to 1875. There was plenty of fighting to retain overseas possessions, but little expansion. After 1875, expansion became a mania and this gave a special character to European politics in our time, although there is nothing novel about land-hunger in all its forms.

For after all, as an American scholar observes: 'Contemporary imperialism is simply the most modern form of that primitive drive for power which had led kings and nations onwards ever since the pharoahs upon the path of ever-increasing masses of territory and of political power.' And yet there was something new and dangerous, as Rosebery indicated. And that was the pace of the drive and the number of the competitors. Whether, granting this truism, emphasis should be placed on political power, which, as Milner argued, is prized as a means to wealth, or on wealth which Rhodes regarded as a means to power, is of little moment, since wealth and power are reciprocally end and means.

In any case, the British public and their leaders threw themselves into the drive for power and pelf with exceptional zeal after 1870. The trading character of the movement was strongly accentuated. 'The Empire is Commerce, Commerce, Commerce,' insisted Chamberlain, and ever fewer grew the dissentients who denied that trade follows the Flag. Less and less did Cobdenite antagonism to wider frontiers act as a restraining influence. Men forgot that commerce with America flourished more abundantly after the Flag was hauled down. They became sceptical of the Free Trade doctrines of the Manchester School, which laid stress on the benefits of unfettered exchange of goods and focused attention on the loss incurred by overseas commitments. These doctrines had prevailed throughout the central half of the nineteenth century, and continued to colour the views of the Liberal Party even when the pull of overseas interests created the Liberal Imperialist wing, led by Rosebery, Asquith, Haldane and Grey. But as foreign trade grew, as the exchange of commodities became more diversified, as consumers' goods ceased to play the leading role in European exports and took second place to capital goods and the export of capital itself, the merchants, manufacturers and financiers concerned in the maritime countries espoused a vigorous trading policy in the overseas field. Interests abroad were most effectively established and protected where European nationals were guaranteed rights to trade with and develop the resources of backward peoples through agencies supported by their home governments and the armaments necessary to enforce their claims.

Whether these 'interests' were ever as commanding and lucrative as they seemed is more than dubious. Certainly the Boer War and two World Wars, dragging on evilly into the Cold War, to cap thirty-eight wars waged by Britain between Waterloo and 1914, have converted the legendary gains of the imperialist centuries into

a gigantic loss, moral and material, for us, as well as for the vanquished. The men, therefore, who disputed the wisdom of devoting
so much blood and treasure belonging to, and exacted from, the
enemy of the hour far more than to ourselves have been abundantly
justified. It was Asquith himself who during the Tariff Reform
controversy pointed out that the 'vital interests' which cost us and
other peoples so dear never yielded a profit of more than a fraction
of the twenty per cent of our national turnover which our total
foreign trade constituted at its peak. The fashion has changed in
the Liberal camp, as in that even of the Socialists. The lesson
taught by our ablest economists fifty and eighty years ago, and
reinforced by eminent Americans, notably Professor Parker Moon
of Columbia,[2] is just ignored. Nobody could guess from the language
of our rulers in politics and in the Press that among scientific
economists for generations it has been common knowledge that
imperialism is a game that does not pay. As Professor Parker Moon
writes—'the doctrine of exclusive and monopolistic imperialism is
being more fervently preached in Europe today than ever before.'
For about the 'strong citadels of self-seeking imperialism . . . there
hangs a mist, obscuring unsightly facts and lending glamor to
illusions. It is no more than a fog of Mid-Victorian misinformation,
accumulated in the form of prejudice and venerable sentiment.'[3]
This is the fog that Liberalism in vain tried to dissipate. A great
Liberal like Bernard Bosanquet during the First World War
diagnosed this self-seeking as the disease which bred the evil.[4] For
the vice of the whole imperialist movement, was, as he declared,
that at heart, it was, and is, never co-operative and peaceful. More
effectively than any other national delusion, it converted the world
order into the *bellum omnium contra omnes* which reason abhors.

On this aspect of the subject Rosebery himself was frank:

> For the last twenty years, still more during the last twelve, you have
> been laying your hands, with almost frantic eagerness, on every
> tract of territory adjacent to your own or desirable from any other
> point of view which you thought it desirable to take. That has had
> two results. . . . The first result is this, that you have excited to an
> almost intolerable degree the envy of other colonizing nations, and
> that, in the case of many countries, or several countries rather, which
> were formerly friendly to you, you can reckon—in consequence of
> your colonial policy, whether right or wrong—not on their active
> benevolence but on their active malevolence. And, secondly, you

have acquired so enormous a mass of territory that it will be years before you can settle it or control it, or make it capable of defence or make it amenable to the acts of your administration... In twelve years you have added to the Empire, whether in the shape of actual annexation or of dominion, or of what is called a sphere of influence, 2,600,000 square miles of territory ... to the 120,000 square miles of the United Kingdom, which is part of your Empire, you have added during the last twelve years twenty-two areas as large as the United Kingdom itself. I say that that marks out for many years a policy from which you cannot depart if you would. You may be compelled to draw the sword—I hope you may not be; but the foreign policy of Great Britain, until its territory is consolidated, filled up, settled, civilized, must inevitably be a policy of peace.[5]

Here, be it noted, we have no reasoned apology for British acquisitiveness in the late Victorian epoch. The process, indeed, was hard to defend, for it was prompted by no natural land-hunger, no aching for *Lebensraum*, no intolerable pressure of over-population, *that* having been relieved by earlier conquests and annexations which offered huge empty national homes in the Dominions. But, while he glosses over the seamy side of the 'deeds that won' these twenty-two areas as large as Britain itself, he does lay stress on the inevitable concomitant of modern white expansionism, its costly militarism. Increasingly in the seventeenth and eighteenth centuries the fleets and armies of Europe took their toll of life and treasure both at home and overseas. After Waterloo there was a respite, and through the nineteenth century Britain won many a cheap victory over backward peoples; yet the interminable chain of colonial and other wars was an expensive adventure and added myriads to the total of a 'million dead' lamented by Kipling. As regards calculated gains, even when spectacular, like Hong Kong or the Koh-i-noor, such profits are disreputable and bloodstained. Yet, although the waste in men and money was grievous from first to last, it was not till the destructive implements of the machine age became common property that the menace of mutual ruin reared its head. Rosebery, as we see, spoke out but what was the response? Hobson comments:

After these words were uttered, vast new tracts of undigested empire were added in the Soudan, in East Africa, in South Africa, while Great Britain was busily entangling herself in obligations of

31

incalculable magnitude and peril in the China Seas, and the prophet who spoke this warning was himself an active instrument in the furtherance of the very folly he denounced. Imperialism whether it consists in a further policy of expansion or in the rigorous maintenance of all those vast tropical lands which have been earmarked as British spheres of influence—implies militarism now and ruinous wars in the future. This truth is now for the first time brought sharply and nakedly before the mind of the nation. The kingdoms of the earth are to be ours on condition that we fall down and worship Moloch.[6]

Writing seven years after Rosebery sounded his warning,[7] Mr Hobson had as an aid in penning his unerring forecast the very war to which Rosebery pointed but did nothing to avert. The sin and folly of the Boer War make a formidable text in Hobson's impeachment of militant imperialism. It also sheds light on the play of real motives and interests which governed British policy in the later Victorian era and, persisting unchecked through the next fifty years, led to Armageddon and bankruptcy. That the nation fell down and worshipped Moloch during what the peoples of Asia regard as Europe's civil wars who will deny? And what British subject will pretend that as a result of this worship of Moloch the kingdoms of the earth are ours?

And yet, although the edifice of national pride, glory and greatness reared by certain white peoples, one after the other, has crashed never to rise again, the deity which lures them to final doom is passionately adored by multitudes today. That the ardour of the cult finds cooler expression in imperialist circles is natural. But though shorn of its brightest jewels this 'blessed and splendid dominion' is still the object of the emotion and the *latreia* which were rampant in Rosebery's heyday. Archbishop Lang, for instance, conferred on the Moloch-worship of his own generation the blessing of the Church, and outdid Rosebery in his ecstatic eulogy of our divinely-appointed imperium by according it the sanction and the status of the National Faith. The cult which Hobson condemned as 'Moloch-worship', Lang saluted as *Imperial Christianity*, sublimely indifferent to the holocausts which the cult demands of its worshippers. Such a burlesque of the teaching of Christ truly confounds a simple European who has heard of The Cross and finds *it* difficult to square with obliteration bombing.

Chapter Two

IMPERIAL CHRISTIANITY

LET US TAKE as typical of alert and progressive Christian thought the position adopted by an eminent Churchman, the Scott Holland Lecturer in 1946.[1] His main object was to trace the evolution of sociology in the Church of England, 'From Maurice to Temple', and in his survey he had naturally to reckon with the economic movement which provided materials for theorists, economists, moralists, politicians, and even theologians to build upon. In this economic movement, of course, world trade had played the spectacular part.

Writing forty years after Hobson, and having witnessed the consequences of the national apostasy deplored by him and his school, how did the modern Churchman react?

In the first place he laid it down that with the outbreak of the war which Hobson, and less definitely Rosebery, had foreseen, our world entered upon an era of disaster. The war of 1914, he declared, marked the end of an era and was 'in fact . . . the logical upshot of an expansion inspired by a combination of nationalist ambition, organised avarice, and a frustration which drove the industrialised "Powers" into world markets to compensate themselves for failure to dispose of a sufficiency of goods to their own nationals'. Such was the net result of Mr Reckitt's reflections, echoing the anticipations of the school of Hobson; and in order to explain the ethical collapse which conditioned the policy of our rulers he quoted Scott Holland: 'A limitless desire for riches, for power, for pleasure, has run like a flame through the Nations . . . and the result is that all Europe is at war.' And even more startling: the war instead of promoting a higher world order 'only produced a new idolatry more devastating than the old. Moloch supplanted Mammon.'[2]

Here then we learn from progressive Churchmen what prudent economists tried to teach the politicians, our rulers, before the catastrophe. In 1914 Europe entered upon an age of violence and 'organised avarice' leading to the enthronement by our rulers of the double-headed deity, Mammon-Moloch, or Mammoloch, under whose malign auspices the Great Powers rattled back to worse than pagan practice. What makes the lapse into the new barbarism so ominous is that the Christian Churches, collectively and officially, have compounded the felonies of Mammoloch to such a degree that they have connived at the whole programme of the militant expansionists, including organized starvation of sister nations and obliteration bombing of glorious cities, every abomination up to Hiroshima and Dresden. They have refused even to condemn preventive blitzing with A bombs or H bombs.

The Church of England, the Nonconformist Churches and the clergy at large are solid with the government of the day whenever it is considered desirable to resort to arms. Examples of this habit are too numerous to mention and it would be tedious to recite specimens of the ordinary kind. But there is a glaring, almost ludicrous instance in which a national Church not merely, as usual, endorsed a great war but with rare candour admitted the material reason for it.

The example is taken from the records of the Church of Scotland and deserves to be pondered. Fully two hundred years ago (May 1756), the Church of Scotland in its General Assembly announced that the Seven Years War, then in its infancy, was due to 'Your Majesty's just resentment of the encroachments of the French in America'. And to mark the *justice* of the resentment, the Address to the Throne adjured 'The Righteous Governor of the Universe' to 'favour our righteous cause'. So far so good. But at the close of the war, when victory called for jubilant utterance, this proclamation of 'our righteous cause' was felt to be too tame and in framing the Address of Congratulation for V-F Day this is what was concocted:

> By a definitive treaty with your enemies, the great objects for which war was undertaken are attained; the possessions of chief conse-quence to Britain are secured; new sources of commerce are opened; and territories added to your crown more extensive and of greater value than have been acquired by any nation since the division of Europe into great kingdoms, and the establishment of a balance of power, have put a stop to the rapidity of conquest.[3]

In the flush of victory the Scots Churchmen thus dropped the mask of piety and congratulated the Monarch not on crushing

'France, the formidable enemy of the religion and liberties of our country', but on adding vast possessions to our Empire and capturing new trading areas. Not much of a Holy Crusade in such a manifesto! This is merely the official avowal of war aims in the Scots capital by the national Church. The Church of England in Convocation is more closely identified with governments than is the Church of Scotland and its partnership with the Crown in all wars is automatic and certain. In London the bishops could never stray into the pacificist camp. Can we say that in modern Edinburgh there has been any change for the better in the past two centuries?

To settle this point we turn to the Church Assembly of May 1940 and what do we find? On the day appointed for the discussion of the Second World War we have two sessions. The first concludes with a declaration that 'War is contrary to the mind and spirit of Christ': but at the second meeting the same Churchmen 'rejected the pacifist contention that participation in war was necessarily contrary to the will of God'.

No amount of sophistry can hide this crashing contradiction. Not even a theological assembly, accustomed to doctrinal subtleties, could honestly affirm in one day first the assertion that war is contrary to the mind and spirit of Christ and secondly the dogma that war is in harmony with the will of God. Never were men more hopelessly impaled on the horns of an inescapable dilemma. And it could not be otherwise.

For in a word the Scots Church in 1940, as in 1756, was confronted with the veritable impasse which has confronted every Christian assembly that debates the ethics of any war at all. Before, during and after each conflict the acquiescence or complicity of Christian communities is challenged by an indomitable nucleus of pacificists, fortified by the example of our Quakers and lately by the triumph of *Satyagraha* or non-violent resistance on a grand scale, who insist on applying the acid test to the conduct of their compromising brethren.

And what is the acid test?

As we shall see in due course, there is a prima facie case against war which no professing Christian can ignore. Without the Sermon on the Mount, Dying to live, *not* Killing unlimited, Self-sacrifice, *not* Self-seeking, The Cross to be borne by the strong, *not* to be thrust upon the weak, what becomes of our common Christianity?

35

Love your enemies is the antithesis of war to the knife, obliteration bombing and unconditional surrender. And yet our Churchmen, at every gathering where a national war is proclaimed or victory is applauded, assert the righteousness of frightfulness. They are capable in our time of invoking the Will of God to confound the Spirit and Mind of Christ! All in the space of a few hours.

The same procedure is fashionable whenever the issue is raised. Frequently, it is dodged by a discreet silence. Indeed, since, according to the League of Nations' count, the British Government waged war during sixty-four years in the century after Waterloo, the eternal theme of perpetual war for Righteousness would have become farcical. But as a screen for the grim and real purposes of wars of annihilation, the plea of the Good Cause, of God and the Right, is more than ever an indispensable agency in winning over a nation to the worship of Moloch.

For every decade invents fresh horrors to grace the sadistic rites of the 'new idolatry'. And these horrors demand, if only as soothing syrup, more war flags in the cathedrals, more blessing of the regimental standards, more colours for the coffins, more hymns of hate from the pulpit, more trumpeting of holy crusades. All this to celebrate the reign of 'Moloch, horrid king, besmeared with blood of human sacrifice and parents' tears'. Such is the crowning achievement of our Christian way of life. At all points the clergy have assisted, even to the caricaturing of the Beatitudes by theological sophistry—killing no murder, and the double ethic, the interim and the divine.

And yet during these fifty years there has been a vigorous opposition in all Denominations. The claim of Catholicity has for a section of the clergy been more than a pretence. There have been outspoken preachers who have championed the equality of men in the sight of God, and the implied right of every human society to manage and mis-manage its own affairs exactly like all the others. In a word to be free.

Pseudo-Christian cant, in fact, is hard pressed to conceal the 'Frightfulness of Righteousness' when embodied in total war, war total in content as well as extent, embracing not only the world but every manner of devilry within the wit of man to devise and execute. As the years pass, nevertheless, the pious fraud becomes more and more difficult to maintain. The age-old loathing of massacre is a definite human sentiment, and found expression even in the Establishment long before Mahatma Gandhi showed what the Cross truly signified and put Christendom to shame.

It is fully a century since Maurice in a Lincoln's Inn Sermon spoke out against 'all unrighteous government whatever, all that sets itself against the order and freedom of man', branding such conduct in our rulers as 'hostile to Christ's government' and 'rebellion against Him, in whatsoever name and by whatsoever instruments it is administered.'[4]

And what has been the response in the concrete to Maurice and all who have followed in his footsteps? Simply this: to the 'innumerable crimes for which religion has been the plea for eighteen hundred years'[5] our rulers have added other crimes, some more foul than Maurice in 1846 could have conceived. These, moreover, were all duly sanctified by orthodox morality and religion, although the purpose, the aim, the ideal reeks of Mammon and Moloch and had long been notorious. Was not the purpose of every debauch of mutual murder defined once and for all by the General Assembly of the Church of Scotland in 1756 in the same terms as were used by President Wilson in 1919 to describe his own Crusade?[6] Yet never during these last hundred years has a national Church entered a solemn protest against a single one of these lapses into the ancient idolatry. The cloak of religion has always been thrown over the acts of our war-loving leaders, to further the supposed material interests of our country. Certain it is that never before was there such need for the plea of religion as in the present crisis, the culminating chapter of three centuries of insatiable aggrandisement.

Such are the fruits of imperial Christianity in action!

How much longer the imperial will-o'-the-wisp may continue to entice Christian nations to further orgies of Moloch-worship who can say? It is useless to look for a change of heart so long as the 'new idolatry' commands the devotion of millions of believers who, in the interest of 'organised avarice', stoop to the hypocrisy stigmatised above. Can we wonder, when councils of the churches deny their nominal Lord by a persistent declaration that *this* war is sanctioned by the Will of God—can we wonder that formal religion is widely suspect? A Christianity that after seventeen centuries of dominance flouts the Golden Rule and connives at such violation of the same, surely invites criticism and disbelief. We have seen Quaker placards in the thick of the war urging:

'Do unto other Nations as ye would that they should do unto you' but never has an effective condemnation of a war of obliteration been authorised by any national Church.

This is the shameless apostasy against which a minority have protested for generations. In recent years perhaps Bishop Gore is the most striking example. Although his direct concern was with the apostasy which elevated Mammon above Christ in the class war inside the nation, indirectly his avowal bears heavily on those who have abused the 'banner of Christ' in the international class war. 'I hate the Church of England', declared Gore, 'because it is an ingeniously devised instrumentality for defeating the objects which it is supposed to promote'.[7] Such plain-speaking was common a century ago among Tractarians and Christian Socialists. G. W. Ward for instance is quoted as lamenting that England was 'one vast mass of superficial splendour, covering a body of festering misery and discontent', and that for centuries the English Church had been 'swayed by a spirit of arrogance, self-contentment and self-complacency'.[8] At the Pan-Anglican Congress of 1908, nevertheless, the tide had turned. Gradually on social reform, on questions of wages, housing and labour conditions the Church was so far won over to the side of the workers that Temple was able to dogmatise and identify Socialism with Christianity. 'The alternative', said he, 'stands before us—Socialism or Heresy; we are involved in one or the other.'[9] *Extra socialismum nulla salus!*

This glimpse of the clerical attitude towards the perennial class war would be misleading, nevertheless, if it ignored the resistance movement to the aspirations of the masses. In August 1908, an editorial in the *Church Times* denied that the Socialism of the Congress was all that the zealots claimed and actually assailed the morale of the workers in uncompromising terms: 'Their greed, their self-indulgence, their dislike of obedience, call for stern rebuke. By administering such reproof in the spirit of love much more than by adulation or by pulpit-babblings about the tyranny of capital will the Church be furthering the "welfare" of the poor.'[10] The Church was not a unit in the controversy, but it had travelled a long way between 1846 and 1908.

In 1846 churchgoing had become little more than a badge of respectability awarded by a 'black dragoon' in every parish to those of the well-to-do who felt the need of his ministrations.[11] According to the *Official Census of Religious Worship* (1851) only an 'absolutely insignificant . . . portion of the congregation was composed of artisans' and below that level seemingly the proportion was nil. Neglect of religion, moreover, was due, not to 'a degraded condition' but chiefly to active hostility to its guardians, especially to the Church of England, regarded as 'part of the system of aristocratic government'.[12]

Within seventy years there was a 'sea change' in the dominant attitude of the clergy towards the chronic struggle of the disinherited against the privileged few. The labours of Maurice had borne fruit and his scathing philippics on the cold-hearted prelates were if possible surpassed in virulence by cohorts of imitators.

On their showing, the banner of Christ under which the Anglican clergy previous to Maurice, with rare defections, marched, was a blind. As the century of reform advanced and the orthodox majority diminished in numbers and influence, the Church which arrogates to itself more and more the function and title of 'The Body of Christ' championed more openly the cause of Lazarus in his struggle with Dives. By 1908 the 'mind and spirit of Christ' came to pervade His 'Body' sufficiently to enable the progressives to take the lead and exalt 'Christian Socialism' as the true faith, with a strong suggestion that conservatives were tainted with *heresy*.

Thus the Pan-Anglican Congress at last wrestled with the secular problem of social justice in the microcosm of England. The agelong injustice under which the under-privileged groaned at home was now a special concern of the most energetic section in the Established Church as well as in the Free Churches. But since the eighties the parallel conflict in the macrocosm, the foreign field, had become vastly more fateful than any domestic dissensions. The day was at hand when the supreme question, not of justice inside the nation but of justice between the British nation and 'the foreigner' was to be thrust on the attention of all, clergy and laity and non-members alike.

The world was shrinking rapidly as space was being annihilated and 'my neighbour' was on the doorstep demanding recognition. The international situation offered a magnificent arena for leaders in the Church as well as in the State. It was for the clergy to create the atmosphere in which not merely fair play but even a tincture of altruism might reduce friction and ill will. Here it was that the Church should have countered the flag-waving of the jingoes by displaying 'the banner of Christ'. Yet it was precisely in this province, in the fostering of goodwill and co-operation that, although there was a measure of awareness that it was part of the mission of the Church to propagate fraternity and equality abroad as well as at home, the clergy practically effaced themselves. They took no active interest even in the philanthropy of Wilberforce. Among his fellows he was nearly a bird alone, and because his life was devoted to the abolition of slavery in distant lands he was dismissed by Cobbett as a 'canting humbug' and disliked by radicals for his tolerance of the 'appalling abuses' at his door.[13]

The pitiful hoax by which our people have been lured on to orgy after orgy of Moloch worship should have been detected long ago. The 'banner of Christ' employed in his service no doubt has borne many a 'strange device'. Why these devices, these slogans, were not disowned at sight as lures invented by Antichrist, a more familiar demon than Moloch, is hard to understand in the Cold War age when their real meaning has become transparent. *Fight the good Fight*, *Onward Christian Soldiers*, *The War to end War*, *The Battle for Freedom*, *War for Security*, *War against Militarism*, *War to defend Small Nations*, *War for Vital Interest*, *War against Autocracy*—these are the alleged war aims which twice in a generation have been not merely trumpeted round the earth but achieved triumphantly at an astonishing price. Is it not preposterous that our people could be deluded by such fustian?

Whether preposterous or not the delusion was, and still is, very real. Moreover our leaders in Church and State, with hardly an exception, have masqueraded successfully as ministers of the 'Prince of Peace' and *twice* have bestowed on Europe an utterly bogus 'Peace of Righteousness'. There are, however, signs that we do learn by suffering, and are beginning to admit that the triumph of Moloch is a tragedy for the nation. 'Even an infant knows a thing when it is done,' says a Greek proverb; and surely we must all agree that in two frenzied orgies of insensate bloodlust our leaders have *done one thing*. They have murdered Peace. *Si monumentum requiris circumspice!*

Is it conceivable that Rhodes today could seriously repeat his famous utterance? 'We, the English-speaking people, have the power to gather the whole civilised world into one great Empire: every inch of it that is fit for white habitation.' 'It's our duty to build up this irresistible power. When once that is done, war, man's greatest misfortune, will become impossible.' Would Rhodes not at least express himself differently?

Certainly the other nineteen-twentieths of the race evince no passionate desire to be dispossessed by the English-speaking twentieth. Nor do they bow down before that twentieth as before their betters. Rhodes, moreover, was not entitled to speak for more than a fortieth of the race, seeing that the United States was satiated with territory and frowned upon all European aggression. By far the larger part of the English-speaking community was, therefore, antagonistic to the empire-builders. If we desire a concise and moderate expression of United States sentiment, why not accept as definitive the famous speech of the illustrious American, Daniel Webster, delivered in the Senate, May 7, 1834? On the question of principle, not of specific injuries inflicted by the English, he declared that Americans had raised their flag 'against a power to which, for purposes of conquest and subjugation, Rome, in the height of her glory, is not to be compared; a power which has dotted over the surface of the whole globe with her possessions and military posts, whose morning trumpet, following the sun and keeping company with the hours, circles the earth with one continuous and unbroken strain—of the martial airs of England'.

In the light afforded by this dubious tribute of an eminent American let us attempt, as British subjects under special and world-wide scrutiny, to see ourselves as others see us.

What the outside world, the Americas, Asia, Africa felt about our empire was never a secret except in England itself, where understanding was swamped by insular complacency. As we have noted, Professor Parker Moon and Daniel Webster both reflect in measured language what Americans of good will have always thought of the 'wider yet and wider' complex. This habit of thought, indigenous in the U.S.A., does not change. Even partnership in two world wars counts for little. Except in the crisis how much did the bond between Stalin, Churchill and Roosevelt signify? Indeed it appears that Roosevelt was so little enamoured of British *pleonexia* that shortly before his death he warned his Secretary of State, Stettinius, that Britain would try to take land anywhere in the world even if it were only a rock or a sand-bar, and assured another Minister that the British, in order to fulfil their programme, were anxious to get America into war with Russia.[14] Similarly, when the

United States entered the First World War, the Secretary of the Navy had instructed Admiral Sims never to forget that, had duty required, he would have fought with as much zeal against England as he would now display in fighting by her side. Who does not remember Kipling's experience during his American sojourn when, helped by his American brother-in-law, he came to the conclusion that the steel hoop that held the States of the Union together was hatred of England? When the fog and dust of war have cleared, we may rest assured that new friendships will arise and old animosities will revive. And most decisive for us, an island folk with a unique record, will be the long repressed uprising of the subject races, already so menacing. Now that we are an occupied country, bankrupted twice in one generation, it behoves us to appraise very soberly the probable reaction to paternalism in any form, particularly in Asia and Africa, where colonialism is being resorted to as an antidote to revolution.

Indians like Rabindranath Tagore, Jawaharlal Nehru and K. M. Panikkar, not to mention Gandhi, and Chinese like Sun-yat-sen and Lin-yu-tang, have published their views on British annexations. Africa too has her interpreters, both coloured and white, and these will be glanced at in due course. But first we must touch on Asia: *ex Oriente lux.*

What then is the endemic Indian view of the British Raj and its liquidation?

In the first place the Indian man of letters is free to make his views known to all the world. The ablest historians and publicists are no longer muzzled, and their reading of Indian history differs *toto coelo* from the current British version. The policy of *divide et impera* motived by *pleonexia* and corrupted by racialism is the burden of their message; and not the least offensive phase of the Raj, we are told, has been the boycott of native history written and taught by Indians. They are taking full advantage of their liberty to fill the vacuum, and their revisionism is drastic.

We observe, for example, the pillorying of all British or European claimants to racial superiority. Whether it is a Foreign Secretary to the Indian Government, like Seton Kerr, who declares it to be the 'cherished conviction of every Englishman in India, from the highest to the lowest, . . . that he belongs to a race whom God has destined to govern and subdue', or whether it is Kitchener asserting that 'it is this consciousness of the inherent superiority of the European which has won for us India,' the spirit which emits such boasting is abhorrent to native self respect and is held up to derision.[15] The Indian, moreover, insists that in spite of superficial alterations and concessions this racialism remained the official doctrine and the basis of the Raj until the evacuation. In the opinion of the Asian, in fact, the charge of racial aggression is one that can be neither palliated nor denied.

'Even at the end of the nineteenth century', we are informed, 'the Europeans—even the most progressive among them—were convinced that their superiority was divinely ordained and was safe at least for centuries to come.'[16] So writes K. M. Panikkar, formerly Indian Ambassador in China and Egypt, with the assurance of a man of affairs and a scholar, passing judgment on his late masters. And what he and other Asians are publishing already is but a foretaste of the vast literary output by which the free peoples of the Free East mean to contest the supremacy of European culture. Is it not obvious that the history of Asia from Vasco da Gama (1498) to the British evacuation of India (1947) is predestined to occupy the energies of many Asiatic Gibbons for centuries? Pandit Nehru himself has commented on the 'resentment felt by Indians at being forced to study in their schools and colleges so-called histories which disparage India's past in every way, vilify those whose memory they cherish, and honour and glorify the achievements of British rule in India'. Further, he quotes an Englishman, 'well acquainted with India and her history,' as declaring that 'our writing of India's history is perhaps resented more than anything else we have done'; hinting with undisguised irony at sundry redeeming passages, when, for instance, Edward Thompson relates how 'one remembers the early history of British India which is perhaps the world's high watermark of graft'.

Enough has been said to suggest that the Asian view of European dominance since Vasco da Gama as an epoch of repression and exploitation is worth our most earnest attention. Also of vital importance for white peoples is the Asian verdict on the World Wars which speeded up Asian and African liberation. It is certainly salutary to be told by these observers that both are simply civil wars in Europe waged by rival nations with the object of monopolising overseas possessions and trade. The day is coming when Asian literature will reflect a truer view of the conflicts than the version hitherto fashionable and will prove a vehicle for the scientific and academic historiography now struggling to the light.

The part which Africa plays in this revisionism need not long detain us in this slight sketch. Europe is being called to an accounting everywhere at last. Morocco, Tunisia, Algeria, Egypt, the Soudan, Kenya and the All Red Zone, including German East Africa; in West Africa the Gold Coast, Nigeria and other divisions of the continent have been galvanised into new life and new ambitions. There is a considerable literature of upheaval and bitterness of which Mrs Paul Robeson's *African Journey* is a sample. Similar in tendency is *The Sun is my Undoing* and *The Twilight on the Floods* by Marguerite Steen. Again the picture of millions of negroes killed in slave hunts and millions more shipped off in 'hell-ships' to a fate worse than death gives a faint idea of the wrongs suffered by the black race and stored up in the African race memory. What the day of reckoning may bring who can foresee? The outcome of all this feverish unrest will be very different from anything imagined by the empire-builders.

To a people indoctrinated for centuries with the *Herrenvolk* thesis, long resented by our subjects and scoffed at by our rivals, it has been impossible to impart prudence by persuasion and wise counsel. What was destined to deflate the swollen expansionism of the Rhodes school was the 'ruinous wars' predicted by Hobson and his friends. Asia and Africa are in full agreement with the latter school.

As our Indian mentor observes with force, it was the wars of 1914 and 1939 that made Western pretensions in Asia ridiculous. 'The war, on the world scale it was conducted in 1914–18, was in itself a great world revolution, and an impenetrable chasm has been created between the days preceding August 1914 and those following November 11, 1918.'[17] In so writing the Indian diplomat virtually restates the position of Scott Holland—August 1914 marked the close of an epoch, and what that portends is more clearly seen by the Asian than by the conventional European commentator. The slump in European imperialism is the grand achievement in Indian eyes of the European tragedy.

Equally striking, for them, was the recantation of the 'mightier yet' gospel by British politicians. 'With the solitary exception of Churchill, there was not one major figure in any of the British parties who confessed to a faith in the white man's mission to rule.'[18] On this dismissal, as a spent force among party chiefs, of the

44

obsolete Chosen Race complex, which distorted official thinking up to the twelfth hour—the evacuation—Mr Panikkar relied much more than the sudden *volte face* in Parliament. That by itself would only show that the House realised the impotence of the British Raj. The rising tide of anti-British passion, as he was aware, had alarmed the bureaucracy and shaken their nerve. The most unthinking Briton in India too sensed the menace every time the polite native greeting was replaced by the rude salutation *Go Home!* The Army of Liberation created by Subhas Chandra Bose and the pro-German sentiment, widely diffused despite Hitler, afforded an added reason for declining the challenge to mortal combat, the monster Mutiny scented by Kitchener long since. As a speaker in the House phrased it: 'We saw the red light.' Likewise two bankruptcies in one generation; the stepmotherly bearing of our Allies headed by the States; the wary surveillance of Stalin and lurking enemies in a dozen directions; all these actually determined the outcome of the 'Quit India' debates. As for Mr Panikkar personally, he had been partly educated in England and was perfectly *au courant* with the insular predisposition to lord it over backward or weaker races. As readily as Wilfrid Blunt or Meredith Townsend fifty years earlier, he recognised the same fixation in leaders of all parties, in Mr Bevin as in Sir Winston Churchill, if less blatant. He understands how that and nothing else endeared Bevin to Tories even more than to Socialists.

But to confess that superiority complex, moral or immoral, when the Empire was in process of involuntary liquidation required exceptional stubbornness. It is, therefore, a distinction of sorts to be singled out as the last of the Diehards. At the same time we are made more clearly aware of the Indian interpretation of our precipitate retreat. It is that our political bosses at last saw the writing on the wall. The game was up. This explains the manner of our going. The scuttle from India, Ceylon, Burma and Egypt implies not so much the demise of a faith inbred in the governing or any other class as a recoil from its public avowal. The lowered tone is what appeals to the Indian observer and his reaction to *that* is a flat rejection of the apologetic based on the thesis of a mission to rule and the white man's burden. The most disconcerting feature of the response to the self-denying ordinance of Westminster is the low estimate of the intention of the heaven-born and the lively resentment provoked by the *spirit* of the Raj.

45

The repercussions in Europe likewise are discouraging to say the least. At the moment few genuine expressions of feeling can be expected. We may not care what the Continent thinks of our imperial Christianity, but our fate will be decided by world opinion, dominated by America, not by what we think of ourselves. How can an island race living in the North Sea learn to think sanely if they are spoon-fed by a popular press tied to a bureaucracy which jealously guards the *arcana imperii* before and during every crisis and releases nothing that damages its own prestige?

It will be many years before the British bureaucracy and public develop sufficient moral courage to stand up to the unvarnished version circulated by Europeans of the deeds that won the Empire and especially of the deeds that aimed at its preservation during the fifty years of the Anglo-French Entente.

On the other hand we may allow ourselves a glimpse of the reaction to our 'mission' among the only people accounted a Power that habitually is classed as Anglophile. These are the Italians, and the Italian whom I select is a diplomat whose reputation in England for kindly wit and humour is outstanding. During the inter-war period *The Laughing Diplomat* and *The Maker of Heavenly Trousers* were household names. Where else should we look for critical and genial appreciation of our undoubted virtues?

We select a passage which touches on the uniqueness of our splendid dominion and the exclusive attitude to sister nations which our heaven-sent mission is used to justify:

> I was much amused at a conversation between Lady Oxford and Leonardo Vitteti, Councillor of the Italian Embassy. She maintained that whereas the Italian advance in Abyssinia was morally indefensible, the campaigns that had founded the British Empire could not be criticised on moral grounds.
>
> To which Vitteti rejoined: 'My dear Lady Oxford, I am a Catholic. As such I believe in the Immaculate Conception. But I accept it as a dogma connected with the birth of Christ, not of the British Empire.'

Varé next improves on Vitteti by observing that Lady Oxford's reasoning is that of *the reformed criminal eager to stick to his loot*, illustrating 'the smug selfish policy that denied to a hard-working, thrifty, sober people like the Italians, the possibility of earning their living in their own currency, under their own flag, in under-developed lands beyond the seas'.[19]

Prompted by greed and envy, as when the first imperialist, the nomadic Cain, killed Abel for the sake of his cultivated land, men resort to bloody coercion of their weaker brethren, reducing the survivors to varying degrees of servitude and holding their gains by the same brute force by which they took possession. In the eyes of the subjects, serfs, helots or slaves the master race remains an intrusion, a usurpation, no matter how *just* and *firm* the controlling Power. The usurpation may be long-continued, rendering the brand of Cain more sinister and his yoke more insufferable. So it was even among the civilized Greeks and the less humane Romans of the Republic, notably at Sparta where the perennial threat of a Helot rising evolved the 'purging' machinery of the ruthless *Krypteia*, prototype of all imperial police services. For however masked, relentless repression is the indispensable basis of law and order where there is no consent. Inevitably too, men being what they are, no such system can last for ever.

And yet judicious repression may last long enough to create in the master race the fog described by Professor Parker Moon, a fog so thick that its brightest minds can deceive themselves regarding the ethos of British aggression, comforted by the superior wickedness of Portuguese, Spanish, Dutch, French and Italian imperialisms. But the world is not deceived.

The foreigner does not forget, whether he is a spectator or a competitor or a 'native' subject, that morally the most efficient ruling race is but *'a reformed criminal eager to stick to his loot'*. Similarly even members of the 'superior' race rise above the fog and throw light on the sordid and dark reality that lies behind the 'splendour' of our 'blessed dominion'. Fifty years ago there was an influential body of thinkers who not merely realised the evils of British *pleonexia* but vigorously demanded its reform and eventual abolition. This theme we reserve for fuller treatment to a later chapter; but to correct the foolish notion that only foreigners and ill-disposed persons resented our bloated dominion, attention must be directed for a moment to the active opposition offered at home to militant expansionism by the numerous groups reviled by Jingo propaganda as Little-Englanders. Out of a large mass of vigorous comment published by these dissenters we choose one of the most striking utterances, from the pen of a man of genius, Wilfrid Scawen Blunt, and ask whether in the light of the catastrophe which he foresaw anything more salutary could have been excogitated at the time. The date is January 9, 1896 and the place Cairo:

> The German Emperor has telegraphed his congratulations to Kruger, and this seems to have produced great anger in England. We have now managed in the last six months to quarrel violently with China, Turkey, Belgium, Ashanti, France, Venezuela, America, and Germany. This is a record performance, and if it does not break up the British Empire nothing will. For myself I am glad of it all, for the British Empire is the great engine of evil for the weak races now existing in the world—not that we are worse than the French or Italians or Americans—indeed, we are less actively destructive—but we do it over a far wider area and more success-fully. I should be delighted to see England stripped of her whole foreign possessions. We were better off and more respected in Queen Elizabeth's time, the 'spacious days' when we had not a stick of territory outside the British Islands, than now, and infinitely more respectable. The gangrene of colonial rowdyism is infecting us, and the habit of repressing liberty in weak nations is endangering our own. I should be glad to see the end.[20]

The eighth quarrel on the list, we observe, is that with Germany, and the year 1896, when the feud that came to a head in 1914, we may say, began. To tell adequately how that feud developed has been the ambition of all modern history that deserves the name: and since 1930 the main outline has been unmistakable. It is the rare distinction of Wilfrid Blunt that in the very year of the Trade Panic he grasped the nature of the disease which was eating into the vitals of the Great Powers and strove to arrest it. The prognosis was accurate and penetrating but like Maynard Keynes at Ver-sailles he was in a minority and during the lunatic half century that followed, like all his colleagues he has been in almost total eclipse.

It is for posterity to do Blunt and his collaborators full if tardy justice. Their fame is secure enough. But to reinforce his message we step forward two-and-twenty years, to 1919, when one of the Big Three, a statesman who had more blatantly than any other wrapped up Allied war aims in ideological platitudes, cast aside all pious pretences of a Holy War and a Peace of Righteousness, and acknowledged with brutal frankness the actual motives of the Big Three and their Allies. After Germany lay prostrate, her torment aggravated beyond endurance by the shameless betrayal of his

Fourteen Points, President Wilson threw caution to the winds and proclaimed the Allied objectives. 'Is there any man or woman, let me say any child', he asked, 'who does not know that the seed of war in the modern world is industrial and commercial rivalry? This was a commercial and industrial war.'[21]

Chapter Three

SIR EDWARD GREY AND HIS CRITICS

1. THE LIBERALS, 1914

THE TIME HAS not yet arrived for a final stocktaking covering the political events of the last fifty years, but the forty years from 1900 to 1939 are sufficiently recorded and sifted to become intelligible and even instructive. It is instructive, for example, to note that, whereas in the nineteeth century Europe achieved a degree of power, prosperity and stability never before dreamed of, in the first half of the twentieth century a Satanic spirit entered into the conduct of affairs which led the Great Powers into an orgy of mutual hate and destruction horrible to contemplate.

Confining our attention to the outlook in Western Europe, it is obvious that the mighty task of partitioning overseas territory in Asia and Africa among the Maritime or Atlantic States had been tackled with a measure of success. The tremendous disproportion manifest in the British conquests had, as Rosebery proclaimed, intensified jealousies and bred animosities, but there was no insuperable obstacle to peaceful adjustments of rival claims. At the turn of the century European imperialism was fitted into the wider balance of power in which the United States and Japan were beginning to play leading roles. As Mr Walter Lippmann has observed, an equilibrium was secured on a global scale partly through the impact of the United States in the Atlantic and in the Pacific.[1] Just as the United States in the Far East maintained friendly relations with Tsarist Russia in order to curb the expansionist drive of Japan, so in Western Europe, on the Atlantic Front, friendship was sedulously fostered with Russia in order to neutralise any threat from the naval Powers facing America. Behind Britain, especially, as behind Japan, a friend, or at need an ally, was always cherished by American policy as a guarantee against the misuse of European naval strength during the immaturity of the American Republic.

Within the elastic and shifting, but serviceable, framework

50

of International Mutual Forbearance, later reviled as The International Anarchy, was lodged the famous *Concert of Europe* which the twentieth century was destined to destroy. After 1871 that Concert evolved gradually into a planetary system of two groups, the Franco-Russian Alliance and the Italo-Austro-German Alliance, with Britain moving freely in 'splendid isolation' on the outskirts.

It was in 1904 that Britain began to function as a member of one group, thereby gradually forfeiting her freedom of action and ceasing to behave as a peacemaker on the Continent. The Minister who switched from splendid isolation to interventionism was Lansdowne, but the real work of participation in Continental conflicts was done by Grey, who by an extraordinary and fatal combination of chances had exclusive and supreme control of the Foreign Office for over ten years. The character of that work, and of Grey himself, is accordingly the crux of the great enigma which confronts the historian of the fifty years 1906 to 1956 and beyond.

How did the European débâcle come about? That is the question of questions! Why the linked chain of earth-shaking disasters? If we understand the ten years' rule of Sir Edward Grey we are well on the road to a solution of the enigma.

For that decade is both the prelude and the key to that unique phenomenon, Mr Churchill's grim and ferocious epoch. The epoch is a unit. The First, Second and Third (Cold) Wars form a continuous whole just as much as any tree in the forest. The roots run back, or down, into the Grey decade and deeper, into the trade competition of the nineties: the trunk, branches and foliage represent the malignant growths—the 1914 War, the violation of the pre-Armistice Convention, the Versailles Dictate, the hollow peace of 1919–39, the 1939 War and the Aftermath. It is all one frightful, diabolic outrage, each phase surpassing its predecessor in beastliness, and all deriving from the hideous blunder perpetrated by the ministers of 1914. For the scientific historian and the moralist it is an immense gain that the quintessence of the atrocity is bottled up in, and can be extracted from, the recorded words and deeds of a few 'statesmen'; and for a British subject one man is of supreme significance.

Let us see what Grey took over from his predecessors and how he handled the task which he inherited. He had a free hand (as he stipulated when he took office under Sir Henry Campbell-Bannerman) and since his subordinates, Sir Eyre Crowe and Sir

Arthur Nicolson, were of his own choosing, the responsibility for every decision belongs to Grey. He was in the last analysis the man in whose hands lay the issues of peace and war during the crisis of 1914.

It is only rational to assume that his tenure of office was dedicated to a purpose. In his book *History and Human Relations* Professor Herbert Butterfield is at pains to restate the conclusions reached by research on this vital problem.[2] An American reviewer interprets the argument as a demonstration that since 1914 Britain has been fighting the wrong wars at the wrong time and *with the wrong purpose*. If so, the purpose of Sir Edward Grey was wrong and the purpose of British policy from 1914 has been and is wrong.

Grey himself laid stress on the purity of his motives for dragging Britain into the Continental imbroglio. To preserve the balance of power is, in his usual version of his interventionism, primary. To safeguard British interests is another powerful motive; and there has been ceaseless chatter about an obligation of honour. These alleged motives have been impugned from that day to this.

As regards Grey's *purpose*, did not a speaker in the fateful discussion in the House on August 3, 1914 say the last word on that subject, when he told Grey bluntly that he could only deplore the conduct of our Foreign Office which after nine years had nothing better to show for its labours than *this war*?

What could be more pithy and to the point? Was not the Liberal Government elected by huge majorities pledged to Peace? What mandate did the autocrat of the Foreign Office have to push us into the vortex? Was his 'great' speech more than a tissue of airy platitudes, recriminations, suspicions, trumped-up grievances, later admittedly reduced to unsubstantial differences to be settled round a conference table? And did not Mr Ramsay Macdonald then and there prick the three Grey bubbles—British interests, British honour and the Balance of Power—in tense unanswerable language? 'Your speech,' said Macdonald to Sir Edward, 'will echo in history, but you are wrong. If the country were in danger I would be with you. I am not persuaded. Honour? No such crime is committed without an appeal to honour. It was so with the Crimean War, with the South African War. And what about Russia? Why no mention of Russia?'

Had the House known that within a few months Grey and Poincaré were to sign treaties with the Tsar guaranteeing him

Constantinople, the Straits and other Turkish possessions, there would have been no stampede to battle, no jubilation in the ranks of 'the Jingo party'.

The pact with Russia, signed early in 1915, was published by the Bolsheviks in 1917; but for thirty years it has been ignored so unscrupulously by the popular Press and politicians that Macdonald's stern warning never penetrated to the ear, much less the mind, of the public, and thus, even when Stalin revived the Tsarist claim in 1945, no echo of the 1915 surrender was heard. Suppression of vital truths is one of the greatest triumphs of mass propaganda and on the list of triumphs few can rank above this—the blackout of the betrayal of Stamboul and the Straits to the Great White Tsar.

Allusion has been made to the scanty information gleaned by Grey's opponents from Foreign Office leakages or blunders up to August 1914. By working in the dark he kept them guessing.

The case against him, nevertheless, was strong and in spite of crippling handicaps was strenuously argued by speaker after speaker in speech after speech *from the Liberal benches*—all, with scarcely an exception severely critical of the Foreign Minister's arguments, and actions. On reading these speeches at a distance of forty years, one is struck with the ability and insight of the brave men who, against tremendous odds, attempted in vain to check the avalanche to which Sir Edward that day put his hand. Vivid accounts of the memorable scene were published next day, and richly do they repay a perusal.

'Enter Sir E. Grey,' wrote the *Daily News* correspondent, 'with two red dispatch boxes, well used and worn. Then a cheer—fierce and terrible in its significance—a war cheer for Mr Churchill, welcomed thus by the Tories.' *Fierce and terrible in its significance.* Yes, for although the Tories detested Churchill they had been thoroughly conditioned by the popular Press, captained by Northcliffe, and could be relied upon to vote solidly for the Grey resolution if, as they calculated, it meant war. The opposition, which he was sure to encounter from sincere Liberals, on the other hand, was by cunning tactics half-paralysed in advance. Inside information and reservation of the truth composed the tactics. In such a crisis, knowledge is power and Grey was triumphant because he had the official knowledge to use and abuse.

Thus his theme, expounded in his opening words—'we have consistently worked with a single mind to preserve peace'—could not be refuted or debated as in a true council-chamber where all parties have access to the evidence and the facts. And yet, in the brief hours allotted to his critics, enough of the truth was ventilated to refute every essential contention in favour of 'the Jingo case'. No better way of testing this assertion can be suggested than a re-examination of the Liberal Press, especially the columns of the *Manchester Guardian* and the *Daily News* during that fateful week.

Volumes have been dedicated to the demise of British Liberalism, but rarely has the cause of death been squarely faced. Many ingenious explanations have been offered, and it is sometimes frankly admitted that Grey's war policy killed the Liberal Party. When Grey took the reins from Lansdowne he joined a Cabinet of unusual distinction, elected by an enormous popular majority. His own gifts were commonplace alongside those of the galaxy painted in such glowing colours by men like Gilbert Murray. Apart from his 'patrician' background and pleasant manners, the North Country squire had no special qualifications for high office; nor did he possess the equipment of a Foreign Secretary in the business of diplomacy. He was an amateur, untravelled, insular, unskilled in foreign languages, but in one respect he was fortunate. His tenure of office coincided with the decade in which the Liberal Party succumbed, as he had done himself, to the imperialist *Zeitgeist*. He was a disciple of Rosebery, and outdid him in militancy. Bolstered up by Asquith, Haldane and Harcourt he made of the Foreign Office a one-man show, coached by subordinates of his own choosing who accentuated his worst weakness.

This was the man destined to lead England down the slippery slope in a wanton and senseless conflict. As Mr Edmund Harvey stated in 'a wonderfully impressive, because so just, so calm' speech: 'No people's war,' said he, 'a war of men in high places—bureaucrats.' And Grey was precisely the man, the misfit in a high place, fated to produce a war of the bureaucrats. For if ever the Foreign Office was entrusted to an astute politician and doctrinaire it was during the prelude to Armageddon. He liked to pose as one pining for the serene life of a country gentleman, and yet he took pains to keep a footing in the Cabinet, and seemed to have a certain following on the Liberal benches. His chief talent was a flair for the party game. He was at home in the moral commonplaces of Gladstonian Liberalism, and gave the impression of being an ardent lover of the *Pax Britannica* which he betrayed. In his private life he was impeccable. *Integer vitae scelerisque purus* might have been his epitaph had he not been Foreign Secretary in a restless era. Universally regarded as *capax imperii* had he not ruled.

It is with capacity alone that his critics are concerned. Though he may have been a paragon in all other respects, what matters was his fitness to rule British foreign policy, fitness to shape and administer it. If so, what qualifications for his task, besides the surface attraction noted above, did Grey possess? Did he first and foremost conform to the type of ruler regarded as safe by all thinking men since Plato? As Foreign Secretary did he manifest the philosophic quality that stamps the *statesman*? Was he absolutely veracious, open, sincere and impartial? Was he free from bias in his judgments of sister nations? Did he lean unfairly to one side or the other in the disputes on the Continent and overseas? Was he a big man, or was he shallow and pettifogging in his conduct of affairs? If it be granted that people will never be happy until philosophers are rulers or rulers are philosophers how would Grey stand that test?

In coming to a decision about the statesmanship of Sir Edward it is pertinent to settle what precisely the *Manchester Guardian* and its collaborators were fighting against when (August 4) it called on 'all good citizens to oppose to the utmost the participation of the country in the greatest crime of our time'. Such was the voice of authentic Liberalism. How easy it should have been to listen and rally to the summons! For all that the *Guardian* urged as an alternative to *the greatest crime of our time* was a policy of neutrality.

What could be more statesmanlike than the *Guardian's* article on Monday, August 3?

> Saturday and Sunday were the fateful days of a century. On Saturday, Germany declared war on Russia. Early the next morning her troops invaded Luxemburg and in the course of the day they are alleged to have crossed the French frontier at two points not specified. The war party in England will use these facts to work up feeling against Germany as the aggressor and the violator of international law; but sober Englishmen, while grieving that Germany should have thought fit to take this frightful responsibility, will not let German military opinion of what is best for Germany affect their own judgment of what is best for England. *Germany was not free to choose*; whether war was to come depended not so

much on what she did as on what Russia meant to do. Having convinced herself, and not without cause, that Russia meant war, she conceived that her policy was one for her soldiers to determine on purely military grounds. And they held, it would seem, that as war had to come, it was Germany's duty to take advantage of the initiative that her superior system of organization gave to her. She seems to have begun the fighting, but not, assuredly, with a light heart. Germany's position is graver than it has been since the days of the great Frederic. With the genius and the brilliancy of France on the one flank and the overwhelming numbers of Russia on the other, she felt herself fighting against odds for her very existence. Her only chance, she probably reflected, lay in taking her enemies in detail and in flinging herself on the other before they were fully prepared. It was a desperate calculation but so is her case. From Italy she will get no help and Austria will be hard put to it. Sooner or later she will bear the whole brunt of the war with Russia and France at once. And she was uncertain of the neutrality of England. Therefore she decided to strike the first blow. *We deeply regret it, but we understand.* Nor shall we apply a harsh judgment to what man or nation does for very life's sake.

The case against Grey is truly black when precisely stated. For in reality his worst offence was not that he participated in the European War instead of standing aloof. If we study his conduct of affairs from 1906 to 1914, we are driven to conclude that he did nothing effective to prevent it.

Professor Butterfield has focused attention on the sophistry in which the real problem has been involved.[3] He relates how his teacher, Professor Temperley, in his last historical paper asked the question: 'Was Grey *justified* in steering the country into the War?' and answered 'Yes!' There was, however, the other problem—was he *wise* in so doing? But while he suggested, he never dealt with that knotty problem, although the gravamen of the charge against Grey lies where his Liberal critics in 1914 placed it.

Although a mediocrity, Grey had the presumption, when entering the Cabinet, to stipulate that Campbell-Bannerman should agree to clear the decks for him by entering the House of Lords—and, when frustrated by the Premier, demanded a free hand in foreign policy. After Asquith took over the reins no stipulation was needed. Grey had no fear of his new Leader and along with Haldane and Harcourt formed a quartet who in the foreign field could make decisions and enforce them behind the backs of the Cabinet, the Commons, the Party and the country with complete irresponsibility. Their group had a right wing foreign policy, indistinguishable from that of the Opposition, but as a minority in their own Party they had to dissemble in order to gain their end.

In spite of the overpowering desire to fall into line, the *Manchester Guardian*, when the war was on, and the 'time was passed when the effort to prevent this country launching into the dreadful conflict could be of use,' did its duty fearlessly:

> We place on record our conviction that it would have been possible and that it would have been just and prudent and statesmanlike for England to have remained neutral. We shall record that a mistaken course of foreign policy pursued over ten years, had led us to the terrible conflict in which we are now engaged.

On the previous day the same paper had summed up the situation in equally memorable language:

> The real argument put forward by Sir E. Grey is that of our interests. He declared that our vital interests were bound up with the neutrality of Belgium and he drew a picture of all the neutral states of Northern Europe being absorbed by Germany. The picture does not persuade, because we see no probability of its ever representing the facts, and while Sir E. Grey asserted our vital interest in Belgian neutrality he did not prove it, and with infinite regret we must confess ourselves unconvinced.

Here then we have the Liberal answer in August 1914 to the question mooted by Temperley. Although the Liberal Press was taken by surprise and possessed not a tithe of the authentic documents at the disposal of our contemporary experts there is none of the temporising affected by Temperley and some of his English disciples. The *Manchester Guardian*, the *Daily News* and other organs declared that it would have been *just* and *prudent* and *statesmanlike* for England to have remained neutral. The last ditch efforts of British historians, whether official, partisan, academic or independent, to blur the *Message of the Documents* reflect little credit on their propaganda when set beside the forthright condemnation pronounced by Grey's own Party Press on the course of foreign policy pursued over ten years by their own Minister.

On August 4 again, the *Manchester Guardian*, commenting on the 'great' speech which launched the country into the vortex, displayed a degree of realism and sagacity which under the circumstances is utterly admirable:

Sir E. Grey's speech last night, for all its appearance of candour, was not fair, either to the House of Commons or to the country. It showed that for years he has been keeping back the whole truth and telling just enough to lull into a false sense of security, not enough to enable the country to form a reasoned judgment on the current of our policy. This long course of disloyalty to popular rights is not atoned for by the deathbed confession of last night. It is a mockery to throw on the House of Commons the responsibility of deciding in circumstances of great excitement on a policy that has been maturing for years. . . . A minority did protest, and nobly, against the incompetence and secretiveness in the conduct of our foreign affairs, which now threatens to wreck the moral and material progress of half a century.

The *Manchester Guardian* and the noble minority who protested against Grey's incompetence and secretiveness and his disloyalty to popular rights, deserve the homage and gratitude of the nation as no minority ever did before or since. Is it not strange that this splendid page in the story of British Liberalism has been blotted out, with the connivance of the dwindling but still considerable remnant of those who cling to the name?

It is here that we find the secret of the Liberal débâcle which has tormented a section of our politicians since Labour has reared its head. Sir William Harcourt's gibe, 'We are all Socialists now', recorded the conversion of Liberalism to Radicalism in home affairs. Death duties and Old Age Pensions were important instalments of the Welfare State, and, had the World Wars been averted, the country would have witnessed steady progress in social reform, without the rigours of penal taxation and the crushing load of a debased currency.

During the late War, a Chancellor of the Exchequer boasted: 'We are stoney-broke and I am proud of it,' but two bankruptcies in succession wiped out the possessing classes more effectively than the French Revolution wiped out the French aristocracy. The proletariat could have achieved a higher and more secure standard of living without bleeding the bourgeois white, and the Liberal Party was actually all set for drastic reforms when the Imperialist wing took the turning that led the nation into 'the terrible conflict in which we are now engaged'. In so doing the Liberal Party deserted its principles of limited foreign commitments, the policy of Gladstone, Cobden, Bright and the Manchester School—

frequently rivalling the Tory militarists in ruthlessness. The apostasy of the Liberal Press and Party after the magnificent stand of July and August 1914 has been a story of squalid deterioration. Rosebery, 'the member for the Stock Exchange', paved the way for Grey and his successors at the Foreign Office. They have faithfully hewed to the line, obeying the 'blessed word continuity'. The keynote is the same whether Eden, Ernest Bevin or Churchill is at the helm. *Germany the criminal nation; Germany twice in a generation.* The habit of falsehood, as Morel asserted long since, has become a disease, and the disease is incurable, because there is no Party Press to ventilate rational and methodical criticism. Continuity of foreign policy is laudable when the particular policy is sound, utterly disastrous when the foreign policy is wrong. Grey's policy as enunciated in the 'famous' speech has echoed in history, but, as Macdonald declared, *he was wrong.* Within a week or two the voice of criticism was nearly silenced, and even the Labour leaders were shipped into line, taking on the function of accessories after the crime from the Liberal Epigoni. Free and independent criticism adequately backed by Labour would soon have corrected the habit of falsehood among the men who hold the reins of power among us; but, as the Liberal Press before the apostasy protested, the party leaders, our rulers, were hand in glove with the Money Power, and, the more the Popular Press extended its sway, the more the bureaucrats employed it to accomplish their designs. The example of the Northcliffe Press was followed by other Press barons, whose finances rested on commercial advertising and sport, plus Stock Exchange activities. When one Party establishes an ascendancy or a monopoly, the opposing Party may growl or even secure the appointment of a Commission to report on malpractices. But, as all parties derive the sinews of war from the same commercial advertising and a general pandering to the foibles and vices of the community, the real crux of the mischief could never be named.

The Popular Press, indeed, leagued with the bureaucracy and drawing its inside information from the Foreign Office, forms a chorus of perpetual assent to the policy favoured by the Money Power. To restore free criticism the only remedy is a separation between the two functions performed by a modern newspaper. As an advertising medium each paper earns the revenue which maintains its fabulous circulation, creating the corps of millionaire proprietors who mould public opinion and establish a permanent oligarchy in our midst. The place occupied in this oligarchy by Northcliffe is broadly speaking held by Beaverbrook, whose methods as a propagandist have been described by his former henchman Mr Peter Howard and which apply fairly well to other members of the oligarchy. The net result is the virtual extinction of the freedom of opinion which did, on the whole, redeem the Press of the nineteenth century. As someone remarks, freedom of thought and speech is almost valueless unless it is possible to disseminate fair criticism. It has, therefore, been farcical to speak of freedom of opinion in these islands since the monopoly enjoyed by the oligarchy in the foreign field has been established. And always we must bear in mind that this monopoly has been steadily used to serve moneyed interests, especially those of International Finance and Imperialism.

An inspection of typical editorials printed during the whirlwind fight for neutrality will show that what was for bureaucratic Liberalism its darkest hour was also Liberal journalism's most splendid crusade.

To bring this home to all of us, Liberal, Tory or Socialist, we conclude this survey with an editorial of the *Manchester Guardian* of July 28, 1914, answering an article in the *Times* of July 27. The contention which the *Guardian* refutes is the theory that peace in Europe could best be maintained by 'our identifying ourselves with one side or the other in this dispute'.

'Should there arise in any quarter,' wrote the *Times* of yesterday, 'a desire to test our adhesion to the principles that inform our friendships and that thereby guarantee the balance of power in Europe, we shall be found no less ready and determined to vindicate them with the whole strength of the Empire than we have been found whenever they have been tried in the past.' This is mediation with the sleeves rolled up. It is far more serious, for it seems to mean that if Russia, Germany and France start fighting we must start too. *The whole future of England depends on the suppression of that spirit. It is war to the knife between it and Liberalism. Either it kills us or we kill it.* Why should Germany choose this, of all times in the world, to test what the *Times* calls the principles of our friendship? As though she would not have enough trouble on her hands, with Russia and probably France against her, should it come to war, without testing anything else. And as though the disturbance of the balance of power — the foul idol of our foreign policy, as Bright once called it, that has done incomparably more harm than any worshipped by the heathen—were not likely to come from the other rather than from the side of Germany.

2. THE HISTORIAN AND THE FOUR PRINCIPLES OF POLICY

AFTER THE REVELATIONS given to the world by international scholarship in the thirties, Grey's alleged motives fell into utter disrepute. For a few years, as Professor Butterfield reminds us, real history of a fine quality held the field, but in the stress and strain of the Hitler lunacy we have witnessed a throwback of gigantic proportions. Therefore, not only is it impossible to discuss freely and sanely the events of 1939 to 1959 but the world press and propaganda have conspired to boycott the revelations of the documents relating to the entire pre-Hitler era. There has been a reversion, as Butterfield indicates, to the primitive credulity of 1914–1920. But as he also contends, the historiography of the late twenties is so scientific and authoritative that no serious answer is forthcoming. The legends of the first war period have been analysed and found to be mere propaganda. Admirable digests of the superabundant evidence are accessible in *The Origins of the World War*, by Professor Sidney Bradshaw Fay of Harvard, and in similar volumes by scholars of international fame. They had the impregnable rock of State Papers to build on.

All the more brilliant, then, must appear the earlier vindication of the just cause by the loyal exponents of Liberalism in the darkest hour of British propaganda.

Let us take, as the most memorable example of the post-war revulsion, the invaluable 'Conversation with Lord Grey,' February 14, 1929, when the policy, which on August 4, 1914 plunged England into war, was sifted nearly to rock bottom.[4] The interview granted by the autocrat of the Foreign Office to one of the official editors of the British Documents, Dr G. P. Gooch, dealt with principles of policy, and covered part of the ground reclaimed from the morass of political polemic since 1919. Accepting as authentic the *Message of the Documents* extracted from the archives of the Six Powers, the message which quashed the verdict of Versailles, we note how bit by bit the case presented by Grey crumples up before the cross-questioning of his indulgent critic.

In the opening passages Gooch suggests that Grey followed three, or rather four, principles in shaping his foreign policy.

The First Principle of Policy

There was first and foremost, supremacy at sea, a principle which Grey accepts as his very own, with the proviso that the two-power standard, essential to supremacy, did not embrace the United States. In so doing, of course, Grey discloses that in deciding what constituted a two-power standard he was guided by his estimate of the attitude of the Great Powers. Two keels to one was not a simple mathematical formula, but was a ratio determined by his conception of political friendships or antagonisms. On this point Grey should have been closely questioned.

For he had prefaced his 'Conversation' with a concise statement on the same page, namely, that 'three deep-rooted antagonisms—the Franco-German feud about the Rhine provinces, the Anglo-German dispute about the fleet, the Austro-Russian rivalry in the Near East', rendered it 'impossible to avert the catastrophe in 1914'. In so writing he drew attention to the axiom as he saw it, like myriads of others, that *the Anglo-German strife was about battleships*.

Certainly, apart from the dispute about the fleet, and the trade that follows the flag, no British subject had any imaginable reason to fight Germany. If we are to follow Gooch, no compelling inducement to join an anti-German bloc existed in 1914, except the objection to a strong German navy, and even that ground for belligerence looked trivial after the 10 to 16 ratio was agreed, and the naval conventions with France and Russia doubled our excess in sea power. The stubborn fact, indeed, remains that at no date since 1066 was the supremacy of England at sea menaced by Germany in such a way as to earn the fear or hatred of the island thalassocrats. There was even a sharp reminder that the Tsar was the secular enemy by sea as well as by land, when off the Dogger Bank in 1904 Rojestvensky's fleet appeared to clash with a British squadron: but even then no tremor shook British nerves lest Germany should intervene. Accordingly the Grey-Gooch dogma of 'a deep-rooted antagonism centred in a dispute about the fleet and rendering it impossible to prevent the catastrophe in 1914' is fantastic.

The further suggestion that England was *compelled* to join the Franco-Russian alliance to prevent a possible combine of that bloc with Germany against us is no less fanciful. The enigma therefore stares us in the face—why did Grey come to believe that an imaginary threat, the German invasion bogy, justified him in jockeying England into the false position into which he lured the nation blindfold in August 1914? If he really thought that a Franco-Russian domination of Europe would bolster up England's far-flung Empire, surely his mind was deranged, his intellect, never brilliant, quite obfuscated by passion. It is, in short, to 'the appalling prejudice against Germany with which in December 1905 Sir Edward Grey entered on his eleven years' control of Great Britain's foreign policy'[5] that we must ascribe this atrocious blunder and all that flowed from it.

The intensity of Grey's 'appalling prejudice' is exactly what he and his defenders are obliged to conceal behind a smokescreen of high-sounding professions, and since, apart from his pet aversion, his policy makes no sense, we must not look for rational judgment in his apologetic. Even in this striking interview, each of his four 'principles of policy' should be analysed and judged on their intrinsic merits, not accepted as self-evident postulates. This applies notably to the first principle, the old assumption, namely, that because for some decades after Trafalgar Britannia's boast reflected an actual position at sea, 'this happy breed' had some moral right to rule the waves in the twentieth century.

Here we are confronted with the dogma, established by a thousand agencies in these islands, but accepted nowhere else in the world, the claim that we British have a right through sea power to hegemony. What that claim amounted to in the schools of Ruskin, Rhodes, Rosebery, Kipling and all the jingoes has already been touched upon: in 1929 a less strident note was in fashion. Gooch is content to affirm that England was a satiated Power, and that she welcomed the 'new departure' authorised by Versailles. 'Our period of expansion, which had lasted for three centuries, was at an end. As a fully satisfied Power, possessing a quarter of the earth's surface and population, it was natural that we should welcome what appeared to be a stabilising influence in the life of the world.' In so writing Gooch was aligning himself with Curzon who in 1921 announced: 'To keep what we have obtained, sometimes against our will; not to seize anything else; to reconcile, not defy; to pacify, not to conquer' was, as he read it, 'the lesson of the time'.[6] But even these two mentors missed the moral which to the great community of subject natives and their sympathisers in five continents transcended all other imperatives in our age.

For surely the lesson of the time was not that the limits of expansion had been reached by us and that perforce we must try to freeze our frontiers. A new wind was blowing, carrying the message voiced by the October *Quarterly*, 1943: 'Since quite common men have souls, no increase in material wealth compensates them for any arrangements which may insult their self-respect and impair their freedom.' The Thirteen Colonies had pointed the way when they nailed the banner 'no taxation without representation' to the mast. The Boer Republics followed suit with 'no suzerainty without consent'. Now the game was nearly up. The imperial flags of Europe were soaked with the blood of the ruling races and not merely with the blood of the subject peoples. Treasuries had been emptied to pay for mutual massacres of white men. Bankrupt nations cannot run empires. And most ominous of all was the resurgence of Asia and Africa on the waves of liberty, fraternity and equality.

This meant a revolution which let loose the pent-up energies of vast populations after centuries of repression. The best informed and fittest judges of European exploitation were free to discuss the system and improve on the history evolved by its advocates and defenders. And the best exponents were drawn from the races who have suffered from, not profited by, foreign rule. They have been quoted in these pages, scantily but sufficiently to confirm and extend the findings of previous British and American specialists who have studied the record objectively. So now we may aptly inquire, with their assistance, what broadly speaking were 'the vital interests' on behalf of which the dogma 'supremacy at sea' was asserted, regardless of consequences, by Grey and his colleagues. That these 'vital interests' were the alleged inspiration of the two crusades waged by Britain since 1900 is a truism that cannot be refuted. But it can be dodged by politicians and their supporters. Although Grey was noted in his day for his frank advocacy of the obligation resting on a Foreign Secretary to employ all the resources of power and prestige at his disposal in pushing British commerce, in the spirit of Chamberlain's 'empire is commerce', no attempt was made by Gooch to discover whether he had any sympathy for the view that, if peaceful commerce failed to stand up to foreign competition, resort may be had to war.

Partisan as he was of naval supremacy, did he endorse the monstrous contention of Sir Alfred Mond, one of his most influential supporters, that a million pinpricks inflicted by German commercial travellers constituted the greatest *casus belli* the world had ever seen? Or the similar declaration made after the war by one of its promoters, Mr Bonar Law? On January 2, 1923, he vowed: 'If an earthquake were suddenly to swallow up the whole of Germany, we ought to gain materially, and not to lose, because Germany was a rival—a competitor to a greater extent than she was a customer.' Does not this utterance shed a lurid light on 'the honour and security of the United Kingdom', to safeguard which he urged Asquith to make war when the issue was trembling in the balance on Sunday, August 2, 1914?[7] Did not Bonar Law show his contempt for the just cause by acknowledging, nine years after the crime, that he and the Tory party cared for one thing supremely—the ruin of a trade competitor, with the object of securing our export position?

Are then Asians and Africans mistaken when they charge us and Europe generally with materialism and greed, and of infecting the whole world with the disease?

In the twentieth century the formula 'supremacy at sea' was obsolete. Even the two-power standard which the two men preferred was preposterous. Two keels to one became a mere slogan for the Navy League and degenerated into a pretext for jingoes to vilify a trade rival. This and much else must have been uppermost in the mind of Grey from the day Cambon began his tireless campaign. Having published, as the official policy of the Entente Cordiale, England's decision to support France in all parts of the world, he was certain that if France went to war with Germany the fleets of France and Russia would convert the ratio automatically from two keels to one to more than three to one.

It is certain also that he was satisfied by reports from the Army and Navy Chiefs regarding the essential facts. He was sufficient of a business man and an arithmetician to draw his salary as director of a railway. And since the two-power standard was an affair of sums he could not plead ignorance of the elements. He was one of a group including McKenna, Lloyd George, Haldane, and later Churchill, who month after month had to study charts and tables in the course of their routine duties. The nation was deluged with garbled statistics, and Grey by a stroke of the pen could have put an end to the frenzied controversies about inadequate defences.

Here then was a golden opportunity for Dr Gooch to elicit from Grey his reply to the accusation of the *Manchester Guardian*, which charged him with disloyalty to the nation. The disloyalty was that of keeping back the truth about Anglo-German relations from 1906 to 1914; and the basic truth of those relations was that the dispute about the fleets was a fraud and known to be such by Grey.

The two-power standard, Grey's fetish, was never safer than during the period of panic. Every naval officer from Sir John Fisher down was thoroughly aware that the German navy never for a moment jeopardised that standard.

Not even Dr Gooch was able to excogitate any serious ground for a conflict except the dispute about battleships; and yet in discussing the one decisive factor in that 'dispute' neither Grey nor Gooch ventured to embark on a few figures. To exclude from an argument about supremacy at sea the strengths of the actual rival fleets was absolutely farcical.

These statistics have been condensed in the following Table[8], drawn up to show the expenditure of the Four Great European Naval Powers from 1900 to 1913.

	Britain	Germany	France	Russia
1900	£26,000,000	£13,026,000	£14,918,000	£ 9,410,000
1901	£29,520,000	£14,716,000	£13,774,000	£ 9,886,000
1902	£31,030,000	£12,526,000	£11,943,000	£10,668,000
1903	£31,170,000	£11,482,000	£12,188,000	£12,106,000
1904	£35,476,000	£11,790,000	£11,719,000	£11,998,000
1905	£36,830,000	£14,814,000	£12,640,000	£12,399,000
1906	£33,300,000	£17,148,000	£12,236,000	£11,862,000
1907	£31,434,000	£25,073,000	£12,628,000	£ 9,319,000
1908	£31,141,000	£17,024,000	£13,251,000	£ 9,933,000
1909	£32,188,000	£20,518,000	£13,908,000	£ 9,799,000
1910	£35,807,000	£22,400,000	£14,545,000	£10,188,000
1911	£40,386,000	£22,028,000	£16,755,000	£12,842,000
1912	£42,858,000	£22,957,000	£18,675,000	£18,794,000
1913	£44,365,000	£23,055,000	£18,452,000	£24,245,000
Totals	£481,505,000	£248,757,000	£197,612,000	£173,449,000

The first arresting datum yielded by the above Table is that from 1900 to 1913 Britain spent a total of £481,505,000 on her navy, as against a total of £248,757,000 for Germany. On the average, then, during the fourteen years Britain spent almost twice as much as the Kaiser.

Secondly, in the same period, the French total expenditure amounted to £197,612,000, and the Russian to £173,449,000, thus bringing the total for the Entente up to £852,566,000 as compared with £248,757,000 for Germany. This calculation by itself makes a mock of the Versailles charge that Germany sought to dominate the world.

So far, therefore, as the dispute about battleships was concerned, the rare overtures made by Grey to Tirpitz were contemptible gestures so long as, in fixing a ratio, the pressure exerted by the expanding navies of France and Russia was rigorously excluded from discussion. Tirpitz would have been an imbecile had he accepted a fleet ratio based on the supposition that, if war came, his sole antagonist would be the British member of the Entente. As early as July, 1905, Delcassé—speaking for the French Fleet—stated that: 'The Entente between the two countries and the coalition of their navies, constitute such a formidable machine of naval war that neither Germany nor any other Power would dare to face such an overwhelming force at sea.'[9]

To quote in answer, the preamble to the Fleet Law of 1900 which professed to aim at a German navy of such strength that, even for the most powerful naval adversary, a war would involve such risks as to make that Power's own supremacy doubtful—to quote that preamble as evidence of a German plot against England's fleets is utterly nonsensical. In September, 1911, for example, Fisher knew quite certainly that 'the Germans are in a blue funk of the British Navy' and about the same date wrote to Esher that there was not the least likelihood of war because 'England was far too strong'.[10]

In short, on Grey's part there were never any genuine *negotiations*. In the few parleys which he authorised he held all the trumps and could afford to talk peace with an air of bland goodwill while coldly brushing aside three-quarters of the relevant German case. Actually when the Kaiser in perfectly good taste drew Lord Tweedmouth's attention, in a private letter, to the strategic position of Germany at sea, Downing Street connived at the storm in the press as though an attempt had been made to sabotage England's defences in the North Sea.

Never was the supremacy at sea endangered by the Kaiser's navy during those fateful years. It would have strengthened Liberalism in the country if the salient facts had been made public and if the furious dispute about battleships had been exposed officially as a scandalous ramp. Nothing could have been easier, for example, than to inform the country regarding the work done by Sir John Fisher at the Admiralty during the Grey régime.

It was he who counted, as Von Tirpitz and the Kaiser realised. His appointment was announced on October 21, 1904, but previous to becoming First Sea Lord he was intimate with Lord Esher (a very influential member of the Committee of Imperial Defence) and Balfour, the Prime Minister. Thus Lansdowne's Entente with France played into his hands; and soon he drew up his grand plan on the Nelson model, except that the intended prey was not the might of Denmark's crown but the young German navy. His plan, naturally, though concealed from the Cabinet and the British people was no secret in Berlin. In London too, behind the scenes, there was no reserve. In a letter to Esher, dated October 7, 1907, Fisher was quite outspoken:

> In regard to the 'Invasion Bogey' about which I am now writing to you, how curious it is that from the German Emperor downwards their hearts were stricken with fear that *we* were going to attack *them*. . . . Here is an interview between Beit and the German Emperor given me at first hand immediately on Beit's return from Berlin.
>
> Beit: 'Your Majesty is very greatly mistaken in supposing that any feeling exists in England for war with Germany. I know both Mr Balfour and Sir Henry Campbell-Bannerman are absolutely averse to any such action. I know this of my own personal knowledge'.
>
> The Emperor: 'Yes, yes, but it doesn't matter if either of them is Prime Minister or what party is in power. *Fisher remains!* That is the vital fact!'[11]

That the Kaiser judged correctly is only too evident. The soothing syrup supplied by Asquith and his ministers had no more value than Beit's assurance regarding Balfour. They could lull the suspicions of the British public but not of the Germans. There were too many ominous facts and threats covering the whole period. Lloyd George summed these up in his *War Memoirs*:

> Throughout the whole period of the shipbuilding competition between Germany and ourselves for the past ten years [1904–13],

we had always forced the pace by increasing the size of the ships, the weight of the guns, and the speed of our vessels, beginning this fatal competition with the laying down of the first Dreadnought in 1904.[12]

This statement by Lloyd George cannot be repeated too often and for extra measure it may be recalled that in February, 1914, Grey himself, after explaining that British naval expenditure was 'a great factor in the naval expenditure of Europe', had the effrontery to allege that 'the forces that are making for that increase are really beyond our control. I will admit that we had some responsibility in building the first Dreadnought. No doubt we are open to the criticism that we set the example.'[13]

The pose should be noted, particularly the suggestion of impotent sorrow over the increases in naval expenditure, which his party and he were pledged to reduce, and the absence of malice prepense. Although his record at every turn in the advance to war belied his professions, he succeeded in bluffing his critics, assisted, of course, by their will to believe *him*.

The Jingo Press applauded every provocation offered to Berlin, and bragged about their motto 'Germany on the Brain'. Never a hint was dropped by the Northcliffe Press that the advice given by the Admiralty to the nation to 'sleep quietly in their beds' was authentic and wise. The people remained in the dark all through: and when in 1919 Fisher's revelations were published only a small minority even of the Liberals took them to heart. Nor were the Socialists much more alert. The country at large never shook off the fatuous belief that the Kaiser's fleet was as great a menace as the fleets of Philip II or Bonaparte had ever been.

When Balfour, then, spoke to Ambassador White, the emissary of Elihu Root, in 1907, of our being fools not to find a reason for declaring war on Germany before she built too many vessels and took away our trade, he meant merchant vessels, not battleships. But that *reason* could not be advanced in public nor defended before the world: so that he concentrated on 'men of war' as the provocation. The panic set agoing by Mulliner was quite to his liking; and he had no scruple about heading the agitation when the *Navy League Annual* was protesting that it was 'one of the most pretentious pieces of parliamentary humbug ever practised on the electors'. The mendacity was too much for Fisher likewise, and he protested vigorously in a letter to the King:

> Now this is the truth: England has seven 'Dreadnoughts' and three 'Dreadnought' battle-cruisers—total ten 'Dreadnoughts' built and building, while Germany in March last (1907) had not begun even one 'Dreadnought'. It is doubtful if, even as late as May last, a German 'Dreadnought' had been commenced.[14]

Had a whisper of this reached the public in 1907 instead of 1919 it is easy to calculate the effect on Anglo-German relations. Not even Balfour could have stood up to such an exposure. Instead, there were the usual party recriminations and Fisher was driven to console himself with the reflection:

> I humbly confess I am neither a diplomatist nor a politician. The former are senile, the latter are liars.[15]

Blunt aspersions of lying are frowned upon in political controversy, and seldom are circulated unless the accused is a foreigner. All the more necessary is it to give due weight, in discussing the Anglo-German 'dispute', to the official utterance of the First Sea Lord, the man who since October 1904 created and ruled the British Navy—and could size up the dishonesty of his political bosses. In the home field the savage laws of libel acted as a damper on candid realists, but there was no curb on the libellous inventors of offences charged to Germans from the Kaiser down. Their invasion bogy was a fraud based on a phantom, an invasion scare cooked up to aid them in fomenting the fear and hate required to send the nation mad and generate the complex 'Germany on the Brain' which, in this full-dress interview, the two men in England best equipped for the task vainly tried to present as rational. What Grey sought, in formulating this first principle of policy, was to show that the Kaiser's fleet was such as to 'render war inevitable', without disclosing what the relative strengths of all the big navies concerned actually and potentially were. Nor is what follows less remarkable.

The Second Principle of Policy

Having disposed of the first principle of policy—supremacy at sea, or two keels to one—the two experts next addressed themselves to the second principle, defined as 'opposition to any power which established a hegemony in Europe'.

The false assumption that Germany established a hegemony in Europe at any time between 1871 and 1914 offered an excellent text for a really fruitful 'conversation'. No one knew better than

70

Dr Gooch that Germany had never been sufficiently united to wield any hegemony previous to 1871 and that, while the defeat of France brought relief from invasion for a few years, that immunity was guaranteed by nothing so securely as by the 'strong right arm of Bismarck'. Accepting further, as we must, his analysis of the situation under Wilhelm II—the three deep-rooted antagonisms, Franco-German, Austro-Russian and Anglo-German—as causes of an inevitable war, we are obliged to conclude that the function of a pacific Foreign Secretary pledged to Peace, Retrenchment and Reform, was to deter the Austro-German alliance and the Russo-French from a resort to arms. That meant in the first place a balancing of strengths guided by the most reliable official estimates then accessible to the Committee of Imperial Defence.

Grey and Gooch had agreed that the compelling reason for England's joining the aggressors in 1914 was the dispute about battleships, but abstained from thrashing out the merits of that dispute, giving a wide berth to mathematical ratios. For one thing both were Liberals and for twenty years as party men were alive to the determined effort of their Tory antagonists to brand them as Little Englanders. The entire stock-in-trade of the Tory propaganda, apart from Tariff Reform (which chimed in with the Rhodes gospel), had been the German menace, and every nerve had been strained to distort the picture by false statistics, such as those denounced by Fisher. The harm done to Liberalism by the diatribes of Balfour, Northcliffe and Bonar Law who spread the fear of German invasion should have prompted Grey to stamp out the lies: in which event the bogy of a Germany hegemony would have vanished into thin air.

If Grey had been swamped with statistics from the Army and Navy to the effect that the British, French and Russian armies and fleets were relatively weak instead of overwhelmingly strong, his bugbear of German hegemony would have been explicable. Either Grey was profoundly deceitful on this vital issue or he was the dullest of men. Good Liberals in 1912–14 considered him to be 'the worst Foreign Secretary England ever had'. Gooch, aware of these views, doubtless felt that to delve into the substrata of his friend's mind would be a delicate task. Hence his neglect of a golden opportunity to learn from his own lips why Sir Edward had stultified himself for nine years by barking up what he knew to be the wrong tree.

71

That Dr Gooch refrained from touching on this tender topic is all the more peculiar since, long before 1929, the literature on the subject was superabundant and scientific. Further as editor, along with Professor Temperley, of the *British Documents* he could not have overlooked several of those confidential minutes which, in spite of the severest censorship, stray into archives and when released disclose secret motives and intentions.

Of these illuminating documents he could have selected, for instance, the amazing dispatch which records the assurance given to Poincaré, as the war-clouds thickened, that, if ever Germany attacked Russia, 'people in Great Britain would be inclined to say that, though Germany might have successes at first, Russia's resources were so great that, in the long run, Germany would be exhausted without our helping Russia'.[16] Under Grey the Foreign Office was obsessed with the belief that Russia was the Power which England should cultivate, because she possessed resources far greater than any other nation in Europe.

This sentiment grew more confident towards 1914. The Permanent Under-Secretary, Nicolson, noted a dispatch of July 18, 1914 which stated that, 'by the end of 1916 Russia would possess an active army greater in numbers than the joint forces of the Triple Alliance Powers' and that 'the Russian Navy estimates now exceed the British ones'. A reason for Nicolson's 'hope that our relations with her will continue to be friendly'.[16] Evidently Sir Arthur's warm feeling for Nicholas II had not cooled since he was recalled from Petersburg to London, a feeling reinforced by awe, inspired by the gigantic military resources of the Romanoff. What more natural, then, when the Tsar was desperately keen to be certain of Grey's support, than that Nicolson should stiffen Grey by a reminder of the danger of losing the goodwill of the All-Highest through lack of zeal in the Russian cause. The reminder, however, was superfluous. Nicolson's chief had long since grasped Nicolson's argument. As early as 1908, he calculated that: 'Ten years hence a combination of Britain, Russia and France may be able to dominate Near Eastern policy'[18] : and at the same time, 1908, Sir John Fisher, confident of English supremacy, exhorted the Tsar to expand his huge armies, not his fleets. That was when the British spokesman informed Russian officials that the British welcomed such an increase in Muscovite land and sea forces that 'in seven or eight years Russia would be arbiter of the situation'.[19]

At this point a cynic might reflect on the agelong apprehension endured by British statesmen who had watched the Russian aggressor pushing out from the Steppes, east, south and west and, since the check at Port Arthur and Tshushima in 1904–5, driving through the Balkans towards the Bosphorus. After 1912, when the rise of Serbia lopped off nearly a half of Austria's military strength, Petrograd was more than ever convinced that the road to Constantinople lay through Berlin and in March 1915 cashed in on the Entente bargain by forcing Grey and Poincaré to yield up Stamboul and much else to the Tsar. What Grey denied to Isvolsky in 1908 he signed away in 1915, simply because he preferred to give the Hohenzollern a fall, regardless of the glaring breach of his second principle of policy—opposition to any power that established a hegemony in Europe!

That the Treaty of March 1915 should have been sprung on the world by Lenin in 1917 only to be consigned to oblivion in Britain is a triumph of suppression worth noting. The only newspaper to publish the Treaty was the *Manchester Guardian*. Little wonder that secret diplomacy still rules in Britain and the public has to listen to the drivelling tale of German War Guilt in 1914!

Yet, as we have seen, Grey came very near to a full confession in this same interview, when he informed Gooch: 'I agree that neither the Kaiser nor Bethmann nor Jagow wanted war.'[20] This unqualified admission indeed is the weightiest utterance of Grey's career. It demolishes with an unceremonious kick the edifice of lies foisted on Europe by the Versailles Dictate, an edifice resting on the blatant thesis that *the Kaiser did want war*, prepared for it and pushed Austria into it.

The addendum, moreover, supplied by Grey sheds a precious light on his own mentality. In a naive afterthought it occurred to Grey to wonder why, seeing these men did not want war, they allowed themselves to be drawn into a conflict they sought to avert. In Grey's opinion the Kaiser simply 'blundered' when he stood by his ally in the hour of need. Gooch, however, pointed out that the German Government was genuinely afraid of losing their only dependable ally, and dared not press Berchtold too far.

'But why should they be afraid of Austria? What could she do?' Such was the argument advanced by Sir Edward.

Why, nothing of course! Anyone could see that. Left to the tender mercies of the Bear and Serbia, Austria would have been a mangled corpse within a few months, unable to *do* anything. But, after all, the Kaiser and Francis Joseph were allies, and so Gooch had to remind his friend: 'Germany was convinced that the Alliance was at stake and she dreaded isolation.' A poor enough answer, since the question was not, what could Francis Joseph *do*?—but what would the Kaiser *be* if he deserted and stood by while Cossacks wreaked their spite on Vienna?

Surely English morale touched near bottom in 1929 when neither speaker had the courage to admit that Germany was in honour bound, apart from interest, to defend Austria. For only fifteen years had passed since, in his epoch-making oration, Grey had agonisingly pleaded both honour and interest as his grounds for joining the aggressors; conscious too that his own honour, not the honour of Britain, was involved. If ever a British Minister, therefore, stood naked in the Court of Clio, it was Lord Grey when he tore off the rags of 'the free hand' and 'no commitments' imposture—the legend of 'the Kaiser's war'—and suggested that the *principle* of opposition to the hegemony of any power in Europe *justified* his attack on a Kaiser whose dire offence consisted of a refusal to throw honour and interest to the winds.

It has not escaped notice, finally, that Grey's notion that the Kaiser, poor man, was not astute enough to perceive that he could *quite safely* leave his venerable ally in the lurch is perfectly in line with one of the most pitiful arguments in his 'great' speech of August 3; to the effect that, if England stood aloof in the impending struggle, Russia and France would in due season exact a dreadful vengeance. It did not occur to him then to ask what in the event of a draw or a defeat, Russia and France would *do* to an England with fleets and armies intact. Had he dropped a strong hint that, in his considered opinion, Russia and France without British help could defeat Germany, and that his ambition was to be in at the death on the winning side, the Liberal majority in the House would have hesitated to endorse the *ultimatum* which he had in view.

The Third Principle of Policy

On his third principle of policy, friendship with France, Grey should have been treated to another searching examination. Dr Gooch was not concerned with the rare commodity, Francophilia, based on a taste for French culture, but with the political calculations of a Foreign Secretary who publicly declared that he supported France in all parts of the world. There is no evidence that he loved French literature, society, music, painting, learning or science, or that he preferred the Bois and the Riviera to Fallodon; but he felt the sympathy, which some English professed, for the victim of the third Napoleon's bellicosity in 1870. His father's violent preference for the French cause could easily have been transmitted to any intelligent boy between nine and twelve years of age; and what his father failed to impart, his grandfather, Sir George, in the following eight years, being *in loco parentis*, handed down. These were the years when politically minded families were mostly warm partisans, like the Cecils, of German unity, while the pro-French section made up for their small numbers by the intensity of their prejudice. It would have been strange if the Fallodon atmosphere left the youthful heir at twenty impartial in politics, domestic or foreign, and the attempt to ward off the charge of bias in the Alsace-Lorraine controversy by alleging Edward's indifference merely deepens the mystery of his anti-German complex. His own claim that in 1892, when he took a junior place in the Foreign Office, aged thirty, he was unprejudiced,[21] if tenable, only makes his conduct more freakish, unless he could demonstrate, from that moment on, that German diplomacy was so wicked as to provoke his righteous hate.

As to this, how far his French leanings were determined by his inherited and acquired 'dislike' of Germany is a crucial problem for his biographers but will not be settled by a recital of his professions: reliance must be placed on his admissions, as the *Manchester Guardian* perceived when it stigmatized the 'great' speech of August 3 as Grey's death-bed confession. Next to the admissions, chief of which occurred in this 'Conversation', come the speeches, dispatches and memoirs sifted and appraised by various schools of researchers who have rescued this 'notable' man from the obscurity of the myth.

The Fourth Principle of Policy

In the endeavour to smooth the path for Grey his questioner hinted at *a fourth principle*. 'You also took over from Lansdowne the policy of a rapprochement with Russia,' said Gooch, introducing, as both were aware, a very delicate theme.[22] For the Triple Entente was always alluded to with bated breath. An Entente

Cordiale with Tsarist Russia, the land of pogroms, corruption, reaction, aggression and autocracy was anathema in the free West and could not command warm support in Liberal Britain. It was a serious matter that Lansdowne inaugurated a settlement of differences, a détente with France, allied with Russia, and promising limited and temporary diplomatic co-operation: much more was it a grave risk to convert the détente into an Entente. Especially dangerous for Grey was the implication reposing in the tie with Russia, the aggressor nation.

It was an article of faith in all sections of the British public that the most brittle stretch of the imperial frontiers, running all the way from the Straits to the Yellow Sea, was at the mercy of the Tsars. The latent antagonism produced along that vast front by the clash of two giant empires grew more and not less intense during the nineteenth century and the anti-Russian role which our rulers had to accept in the Balkans, at Stamboul, in Armenia, the Caucasus, Persia, Afghanistan, Tibet and Northern China was nerve-racking. Every Prime Minister in turn was desperately anxious to come to terms with the Colossus and endless pacts were framed to that end in the Balkans, in Turkey and not least in the arena of the Persian Gulf. But nothing fatal was concocted so long as our rulers adhered to the doctrine of independence, neutrality and non-intervention. More than ever was it essential to stick to the policy of the free hand, the well-tried gospel of splendid isolation, based on the conviction that the European Powers had overcome the principal difficulties inherent in the evolution from medieval empires into independent nations and that, in the Concert of Europe, Britain could best serve the highest of British interests, peace, by helping to preserve the genuine balance of power at a crisis. Friendship was right and proper but partnership was another thing, and safety depended on the wisdom of the British ruler who judged, from time to time, from what power or group of powers the aggression came. It was the distinction of Grey that he made the plunge that Palmerston, Gladstone, Salisbury avoided; the change which, under his aegis, converted the Foreign Office into a branch of the Franco-Russian combine controlled by Paris and Petersburg was made by none other, with the collaboration of Asquith and his Liberal Imperialist group. The outcome of that change was the forty years of turmoil and devastation that followed.

Speculation is rife regarding the meaning of the whole catastrophe. Mr Arnold Toynbee airily views it as a phase of universal history, as a chapter in the long story of *The World and the West*. The two Wars and the aftermaths certainly reflect no credit on the white races who mauled themselves in the struggle: and the global significance of it is fascinating. But unless a commentator bases his reflections on the best available historiography his conclusions can never be very illuminating. The average Englishman wants to know firstly whether the civil wars in Europe were inevitable, and secondly whether the better cause triumphed. It is here that Mr Toynbee is less adequate than some other critics. And we would cite as more useful the Cambridge Professor of Modern History. Professor Butterfield is not merely highly regarded in Britain, he is considered by good judges in America as exceptionally learned and sound. What then is his line?

For him the urgent question is: was the Grey policy in 1914 wise?

In thus probing the sore spot from which Temperley shied away, Professor Butterfield renders valuable service, in so far as he implies that there is a broad issue which has been pushed into the background by the monstrous horrors of the sequel. In a deeper sense than that contemplated by Temperley, the statesmanship of Grey, denounced by Macdonald and the best part of Liberalism in 1914, may obviously be held unjustifiable, and the least Temperley should have done was to justify his own verdict by proving that Grey's action was not only narrowly defensible but *wise*. The glaring fact that Grey was *wrong* is too stubborn and clamant to be upset by a forensic defence that excludes the paramount obligation which exacts from ministers wise counsel and wise direction.

Temperley was mistaken in condoning the Grey policy in 1906–14. It is only the aura of 'nobility' surrounding the figure of Grey that dims the vision of historians who decry the far abler, sounder and nobler figure of his splendid opponent E. D. Morel. Once the conventional bias is overcome it becomes obvious that Grey was actually such as Morel painted, namely a man who betrayed his trust and launched his country into a war to uphold the worser cause. It is ludicrous to contend that intervention was *justifiable* and still more preposterous to contend that it was *wise*. What we behold today is the fruit of eight years of the Grey diplomacy, and no sane man can applaud *that*.

Worse still, there is strong reason to believe that without the compliance of Grey the 'conspiracy against the peace of Europe' would have been nipped in the bud. In effect, certainly Sazanov was emboldened by Grey's attitude and fortified in his determination to make war on the Central Empires in defence of Serbia. Had his resolution not been stiffened by the attitude of Grey and his friends who can say that he would have gone ahead with mobilisation? No war is inevitable apart from the voluntary action of the aggressor and to the last Nicholas II was irresolute; Grey stated that Russia was like a great vessel without a rudder.[23] No sane man wants war in general, but no actual particular war was ever started unless some minister or autocrat sanctioned it. And the men who wanted the European War in 1914 were not the Kaiser, Bethmann and Jagow. Unless this is admitted nothing worth while can be said regarding the greatest calamity in history and the authors of it.

The verdict against Grey remains. His war policy in 1914 was neither justifiable nor wise.

Chapter Four

THE FUNDAMENTAL ISSUE

A FEW MONTHS before the Second World War began, a group of Scottish Churchmen, in a statement issued to the Press, sounded an urgent warning against the Fake Peace Front, which, because it was built on armaments first and on conciliation last, was bound to lead to disaster. 'The worst feature of the situation,' they declared, 'is that attention has been distracted from the fundamental issue—is the *status quo* which Germany and Italy have been seeking by force to change, and we similarly to maintain, just or unjust?'

The warning went unheeded, but the challenge persists, more arresting than ever: 'Less and less is heard of justice: more and more the discredited fallacy that peace can be attained through a balance or preponderance of power masquerades as a well-established truth. But peace with justice is the only peace there is. Anything else is either armistice or enslavement. Until this issue is seriously faced there is no prospect of peace at all.'

It was the *status quo* dictated at Versailles, a Dictate based in form and substance on the notoriously false allegation voiced by Article 231, and rendered possible *de facto* by dishonouring the Armistice Convention on the strength of which Germany laid down her arms, that the Allies refused to redress between 1919 and 1939. And it was because for twenty years they traded on the advantage gained over the enemy that no progress was made towards peace.

Logically it was inevitable that the *de facto* winning side should attempt to pose as *de jure* autocrats, absolute right over the vanquished being established by vehement charges of moral culpability. Tactically could anything be simpler for the victors than to advance their own moral supremacy as a ground for any preconceived wrong they might inflict? To justify the premeditated Carthaginian Peace, they had only to brand Germany as *the aggressor*. How easy it looked!

For in the war of words the Entente had enjoyed a walk-over.

German propaganda had been nearly blacked out, while the Allies romped ahead. The enormity of the crime imputed to Germany made her name a hissing and a reproach. Ever since the 'nineties in fact, when the Trade Panic raged, and British patriots adopted the slogan *Down with Germany!*, war, 'the sin against God and man,' had been tirelessly castigated in the Press, in the Pulpit and on every platform in Christendom. All that was needed now was, in 1919, to convict Germany of responsibility without reserve or qualification.

What a score it would be if the Allied and Associated Powers were to place on record their unanimous condemnation of the Central Empires! And what a triumph if they could induce the Germans to sign the declaration which registered the Allied accusation, and thus convert the unilateral scrap of paper into an authentic diplomatic document ratified by *both* contracting parties!

Yet when it came the triumph was utterly unreal and empty.

For, after all, the business of the Paris Conference was to draw up a Treaty, or in other words an International Contract. The 'Peace of Righteousness' had to be embodied in a document whose terms to be valid had to be *negotiated*. Only so could a Peace Treaty yielding a genuine Contract between Germany and the Allies come into existence. The negotiations, moreover, in this case had to be conducted, if legal and moral at all, 'within a framework': the terms had to conform to the conditions, twenty-three of them, laid down in the pre-Armistice Convention. These constituted a Contract whose nature, as Keynes pointed out in 1919 was *plain and unequivocal*. 'The terms of the peace are to be in accordance with the addresses of the President, and the purpose of the Peace Conference *is to discuss the details of their application.*'[1]

For, as Keynes further insisted: 'The enemy had not surrendered unconditionally, but on agreed terms as to the general character of the Peace.'[2] From which it follows that the vital, the basic pre-condition of the Armistice and its sequel was the Allied pledge to obey the twenty-three conditions underwritten by both sides. That pledge was the governing Contract by which the Allies were inexorably bound as soon as the Armistice was concluded and the Germans laid down their arms. The Contract embodied in the Armistice Terms was a thing apart. *It* was fulfilled, executed and done with as soon as Foch received the German surrender, and its fulfilment in no way exonerated the Allies from the obligations accepted by them in the exchange of documents that preceded the

Armistice. Its fulfilment by Germany, indeed, riveted the obligations more firmly than before round the necks of the Allies.

Nothing could be more explicit than the language of Keynes on this point:

> The circumstances of the Contract were of an unusually solemn and binding character; for one of the conditions of it was that Germany should agree to Armistice Terms which were to be such as would leave her helpless. Germany having rendered herself helpless in reliance on the Contract, *the honour of the Allies was peculiarly involved in fulfilling their part*, and if there were ambiguities, in not using their position to take advantage of them.[3]

How little the Allies heeded the admonition of Keynes and other men of honour is no secret. Not merely did they flout the peculiar obligation of honour incumbent on them; they cast to the winds all the canons and scruples of European statecraft. Their Dictate was a deliberate offence against the civilised code, rendered grotesque by their transparent insincerity, so revolting to Keynes. For not only did they condemn Germany unheard; they indicated and condemned whole peoples unheard and *in absentia*. A verdict of Guilty was recorded even before the Peace Conference met, with the result that none of its proceedings, however masked, could hide its true character. In essence the policy adopted was precisely that pilloried by Plato in his famous castigation of Thrasymachus. Furthermore, if it was a crime, in harmony with the truculent Sophist to confound justice with *the interest of the stronger*, interpreted as the defaming and pillaging of the temporarily defenceless and weak, it was a hideous blunder to trumpet abroad as their excuse the nefarious dogma that the momentary interest of the stronger had *of necessity* to be paramount, and therefore the legality and the morality of a flagitious Dictate must never be examined in the interest of truth and justice. In the German Government's Note of November 29, 1918, the accused proposed to their accusers that a neutral commission be set up to examine the question of responsibility for the War; only to receive a categorical refusal from England on March 7, 1919, to the effect that 'Germany's responsibility for the War was incontestably established a long time ago', and that no answer was necessary.

Nevertheless, it had been decided on January 25, 1919, by a plenary session of the Preliminary Peace Conference to set up a Commission of Fifteen to settle that very question; and on March

29 the report was submitted officially to the Conference. In it the Commission found in Chapter One that the Central Powers had deliberately planned the War and had intentionally made it unavoidable.

To make the position adopted by the Commissioners of the Allies precise and indisputable, it is helpful to repeat the preface to the indictment proper. So eager were they to leave no shadow of a doubt regarding their intention that they abandoned every pretence of giving the vanquished a square deal. As the Germans observed, they forgot that *even the Devil is entitled to a hearing*. The Kaiser was down and had only to be kicked, until he could be hanged. And so at the outset they registered their predetermined judgment:

> On the question of the responsibility of the authors of the war, the Commission having examined a number of official documents relating to the origin of the World War, and to the violations of neutrality and of frontiers which accompanied its inception, has determined that the responsibility for it lies wholly upon the Powers which declared war in pursuance of a policy of aggression, the concealment of which gives to the origin of this war the character of a dark conspiracy against the peace of Europe. This responsibility rests first on Germany and Austria.

And so the impeachment staggers along until it reaches the Covering Note appended to the Ultimatum, of which we give a choice extract:

> The conduct of Germany is almost unexampled in human history. The terrible responsibility which lies at her doors can be seen in the fact that not less than seven million dead lie buried in Europe, while more than twenty million others carry upon them the evidence of wounds and sufferings, because Germany saw fit to gratify her lust for tyranny by resort to war.
>
> The Allied and Associated Powers believe that they will be false to those who have given their all to save the freedom of the world if they consent to treat this war on any other basis than as a crime against humanity and right.

From these pompous and savage pronouncements then, it follows that, in discussing war-guilt in 1914 and after, we are forbidden by the Allied and Associated Powers to inject into the argument any plea of extenuation on either side. With impeccable correctness the Allies take their stand on *whole responsibility on the one side and on the other side none* as the predetermined issue. They grasp the undefined principle of aggression tenaciously and apply it rigorously to the Central Powers. In a quarrel there must be an aggressor, and both sides cannot be arraigned where, as in the World War, 'the responsibility for it lies wholly upon the Powers which declared war in pursuance of a policy of aggression'. Either Germany and Austria or the Allies must be the *authors* of the war, the *conspirators*, the *aggressors*. The alternatives are watertight. In logic the Fifteen Commissioners had found the perfect disjunctive. If the Germans and Austrians are guilty, the Allies are *es ipso* guiltless. Conversely, with equal certainty and finality, if the Germans and Austrians are innocent the Allies are guilty; they are the authors of the war, the aggressors, the conspirators. Such is the governing idea of the Dictate. Such is the theory, the ethic and the logic and the practice of the victors. Accordingly they wasted no time on divided guilt: there could be no sharing of the 'crime against humanity and right'. And if, in fastening that crime on Germany 'first' they have been proved to blaspheme against truth and justice, we have a measure of the 'terrible responsibility that lies at the doors' of the Fifteen and their Allied and Associated Governments. That responsibility is no less terrible because their thesis had been discredited long before 1919. Yet nothing daunted, they registered their platitudes and inventions until they created a morass of mendacity, such that after thirty years of floundering in its slime the pollution of Europe has become a world-wide scandal and reproach.

Such is the judgment on which the Peace Treaty was based; and it is precisely that finding which is repeated in the Introduction to the Treaty and in Article 231. It is repeated moreover in the Ultimatum of June 16, 1919, and in Part I of the Note covering this Ultimatum. These particulars are given here in order to correct the common impression that war-guilt was charged in Article 231 and nowhere else, an impression that played into the hands of the defenders of the Treaty, those 'subtlest of sophisters' and 'most hypocritical draftsmen'[4] who tried to argue later on that the Germans themselves had as early as November 1918 admitted war-guilt, as a ground for exacting from Germany 'compensation for all damage done to the civilian population of the Allies and their property by the aggression of Germany by land, by sea, and from the air'.[5]

Colour was given to this argument by the word *aggression* used in this Lansing Note of November 5, 1918 and skilfully abused by Clemenceau to excuse his brusque rejection of Brockdorff-Rentzau's Note claiming exemption from the authority of Article 231 in settling reparations. If the *military operations* described loosely as *aggression* in the Lansing Note, handed to Germany in November 1918, were admitted by desperate Germans as a reasonable ground for indemnifying the sufferers, that was no reason for saddling them with the very different admission that Germany had caused the War.

What this charge of war-guilt means has been already discussed; but to remove any trace of dubiety we add the interpretation of Article 231 furnished in the authoritative history of the Peace Conference:

> This article asserts the responsibility of Germany and her Allies for causing all the loss and damage suffered by her enemies as the result of the War. This responsibility is a moral and not a financial responsibility. The clause means simply that Germany caused the War.[6]

Finally it interprets the Treaty, as regards finance and reparation, as asserting among others these two theses:

> I. Germany accepts the moral responsibility for having caused all damage suffered as a consequence of the War.
> II. The Treaty specifies what portion of this damage is to become a financial liability of Germany.[7]

Accordingly we may take it that the only basis for reparation demands alleged by the Allies before the Treaty was signed and ever after was simply Germany's moral responsibility for bringing the War about.

In so much, therefore, as the Germans have always repudiated the charge—and rightly as the evidence shows—no subtle sophistry can justify Clemenceau's stretching of the *aggression* sentence in the Lansing Note of November 5 to imply the German acceptance of *responsibility*. And with this collapses the 'most hypocritical draftsman's' attempt to argue that Germany at the conclusion of the Armistice had confessed her war-guilt.

In the German *Professors' Memorandum* drawn up by a Committee of Four, the position was made absolutely definite and again a request for a neutral Inquiry was submitted as a reply to the blunt rejection of Brockdorff-Rentzau's Note. To this last appeal the Allies responded with the Ultimatum of June 16, 1919, which was clinched by the covering Note mentioned above.

Thus did the corps of 'hypocritical draftsmen' flayed by Maynard Keynes crown their labours. And how rapidly Keynes was vindicated the whole world should know. He had his fore-runners, his collaborators and his successors, but in one respect he is unique. He was not only the most brilliant economist at the Conference but he was the only important official who *resigned* as a protest against the iniquity which many knew to be wrong. His masterly indictment, though for practical purposes boycotted by the Control, grows more impressive with the passing of the years and is sufficient of itself to blast the laurels of the Conference. The men who allowed him to resign were glad, when faced by their own financial wreckage, to give him a peerage and send him to Washington to plead their cause. But the hush-hush technique has nearly blacked out his arraignment and the British people have no popular mentors to keep his memory green.

Apparently his endowment was unique among the bureaucrats who acted for Britain at Versailles. It took a man of rare courage as well as superlative talent to grasp the criminal folly of the leaders and their entourage at Versailles and brand it as such instantly; a display of genius and honesty all the more astonishing because in 1919 he harboured the common delusions of sole or substantial German war-guilt. What he would have said had he been familiar with the full evidence on that head is not difficult to imagine. All we *know* is what by sheer insight and natural humanism he accomplished. He was big enough to rise above his load of purely 'British preoccupations' and dedicate himself to the one thing needful—'the assertion of truth, the unveiling of illusion, the dissipation of hate, the enlargement and instruction of men's hearts and minds' as the only means of coping with the 'fearful convulsions of a dying civilization'.[8] That such a man had to resign is an eloquent commentary on the Paris 'nightmare'.

The evidence was there, plenty of it, to show that there were other aspirants to the distinction of bringing on the War who had incontestable claims. At the moment it is enough to recall that Isvolski avowed himself to be 'the only begetter'. *C'est ma guerre*, he bragged, early on, when it looked as though Germany must be crushed like an egg. Poincaré likewise had strong claims. Any

85

Treaty founded *de jure* on a colossal war-guilt lie was bound in the end to be a broken reed. So, in their inmost thoughts must the Big Three have sensed. Wilson's consuming desire to provide machinery for remedying glaring injustices proves that he was ill at ease; but his 'Presbyterian conscience' smote him less painfully as the mephitic vapours of the Conference got him down. As soon as he arrived, indeed, 'the word was issued to the witches of all Paris:

> Fair is foul, and foul is fair,
> Hover through the fog and filthy air.'

The subtlest sophisters and most hypocritical draftsmen were set to work and produced many ingenious exercises which might have deceived for more than an hour a cleverer man than the President.' Thus, with the scene fresh in his mind wrote the keenest observer of them all.[9]

There is reason to believe, moreover, that Mr Lloyd George was never convinced that Germany was the villain of the piece. The day came when he could ease his conscience by confessing that all the ministers—which points markedly to Grey and himself—might be held guilty of manslaughter.[10] Lord Lothian similarly, ex-secretary of Lloyd George, would never have taken his well-known stand during the Hitler crisis, March 1938, had he not been aware that the charge of sole responsibility was a fraud.[11]

And let it be remembered always that it was the bedraggled colours of Germany's unique and exclusive war-guilt that the Allies nailed to the mast and have never hauled down. Nothing less could serve their purpose. That is why for instance, shortly after Versailles, one of the prime movers, Poincaré, reiterated the charge as an ineffable verity:

> Indeed, if the Central Powers did not start the War, why should they be condemned to pay the damages? *If responsibility is divided, then, as a matter of necessity and justice*, the costs must also be divided!

What Poincaré thus scornfully dismissed in *Le Temps*, December 27, 1920, Lloyd George as Prime Minister and spokesman for the Allies equally scouted at the London Conference, the following March. In peremptory fashion he rebuked the German delegates

for their temerity in 'renewing their request for a neutral investigation of responsibility for the War' and so endangering the beloved
Peace of Righteousness and all its works.

> For the Allies, German responsibility for the war is fundamental.
> It is the basis upon which the structure of the Treaty has been
> erected, and if that acknowledgment is repudiated or abandoned
> the Treaty is destroyed. . . .We wish, therefore, once and for all to
> make it quite clear that German responsibility for the War must be
> treated by the Allies as a *chose jugée*.

On March 21 of the same year the American Government, and
on August 31, 1924, the French Government, solemnly returned
the same reply to the dissatisfied Germans, officially identifying
themselves with the 'ruling made by Lloyd George, in the name
of the Allies on March 3, 1921'. All this and vastly more to the
same effect, in order to bolster up a Dictate widely denounced in
America as 'a Treaty that violated every promise' and was bound
'to perpetuate hatred for generations to come'.

Thirty years on, this feverish itching to let sleeping dogs lie is
thoroughly understandable. The argument has gone badly for the
Big Three. Lloyd George could bludgeon the German delegates
at the London Conference in 1921 and could solemnly pronounce
undivided German responsibility a closed question. But he could
not hinder Professor Sidney Fay of Harvard from supporting
the Germans in his classic work, *The Origins of the World War*, and
proclaiming *urbi et orbi*: 'The verdict of the Versailles Treaty that
Germany and her Allies were responsible for the War, in view of
the evidence now available, is historically unsound.'[12]

Nor could the 'closed question' dogmatism hinder Fay's able
volumes from launching not merely American 'revisionism' but
stimulating the world-wide revulsion of which numerous leading
public men even in Britain are witness. Notable among their
judgments is the summing-up of Lord Lothian on March 24,
1938, in his striking address before the Royal Institute of International Affairs, in the course of which he declared: 'I am not
going to argue the war-guilt case here and now, except to express
my own conviction, having read a great many books about the
origins of the War, that *the doctrine of the sole guilt will not hold
water at all*.'

Truly this from the inmost *penetralia* of the House of Lloyd
George bodes ill for the untouchable 'basis upon which the structure

of the Treaty has been erected!' But such pronouncements are only a foretaste of what was in the wind. The chorus of war-guilt repudiation, in tune with which Lothian was delivering his considered opinion, is not hard to imagine.

It is useless to pretend that the wrongs inflicted on the Germans and Austrians from 1914 can be annulled or atoned for by withdrawing the monstrous indictment of the Dictate and substituting a modified charge sheet. The indictment and verdict were translated 'all savage and tartarly' into act and deed, and paraded as the Peace of Righteousness. They have never been bilaterally discussed or debated, never deplored nor disowned. Let us never forget moreover that war-guilt is no matter of theory or dialectic. German war-guilt is the groundwork of the European order created and enforced by the Allied Powers in 1919, the *fons et origo malorum* from 1914 to 1954 and decades to come.

To imagine, therefore, that a few words of regret can wipe away the stain is obviously futile. The clash between their thesis and the Documents is a head-on collision on a track which they laid down rigid and immutable. The message of the Documents wrecked their indictment as completely as events have wrecked the European and world order based on it.

We can lead off, by quoting, as a safe exponent of the reformed history of World War I Dr G. P. Gooch, co-editor with Professor Harold Temperley of the *British Documents on the Origins of the War*. Perhaps the most erudite of native scholars in the field of modern British diplomacy, he has been the official scrutineer of our archives as well. As 'source material' for our purpose nothing could be more relevant than his two works, *Recent Revelations of European Diplomacy* and *Studies in Diplomacy and Statecraft*, the former reaching its fourth edition in 1940, the latter first published in 1942.

His conclusion, of course, could not possibly be new; and yet he is fresh and comprehensive. He is also definite and positive, if cautious and guarded. 'If the documents are studied as a whole,' he writes, 'their message is clear enough.' The Kautsky volumes 'disproved the legend that the directors of German policy deliberately unleashed a general war'.[13]

Such is the unvarnished reply of the leading British official expert to the *lie* denounced in 1918 by Professor Delbrueck. Explicitly and bluntly in the very first page of his *Recent Revelations* Dr Gooch exonerates the directors of German policy from the global and damning crime saddled upon them by the Versailles 'Peace Treaty'. Nor need we be astonished.

To have fathered any other conclusion would have made Dr Gooch a laughing-stock in the world of scholars to which he owes his standing and prestige. How could he have stultified himself by saying less? In 1929 had not he learned from the lips of Grey himself that 'it was a very bad mistake to attribute the whole responsibility for the War to the Central Powers in the Treaty of Versailles?' Had not Dr Gooch also informed his readers that in the same interview Grey 'agreed that neither the Kaiser nor Bethmann nor Jagow wanted war?'[14]

Having found the Versailles verdict 'historically unsound', Fay, the American scholar, had the courage to add: 'It should therefore be revised';[15] whereas, the Englishman shied away from the practical resolve to redress a proved wrong. Instead of ramming home the moral of the reformed history he executed a movement to the rear and contented himself with a transparent diversion.

'The Kautsky volumes,' he declares, 'led us to substitute one indictment for another.' And what is the *Ersatz* indictment? 'They proved William II and Bethmann to have been short-sighted blunderers,'[16] states Dr Gooch, yet if German diplomacy was short-sighted and blundering, Entente diplomacy was nothing to brag about, God wot!

Indeed, if diplomacy is to be tested by its long term results what are the blunders of the men who were defeated, in comparison with those of the group who nominally won the game? We must judge by results, and what are they? There can be only one answer: a gigantic work of ruin without which there would have been no Second World War, and no Third. For the world as it is has been shaped by their decisions.

If we want a sample, observe what happened in Germany in 1953. On February 19 of that year it was widely reported in the Press how, on his first visit to Berlin, scene of the 'Potsdam Guzzle' of 1945, the American High Commissioner for Germany, Dr Conant, delivered himself of a stirring address. Berlin, he declared, was the 'home of brave men and women who continue the traditions of European culture in the face of the attempts of the Soviets to enforce a new type of alien culture and to fasten a tyranny upon free people. . . The United States is pledged to do its part to see to it that this city continues as an unshaken outpost of the Western

World. . . Everyone in the United States knows that here the two contending forces of this mid-Twentieth Century stand face to face. . . The refugees who are daily crossing from the East Zone to the West provide tragic evidence of what all Germany would expect if it were unified on Soviet terms.'

This utterance, for all its bland air, is too obviously a piece of Allied propaganda to mislead any but a simpleton. Dr Conant's hearers are well aware that the short-sighted blunders of Allied 'statesmen' persisted in for forty years, have converted the 'home of the brave men and women who continue the tradition of European culture' into a slum and a cemetery: is it conceivable that an American High Commissioner is unaware that among the top-ranking agents of destruction are two of his own Presidents? Can he erase from his memory Wilson's Fourteen Points? Does he seriously contend that the honour of his country remained un-sullied when eighteen of the twenty-three conditions on which Wilson induced the German armies to surrender in November 1918 were violated by the Big Three in 1919, *with his consent?* As regards Roosevelt and his frightful folly of Unconditional Surrender, not to mention Clare Luce's denunciation *he lied us into the War*, no American can blot these from the record. For twenty years Dr Conant was President of Harvard and had ample leisure to digest the contents of the epoch-making volumes on *The Origins of the World War* published by the Harvard Professor of History several years before Dr Conant entered on the Presidency. The work, as the Dean of American historians observed, is indispens-able. 'Whoever else is read Mr Fay must be read. And it would contribute powerfully to the understanding and peace of the world if all editors, politicians, preachers and teachers were required to read him before opening their mouths on the present state of Europe's tangled affairs.' The refugees who are daily crossing from the East Zone are 'tragic evidence' of the Anglo-American policy of dismemberment and that what all Germany would expect if it were unified on Soviet terms can hardly be more detestable than what the sponsors of Unconditional Surrender intend. For it is not merely what the Occupying Powers in the West Zone intend to do in the near future, when German cannon fodder or at least neutrality is so easily sought, but what they plan for the Fatherland in the days to come that counts. And it is the dread that Russia and Germany may bury the hatchet that strikes a chill into the hearts of the three Western masters. May not Soviet terms be adjusted to suit both sides in the not distant future as they were in the not distant past?

Let us glance at the problem as the Russians saw it as recently as 1939. On October 31, 1939, 'Germany', said Molotov, 'is in the position of a State which is striving for the earliest termination of war and for peace, while Britain and France, which but yesterday were declaiming against aggression, are in favour of continuing the war and are opposed to the conclusion of peace.' Today, we observe, Molotov can point to Unconditional Surrender as a confirmation of his accusation; and he goes on to assert: 'We have always held that a strong Germany is an indispensable condition for durable peace in Europe.' On August 1, 1940, he followed this up by stating: 'We can only reiterate that in our opinion the good neighbourly and friendly relations between the Soviet Union and Germany are not based on fortuitous considerations of a transient nature, but *on the fundamental interests of both the U.S.S.R. and Germany.*'[17]

Three months later Molotov had an opportunity to give effect to this old idea—that German and Russian interests need not clash. The Molotov-Hitler meetings in Berlin early in November 1940 were easily the most important conferences of the Second War and the most dangerous. The critical issue was *mirabile dictu* the same as that which faced Sir Edward Grey in 1908 and again in 1915. What Tsar Nicholas demanded in 1908—Constantinople —and was denied, he again demanded in 1915 and received. Had Lenin not intervened, nothing could have prevented Nicholas from grasping the prize on whose account he mobilised on July 30, 1914. This was the crux of the whole war in 1915 as in 1940 and, if Hitler had consented, as Grey had done, to hand over the Straits to Russia, Stalin's knife, as Mr Ernest Bevin phrased it, would have been at the throat of the Empire. The threat in 1943 was a sharp reminder of the eternal threat to the 'jugular vein' at the Suez.

Had Hitler been a German instead of an Austrian he would have come to terms with Molotov and demonstrated once and for all the inherent workability of a Russo-German settlement on rational lines. Russia, once dug in between the Bosphorus and the Dardanelles, would instantly make the Mediterranean untenable for enemy navies and would automatically become mistress of the Levant, with a stranglehold on Egypt, Mespot and Persia that no grouping of Western Powers could break.

Hitler's gamble in November 1940 sealed his fate; but the underlying community of interests between a reviving Germany and a powerful Russia remains. As a leading expert on Near Eastern problems has expressed it, the German need to reach an understanding is vastly more urgent than it has ever been before:

> Germany will never accept the loss of her eastern territories. But it provides her with a demand upon Poland which Russia—not Poland—can grant when the time comes to establish a *modus vivendi* between Germany and Russia. It provides Russia with a powerful means of achieving an association with Germany and of preventing any association between Germany and western Europe, indeed of sustaining permanent German hostility in the West. *The principal claim which Germany will make, and must make, some day—the claim to her Eastern territories—cannot be met by the Western Powers . . . but can be met, with one stroke of the pen, by Russia alone.*[18]

Since Mr Voigt made this declaration in *The Nineteenth Century and After*, September 1945, nothing has transpired to lessen its weight. Year after year since Mr Churchill went to Fulton and served notice on the Kremlin that the Western Powers repented of the blundering policy they followed between 1933 and 1939, and that they confessed that Germany must be won back, to serve as the front line of defence against Russia, the fear of a Russo-German *modus vivendi* has been the underlying obsession of Anglo-American power politics. The obsession is never openly avowed or ventilated in the Popular Press, and there is a tacit conspiracy to ignore any stray article in a monthly journal which reveals the genuine moving force in modern diplomacy. Thus the entire official and 'orthodox' propaganda effort has to be based on a set of hollow pretences. Nothing that really matters can be plainly and truly presented to the British public on a nation-wide scale. For if the average citizen were permitted to see clearly that both World Wars, as Mr Churchill said of the Second at Fulton, could have been prevented 'without firing a gun or losing a man', he would also perceive clearly that the main responsibility rests on his own leaders, including their collaborators in Parliament and the Press; whereupon there would be a speedy end of warmongering 'at the highest levels'. The public would begin really to understand the tremendous publicity given to the twin 'outposts of Western Culture', Berlin and Vienna, and would identify at length the real architects of the catastrophe which has converted a peaceful and prosperous Central Europe into a quagmire and a shambles.

Now that Marshal Stalin has gone to his account, the Russo-German identity of interests becomes more than ever crucial. Ideologically the gulf between Red Russia and each of the many-hued 'democracies', Germany, France, Italy, even Spain and Britain, tends to shrink and Molotov's assertion of a natural community of material interests between Russia and Germany in particular is incontrovertible. The vast reserves of oil and so forth waiting to be tapped by Russia, with German participation, in the Near and Middle East are simply a prodigious lure, and call for precisely that co-operation which the neo-scientific era invites. A gigantic programme of development in Asia, even if it were sponsored by Russia, China, India, with a friendly Germany on the Western Flank assisting and sharing, would leave abundant room for the Western nations in the Americas, Africa, Polynesia and the Pacific.

The maritime nations of Europe had their three centuries of monopolistic imperialism and the day of reckoning is at hand. Competitive expansionism led to the quarrels over the spoils which culminated in the massacres of our generation. The devastation and carnage wrought by European politicians in two Civil Wars of unprecedented ferocity demand a drastic remedy. As Col. Miksche puts it, unconditional surrender must be replaced by unconditional peace; and whether the Powers like it or not, history and geography have decreed that by a stroke of the pen Russia *can* grant what every German demands as a right and covets more than anything else on earth—the independence and unity of the Fatherland within the old frontiers. In return Germany has only to resume the policy laid down by Bismarck, recognising that the *ignis fatuus* of the *Drang nach Osten* was never worth the bones of a single Pomeranian grenadier, and that the wise course is to accept the 'historic mission' of Holy or Unholy Russia as ripe for fulfilment. Did not England and France bestow on Tsarist Russia the right to annex Constantinople and much besides in 1915? If by such a concession these countries sanctioned the age-long ambition of all the Russias to possess the prize of the Golden Horn (and with it the command of the Straits) celebrated in the Jingo verses, why should any other European nation object? In 1912 to 1914 it was certainly an axiom of Russian policy that the road to Constantinople ran through Berlin, and it was no other conviction that nerved Nicholas to let loose the dogs of war, when the opportunity to destroy the military and economic power of Germany presented itself after Sarajevo.

Consequently Western policy will have to recognise that only by going into reverse in true American style can we escape from the hideous trap contrived by our incompetent rulers since 1904. The men of the Kremlin are free to choose. They may now adopt the plan sketched by our foremost military scientist, the plan whose cardinal feature and objective is the annihilation of England. Neither in Russia nor in Germany can there be any scruple about adopting that objective if war comes. Now that Stalin has gone to join Hitler and Roosevelt we can only guess feebly as to the likely decisions of their successors. We can be certain, however, that there will be no world rising to divert the atomic blitz from the English target. Has not Lin-Yutang promised that China will in due season fight England for Hong Kong?[19] The liquidation of England would not be regretted in Persia nor in Egypt; and already India shows signs of gravitating from the British to the American orbit; so that there are very substantial reasons for condemning the ruling groups who according to the *Manchester Guardian* of August 1914 were plotting to drag England into the Continental conflict. It was no easy achievement to stampede the nation, for the majority detested the bare idea of aggrandising Tsarist Russia, and many good men and true foresaw the disastrous outcome of Grey's manoeuvres.

Chapter Five

THE SECOND CARDINAL TRAGEDY
CHURCHILL

ON MAY 2, 1945 the remnants of the German garrison of about 250,000 men surrendered Berlin to Stalin's armies. Vienna had fallen on April 11, and now the Russian triumph was complete. The Red Tsar had accomplished what the Great White Tsar had tried to do in 1914–17, only to perish by the bullets of Red avengers in the cellar at Ekaterinburg. To that extent the glorified victory over Hitler was a ghastly Anglo-American tragedy, as Churchill duly noted in the title of his final volume.

In due season the Allies were to learn that the triumph was for all but Stalin a mockery and that the only reality for them was the hideous tragedy which thinking men had foreseen, some since 1914 and others since Versailles. The loss of the two Western outposts to the Eastern swarms was the sequel to the Dictate of 1919. Certainly before Berlin fell it was sensed by Churchill if not by Roosevelt that the genuine menace was the Red Tsar, as the notorious Montgomery telegram made plain and the challenge at Fulton, Missouri demonstrated shortly after. Not, however, till 1946 did the Western politicians shed their delusions. But after the prime mover began to lament how we were 'roaming around and peering on the rim of hell' it dawned upon our supermen that the day of reckoning could not be staved off for ever by tags of rhetoric.

Cautiously, therefore, in *The Gathering Storm*, 1948, Sir Winston proclaimed, as though it were something hidden from the profane, that 'the second cardinal tragedy was the complete break-up of the Austro-Hungarian Empire by the Treaties of St. Germain and Trianon'.[1] Apparently he at last woke up to a truth which had been the veriest commonplace of European politics for more than a century—that 'if Austria did not exist she would have to be invented'. As a life-long student of the great Corsican, indeed, he should have known that on October 17, 1805, Napoleon himself had been warned by Talleyrand that the Austrian Monarchy, though enfeebled by its ill-assorted groupings of many races within its framework, was 'an adequate bulwark against the barbarians and a necessary one. In the future the Habsburg Empire will stand with its back towards Europe and its front to the East, thus protecting Western civilization from the aggression of Russia.'[2]

It took Churchill's successor, Eden, some years to ponder the hint in *The Gathering Storm*; but it duly regurgitated on October 6, 1950 in the sapient assurance that 'the collapse of the Austro-Hungarian Empire was a calamity for peace'.[3]

Nobody would guess from Eden's version that his fellow-travellers were at all responsible for the *collapse*. Not a hint that the onslaught on Austria in 1914 was the first lethal blow at 'the adequate bulwark against the barbarians' cherished by Talleyrand-Napoleon in 1805. If British Foreign Secretaries and Premiers are to be excused for ignoring, from stupidity or neglect, the 'cardinal' maxim of European statecraft, propounded in 1805 by Napoleon's adviser and in 1848 endorsed by the 'Father of the Czech nation', Palacky, author of the celebrated aphorism quoted above, one must be left in a state of stupefaction where no more surprise is possible.

For surely an English minister who presumes to attack a political institution vital to the prosperity of Europe should first have learnt something of that institution's function and history. In this case the two ministers who, more than any other politicians, shaped the national policy in reference to Central Europe since 1906, wallowed in the grossest ignorance of everything German, Churchill boasting that he hated even 'the beastly language,' and Grey content to remain an expert in fly-fishing while he fuddled disastrously in *la haute politique*.

When the 1914 crisis arrived, with the Sarajevo murders, Grey professed to be detached, and averred that Austria was entitled to satisfaction; but took care to notify Nicholas II that the British Navy was *mobilised* precisely when (July 24) Russia was taking the decision to back the regicides of Belgrade against England's venerable friend, Francis Joseph. When Churchill ordered the Fleet movements corresponding to the Russian preparatory measures for mobilisation, did he never reflect that he was conspiring, without Cabinet authority, to destroy the only Power that could or would try to save the Austro-Hungarian Empire from Russian aggression, the aggression envisaged in 1805 by Talleyrand?

This matter of ministerial nescience, or wilful blindness, really is of cardinal importance. Grey and Churchill, virgin as they were of higher European culture, which, at its best, 'patriots' reviled as *Kultur*, might be permitted to ride off scot free when charged with ignorance of Continental statecraft, and its high lights in 1805 and 1848. But is it pardonable that neither of the two men who presumed to destroy the ancient Habsburg Monarch had sufficient conscience to examine fairly the one question that mattered? That question of course was:—Who was in the right, Francis Joseph or Nicholas II? What did each stand for? What did the Romanoff aim at and by what means? What did the Habsburg defend?

As we have seen, Talleyrand and Palacky had long ago furnished the answer, and that maxim had been accepted decade after decade until it became not merely a truism but one of the most vital maxims of European statesmanship. The gist of it was proverbial in the pithy dictum pronounced by Palacky, the Czech historian; and its significance was familiar to every tourist who tramped the pavements of The Ring in Vienna, Baedeker's *Austria* in hand, with the motto *Bella gerant alii, tu, Felix Austria, nubes*, a reminder of the relatively peaceful process by which the Habsburgs had built up their Empire.

The stresses to which the Danubian State was subject were proverbial; the Emperor was old and by some was derided as 'The Sick man of Europe', and the vultures were gathering; but the Crown Prince was alive to the dangers and was equipped with a remedy, a remedy in harmony with the most modern Liberal ideology, prefiguring in fact the solution that beckoned to Churchill and Eden in their wishful thinking after 1945. How was it that Grey's collaborators and successors required the lesson of two World Wars and the Cold War to teach them what in 1914 was as familiar to the intelligentsia of Europe as the multiplication table?

Recently the spade work in this arena of controversy has been tackled in earnest. Thanks to the ability and courage of a Czech military historian we at length possess in English a reliable picture of the 'dissolution' of the Danubian Monarchy, lamented by Churchill, Eden and the rest, sufficiently worked out to show how the 'calamity' was engineered.

Colonel F. O. Miksche, in an effort to penetrate the mystery, has examined this phase of the Great Betrayal of 1914 in his penetrating studies of the Danubian federation. The result is illuminating.

He has collected weighty evidence, in the first place, to prove that round 1900 the Habsburg Empire filled its historic role not only with incalculable advantage to Western Europe, but with much satisfaction to the mass of its subjects, *the Czech community included.*

The proof of this internal and domestic success was actually ventilated by Talleyrand's biographer, Duff Cooper, who incontinently upset the current mythology by reporting in the *Daily Telegraph* Jan Masaryk's admission at his table in the British Embassy at Paris that the Czechs had never been so happy as they were under the Habsburgs. This was, as Duff Cooper noted, a tragic confession for the son of Thomas Masaryk to make; more tragic, of course, because, as a consequence of the father's sin, the son was already marked down for a violent death, and saw it coming. And so nemesis took care that the Masaryk family paid the penalty, as did the Romanoffs.

The task for the historian set by the Entente destroyers was facilitated by the astonishing success of the chief mischief-maker Thomas Masaryk. It so happened that this sinister intriguer, who represented a small minority of Czechs, and a still smaller section of his Slovak fellow-countrymen, conceived a consuming hatred of the Habsburgs and devoted himself heart and soul to their overthrow. That a Slovak schoolmaster, a second-rate humanist and a narrow fanatic in politics, was able to exert a strong influence at Versailles is a biting commentary on the capacity of the Triumvirs and their advisers. For Masaryk, when he applied for his permit to leave Austria early in the crisis, on a pledge to return, which he shamelessly violated, had no standing as a delegate. His pose as a representative Czech may be readily appraised from the disclosure of Colonel Miksche[4]—he was a member of the Vienna Parliament, indeed, one of a group of 107 Czech representatives; but, being the one and only Czech Progressive, was in a minority of 1 to 106. The largest contingent was Agrarians 29, next Socialists 23, then Young Czechs 20, Catholics 17, Radicals 10, Conservatives 7 and Czech Progressive 1. The lone wolf, whose slogan was 'smash Austria,' was acutely distressed during his crusade by perpetual reminders that he had no following at home, that the Czech leaders in Austria were sharply opposed to his propaganda and that in 1917 all Czech parties declared themselves loyal to the Habsburg Monarchy. 'Yet the disavowals,' wrote Masaryk, 'were soon forgotten.' The Russian Revolution (October 1917) and the entry of the United States into the war filled men's minds. Since, moreover, his anti-Habsburg jehad appeared to be a thundering success in 1920, when he returned to Prague as the Father of his Country, he took no care to conceal his mania. 'The refrain of my propaganda,' he boasted, 'was *Break up Austria*.' And the amplifiers provided by Allied machinery transformed Masaryk's utterances into the patriotic cries of an oppressed people struggling to be free. Miksche observes that Lloyd George was sufficiently taken in by the arch-agitator to assert that the Czechs were so oppressed by Vienna that the only occupation open to them was coal-mining! Not till 1928, however, did he openly complain at the Guildhall, October 17, that documents produced by Masaryk at the Peace Conference were falsified and that decisions were made on the strength of these falsehoods.

It was not ever thus with Masaryk the Habsburg-baiter. As late as April 14, 1900, in a party programme he announced:

> We believe that the former sovereign independence of our Bohemian Lands is impossible to-day. Our small numbers, our geographical situation, and the fact that the Czech countries are also inhabited by Germans, have compelled us to unite with other nations and lands.

Similarly, in 1908, Masaryk's collaborator Benes declared:

> People have often spoken of a dismemberment of Austria. I do not believe in it at all. The historical and political bonds between the different nations of the Empire are too powerful to make such dismemberment possible.

The *volte-face* of these politicians should be better known; it was so sudden and so complete. In his first approach to the British Foreign Office on April 15, 1915, Masaryk registered his clean break with his past:

> Now Bohemia wishes and hopes that her Russian brethren will soon succeed in occupying the Bohemian and Slovak districts. . . . They must, however, on no account enter Bohemia except to stay.

As Miksche observes, Masaryk expressed a wish that has been granted! But the governing idea is puzzling, for in 1915 an ardent democrat like Masaryk could hardly welcome a Tsarist occupation in place of the easy régime of the Habsburgs.

We can better understand Benes. In 1946 he not only nailed his new colours to the mast: he announced that surreptitiously he had been for four-and-twenty years sailing under false colours:

> We never changed our ideas or our plans, we never participated in any political combination directed against the Soviet Union. We worked methodically. Our endeavours to maintain this 'Eastern' and 'Slav' line were conscious and premeditated; they were based on a new conception of Europe's future.[5]

In 1946, therefore, we behold Benes bestowing his blessing on the Russian occupation *de facto* which in 1915 Masaryk desired to bring about *soon* and for keeps. The two men, that is to say, not merely *schemed* to plant an artificial, brutal Czech minority yoke on the necks of Germans, Slovaks, Hungarians, Ukrainians and Poles (6·5 m, ruling over 7·1 m, subjects) but aimed, the former since 1922, the latter since 1915, at a permanent Russian hegemony to guarantee Czech supremacy. Stalin's legions in 1945 accordingly effected what Masaryk recommended to the British Foreign Office in 1915 and, even if in 1955 they did evacuate Austria, they still stand guard a few leagues from Vienna. Shades of Talleyrand, Napoleon, Palacky, how have their worst fears been realised! And to make the triumph of Stalin more electrifying, Miksche sounds a warning that the relaxation of the Communist régime in the Soviet Union will bring no change in Russian policy towards her neighbours.[6] If and when the Socialist State, which Lenin and Stalin strove to develop through a Communist phase, is an accomplished fact the pressure of the three-fifths of the world's population on the White Front in Asia and Africa may easily become irresistible.

The stakes are, of course, the petroliferous and other deposits of precious raw materials in the Asian Fertile Crescent; the privilege of exploiting these vast stores of natural resources is perhaps the most coveted thing on earth. And the rejection by the Bandung Conference, April 1955, of Colonialism in any form was an omen which points to a recrudescence on a semi-global scale of the Cold War in the not distant future. More grim, however, for Western Europe is the appalling prospect of turmoil opened up by the suggestion that any reconstruction of the Danubian Federal System on Habsburg lines presupposes the homecoming of the Sudeteans. It links up with Mr F. A. Voigt's reminder that Germany will never rest till her Eastern frontier, Dantzig and all, is restored.

When the gulf between Berlin and Moscow is narrowed down, and the *modus vivendi* championed by Molotov in 1941 is adopted by Russia and a revived Germany, the full extent of the 'calamity' detected by Eden in 1950 will be impossible to conceal any longer from the man in the street. The 'Ministers of our Age' will then be relegated to their true position in history. And that position will not be exalted.

The pronouncements of Churchill, Eden, Duff Cooper, Jan Masaryk, belated as they are, must be taken as high lights in the murky propaganda which conditioned the Entente countries, namely Tsarist Russia, Chauvinist France and Imperialist Britain, for the road to ruin. The five men in Britain singled out as the culprits by the protagonist of peace round 1914, E. D. Morel, who vanquished Churchill and drove him from Dundee in 1922 thus clinching his moral victory over the war-makers, were Grey, Churchill, Asquith, Balfour and Lloyd George. It was thanks to their misguided defaming of Germany that the public were infected with the gospel of a wicked Germany led by a fiendish Kaiser, solely responsible for the World War. These were the men who poisoned the wells, declared Morel, and engineered the treasonable conspiracy against England and Europe which bred the whole sequence of disasters from 1914 onwards. The *Manchester Guardian* at the beginning of August 1914 dissected the plot and branded the 'great speech' of Grey on August 3 which propelled England into the maelstrom as his 'deathbed confession', bringing to a focus the tortuous proceedings of nine years autocracy at the Foreign Office. Never before had any minister been so untrammelled and so consistent in concocting a national blunder, hingeing at every turn on a personal mania which perverted high policy in Whitehall to the point of imbecility as the whole world can see, now that it trembles and grovels on the verge of the abyss.

When the Grey clique crowned *The Great Betrayal*, exposed by the Liberal Press in 1914, with the Carthaginian Peace of 1919 they not merely wrecked the Austro-Hungarian Empire but left a vacuum to the North where for 1500 years, as Professor Butterfield pointed out, the German nation held the marches against the Eastern hordes, despite the frequent stabs in the back dealt them by their Gallic neighbours. To uncover the Western fringe and centre of Europe to the Tsarist swarms was the crime of crimes, execrated long before Talleyrand. To clarify that crime is the

101

business of history, and already the spade-work has been done. The second triumph of Revisionism, when the fever and the fret have subsided, is assured; the true story of the fall of the Habsburg Empire is part of the achievement. Thanks to Colonel Miksche and his collaborators the authors of the calamity which overtook the 51 million inhabitants of the Danube Valley have been verified. The evil they uncovered—for which Churchill, Eden, Duff Cooper, Masaryk and Benes were largely responsible—spoke for itself. The men who rode so high at the Potsdam Guzzle in 1945 were already baffled by their own misdeeds and within ten years were at their wits' end.

What has happened since 1945 is that the scholarly verdict of the twenties has been confirmed by the aftermath of *two* World Wars. If the origins of the interminable Armageddon are illuminating, equally illuminating is the 'situation measureless, and laden with doom' which has resulted from the carnage. That situation, etched in by Churchill, can further be elucidated now that Austria has tried to patch up a *modus vivendi*, and in so doing has called attention to Eden's 'calamity for peace'. For at length the implications have forced themselves on the world.

For half-a-century the people of Britain have been fed on poisonous propaganda designed to carry out and justify an atrocious plan, sponsored in the nineties during the Trade Panic by politicians and industrialists, of whom the most influential was Sir Alfred Mond. Elsewhere this crusade has been more fully discussed, and the literature of the subject is enormous. But the authentic expression of that plan is the official indictment of Austria and especially of Germany printed in the Peace Treaty of 1919. The abysmal stupidity of their actions, persisted in ever since 1904 and 1905, when the Great Betrayal began to take shape with the clandestine military and political commitments disguised as Staff Talks, Conversations, Conventions or Understandings, which tied England to France and Russia, must be the theme of European historiography for generations. Already the moral delinquency of the oligarchy is a byword, and is rendered more detestable with every fresh device invented to shield the real enemy in our midst.

Jan Masaryk's deathbed confession, mentioned above, is infinitely more than the repentant avowal of a personal or family blunder or sin. It is a text from which the historian is conducted right into the mystery of mysteries, the enigma of the 'dark conspiracy' against Europe imputed to the rulers of Austria and Germany. What is truly mysterious is the conduct of England's rulers, not the behaviour of the Russians and the French. There is nothing enigmatic about *their* objectives. To anyone seeking for objectives and motives that can be defended as rational and wise the over-riding purpose of the Grey minority in the Cabinet is the enigma. Even if it were conceded that Grey, Asquith, Haldane and Churchill were animated by a loyal desire to promote British material *interests* these were never respectable enough to be acknowledged, still less widely advertised as the *casus belli* by the ministers concerned. That would have ruined in advance the 'slickest ever ethical conjuring-trick' palmed off on the British public at Versailles, where the defamation of Germany reached its climax.

On the other hand the *ethical* pose of the crafty Three who cooked up the witches' brew at Versailles deceived nobody except those who wished to be duped by the grand propaganda stunt. Plato wrote, as we know, to prove that a calculation of material interest is always at the bottom of discord and war. In both World Wars multitudes were stunned by ideological appeals, invented to obscure these squalid calculations and glorify the fiendish ecstasies of mechanical murder. Were not masses of peaceful citizens duped into believing that they were in duty bound to slay their fellow men for democracy, for freedom, for small nations, for a superior way of life, for religion, for honour, for prestige, for anything but the all-embracing national interest?

And yet is it not obvious that all these impulses and objectives are secondary and unessential? The doubter has only to ask what the response to a call to arms would be if each citizen were invited to fight in order to injure the *vital interests* of the *patria*, to learn where we stand. To make the point clear it is only necessary to analyse the last of these 'idealised' objectives to see how fraudulent they are. Let us examine the magic spell cast over diplomacy by the pompous pretensions of *prestige*.

Is not the very word steeped in trickery? It comes into English from Latin through French and reeks of jugglery and deception. That is why it is a catchword of the diplomats. In ordinary usage it connotes distinction based on integrity of character, genius, high achievement; in diplomacy it signifies the distinction conferred by

103

power and its *alter ego* wealth. In international politics the basis of prestige is, moreover, power to kill and dominate. Accordingly when Nicholas II fastened a fight to the death on his neighbour, Francis Joseph, on grounds of prestige, allegedly menaced by Austrian demands on Belgrade, he was simply, in order to enlarge his imperial inheritance, forcing Francis Joseph to forgo his right to defend the Empire against assassins who were plotting to plunder the heritage of the Habsburgs. The claim of Russia to take the Balkan states, being Slav, under her wing, lest her own prestige should suffer, was sheer aggression; and, as Sir Francis Bertie, his ambassador in Paris, reminded Grey, the pretext for assuming such a protectorate, the racial affinity pretext, was 'rubbish'.[7] Moreover, that Grey should propel England into war to bolster up the Romanoff prestige in the Balkans was gross, suicidal imbecility, involving such an unbalance of power as Europe never endured even in the heyday of Napoleon.

That England should be lured into the subversion of that venerable union which by an almost natural growth had combined more than three large communities and their glorious capital cities Vienna, Prague and Buda-Pesth into a tolerant and slowly evolving polity which had earned the name of *Austria Felix*—such a betrayal could only bring on the autocrat of Downing Street the wrath of fair-minded men. And it was not long before Grey was made to feel that of all the fomenters of war he was the most detested by his Continental critics. For the Furies were on his track and his dreams were haunted by the consciousness that he was no saint, and no Solomon. The fact that he never replied to the castigation by Ramsay Macdonald and Edmund Morel in his apologia proves only that he cultivated, as few other politicians have done, the art of reservation when faced with unanswerable charges. We look in vain for a sign that Macdonald's deadly thrusts in the Commons went home, not because he was too deaf to hear or too blind to read them in print, but because he was unable to invent a rejoinder. Similarly he kept silence when his noblest and ablest critic Edmund Morel was gagged by imprisonment on a trumpery charge; and when Morel, the conqueror of Churchill, was justified by the people at Dundee, he issued no challenge to debate on the platform or in the press and even in his memoirs allowed the real case against him to go by default. Accordingly, accepting the judgment voiced by President Wilson and numerous other witnesses that calculations of commercial interest, not always disavowed by the leaders, dictated the London decision for war in 1914, then the enigma appears to be almost desperate, since it is nearly impossible to explain how ministers could seek to advance British *interests* by hacking down the bulwark against Russian aggression at an astronomical cost in blood and treasure and an irreparable loss of national independence and honour, accompanied by bankruptcies, one in 1919 and another in 1945.

One could only imagine that these ministers counted on a picnic such as Secretary Stimson delighted in during three weeks on active service in France in 1918. In his own words, to convey 'the joy of war' he wrote of the killing business as 'a game of wits', spiced by a 'pleasant uncertainty' like that of a 'good grizzly-bear hunt'. There were touches of 'glamour' in that 'quiet sector' of the Vosges for 'under the branches of the firs camp-life went on with all the enjoyable surroundings of an outing in the Adirondacks' and there were especially glamorous contacts with French officers who would 'spread out under the pines a delicious repast, admirably served, with cooking of a kind to which the American army was a stranger'. Stimson likewise had the felicity to order the discharge of the first shell fired against the Germans by the United States Army, listening with 'delight in the roar of the barrage that followed'. Long afterward, in old age, he was still to recall how 'wonderfully happy', he felt throughout the next three weeks, until he had to leave.[8]

Not all those in Washington or London have given themselves away so completely. Churchill has done pretty well in that direction, and what he has omitted to disclose Asquith and other colleagues have generously supplied. Is it difficult to guess how strongly this mentality at top levels influenced the decisions of 1914 and 1939? And this 'sporting' urge to war was enormously stimulated by the conviction at Downing Street in August 1914 that the march on Berlin and Vienna would be a walk-over—a good grizzly-bear hunt. Had they shared Kitchener's belief (which he never, according to Northcliffe, avowed or declared) that the war would last three years they would neither have yielded to the seductive 'joy of war' nor figured out the costs in such a way as to show a financial balance so magnificent as to compensate the nation for its sacrifices.

Nevertheless the two factors, the anticipated 'joy of war' and the miscalculation of material profit, depending on a lightning knock-out, could hardly account for the drive to war at the Foreign

THE ATHENIAN EMPIRE AND THE BRITISH

Office and Admiralty in 1914. One can only imagine that some overpowering and unacknowledged passion obscured the dim intelligence of the ruling clique to such an extent that they blundered as if demented. Such has been the *Message of the Documents*, for twenty years familiar to historians, but still concealed from the politicians and the public by the hidden hand.

The blackout, however, is gradually fading. It is an ancient proverb that man is taught by suffering. The appalling suffering and the fear of worse have promoted reflection in those who look squarely at the conclusion, even if momentary, of the wholesale butchery. *Finis coronat opus* or rather *finis declarat opus*. The world order in 1945 and after is the *finis* which lights up the *opus* of the preceding forty years. Let us concentrate on this glorious triumph and see, not in general terms but in statistical form, what the policy of blood, sweat and tears has in a generation yielded. When Bernard Shaw explained[9] that our sorrows were due to the failure of our countrymen to feel deeply the murder of an Austrian Archduke at Sarajevo he touched a sore spot, but it was easy to pass off the reminder as a jest. If he had lived to examine the Report issued in November 1950 by UNESCO he would perhaps have left a sting of a more rankling kind.

Here is a summary of the destruction caused by the Second World War, traceable to the callous reaction of a handful of politicians to the assassinations of June 28, 1914. The misery involved will be variously estimated, and the tale is far from complete: but it serves our purpose.

According to the report 250,000,000 children throughout the world were starving; and in Europe 60,000,000 children in twelve different countries were in need of help.

At the same time *The International Review of Diplomatic and Political Science*, Geneva, stated the following as the cost of the same World War II:

> 21 million men killed in action;
> 29¼ million wounded, mutilated or incapacitated;
> 21¼ million evacuated, deported, interned or otherwise removed from their homes;
> 30 million homes reduced to ashes;
> 150 million left without shelter, a prey to famine and disease.

Financial losses were colossal. Up to 1946 World War II cost three times as much as World War I: enough to provide a house costing £12,000, furniture worth £4000, a cash present of £20,000 for every family in the U.S.A., Canada, Austria, Britain, France, Germany, U.S.S.R. and Belgium. In addition each town of over 200,000 population could have been allotted a cash donation of £25,000,000 for libraries, £25,000,000 for schools and £25,000,000 for hospitals.

With these figures in mind let us contemplate the 'terrifying statesmanship' immortalised by Maynard Keynes in his castigation of the Big Three after Versailles. For it was in 1919 that the 'calamity' lamented by Churchill, Eden and others in 1950 was brought to birth by their associates and prototypes. Thirty years of the same régime brought the monster to maturity.

It is worth while to note that our rulers, in the Cabinet and the Press, have little to say about instructive figures such as these. To call attention to the dead loss, in treasure and in blood, caused by the total warfare engineered by them for the first time in modern history, the knock-out, unconditional surrender, and victors' justice to follow, all novelties marking the reversion to barbarism— to call attention to the horrible truth that their chosen type of war pays no dividend except inextinguishable hatred and a world of sorrow would lower their prestige to zero. They prefer, when confronted with the urgent problem of stiffening popular morale, to steer their judges away from the question: what do we, the ruled, get out of your thrones of skulls and martial harangues? War profiteering is many-sided and for the promoters lucrative but what do the people gain? On that point Horace spoke for the common man in all ages: *Quidquid delirant reges, plectuntur Achivi.* Yes, 'the rulers go mad; the people are bled'. And as every sober citizen knows in his heart that the bait held out by his rulers, to induce him to go forth and kill his brother, is identical with that which lured on Cain, it would be disastrous for his rulers if he was allowed to see how he was cheated. Hence the tremendous barrage kept up before, during and after every orgy of slaughter to conceal its grotesque absurdity and wickedness.

When the absurdity is multiplied by the reduplication of the menace, to meet which his rulers conditioned him for World War II what can his 'victorious' war lord do but bludgeon him into insensibility by threatening him with the last menace of all, extermination by the Hydrogen Blitz? The menace, however, must be presented as proceeding from a malignant enemy, unprovoked

107

by our rulers; and so World War II is depicted as a struggle forced on the Allies, Great Britain, France, U.S.A., and Russia by 'the sole wicked nation in Europe' led by the Ogre from Austria, *not* as a war rendered inevitable by the chain of follies and crimes reaching from 1906 to 1919, and foreseen by countless observers long before Churchill and Vansittart resumed the defamation of Germany which had paved the way for World War I.

When taken to task for their sins, as sometimes happens, what do our heaven-born statesmen say for themselves? It is remarkable how they deride every imputation founded on evil consequences. These they palliate as 'calamities', like earthquakes or typhoons, something like acts of God or rather the Devil. And when taunted with blindness, as blind leaders of the blind, they deride all prudence as not their prerogative and self-chosen responsibility and dismiss all criticism after the event as hindsight. This is best seen when military blundering is charged against the High Command. Thus the whole row of disasters, Narvik, Namsos, Andalsnes, Dunkirk, Dieppe, Tobruk, Hong Kong, Singapore, Rangoon, the Maginot and the rest can be belittled or converted into splendid miracles or better still ignored. The larger blunders of policy are likewise artfully manipulated and explained away as misfortune that nobody foresaw or could have foreseen at the time.

That is naturally the tactic of a bungler on the defensive, but how feeble it is in the grand controversy of our age, now settled by the *fait accompli* and the scientific analysis of the evidence! From the example of one prudent contemporary critic, member of the British delegation at Versailles, an impartial tribunal could secure a conviction. He has been quoted elsewhere but we have no hesitation about using his contribution further. For Maynard Keynes is a name to conjure with, despite the conspiracy to forget him and the other members of that brilliant school.

In 1922 he followed up his *Economic Consequences of the Peace* by another treatise entitled *A Revision of the Treaty* from which we extract sufficient to prove that, whilst our Big Three and their experts were sowing the dragon's teeth at Versailles in 1919, degrading diplomacy as never before, there were exponents of a higher statesmanship who foresaw the harvest which we have reaped and but for the criminal decisions of the Allied oligarchy would have truly 'saved the world'.

On page 11, Keynes notes as the first result of the League of

Nations influence the 'intensifying of nationalism'. That observation alone makes clear what he calls 'the terrifying statesmanship' of the Paris Conference. Next comes a passage, page 39, which illuminates the danger which he scented in the intensifying of nationalism. Half of the denigration of Germany since 1933 has consisted of a virulent campaign against nationalism in Germany, Italy, Japan (not nationalism in Britain, France, Russia, etc.) and here we find Keynes sounding a warning, unheeded by the founders of the League of Nations and its patrons up to World War II, as Lord Lothian protested and many others perceived.

Keynes went to the heart of the contentious issue debated beyond every other mischief in the past thirty years. Before Mussolini or Hitler or Stalin had emerged he showed how Fascism, Nazism and Communism, which were rooted in an intensified nationalism, were destined to assume a formidable shape in Germany thanks to the terrifying statesmanship of the Triumvirate at Versailles. Like many a despairing intellectual since 1920 he called on all reasonable men to witness, 'how deep a wound has been inflicted on Germany's self-respect by compelling her, not merely to perform acts, but to subscribe to beliefs which she did not in fact accept. It is not usual in civilised countries to use force to compel wrongdoers to confess, even when we are convinced of their guilt; it is still more barbarous to use force, after the fashion of inquisitors, to compel adherence to an article of belief because we ourselves believe it. Yet towards Germany the Allies had appeared to adopt this base and injurious practice, and had enforced on this people at the point of the bayonet the final humiliation of reciting, through the mouths of their representatives, what they believed to be untrue.'

This description of Article 231, the article which stigmatises Germany as the aggressor in the war, tallies with the denunciation of the said Article by Archbishop Temple at Geneva. Article 231, branded Germany as 'the sole and only author of the War', asserting 'the responsibility of Germany and her Allies for causing all the loss and damage suffered by her enemies as a result of the War. This responsibility is a moral and not a financial responsibility. The Clause means simply that Germany caused the War.'[10] And yet, even if it had been true that Germany was 'the sole and only author of the War,' the Allies' claim, based on this proven falsehood, for Pensions and Allowances—an enormous indemnity by themselves—was in Keynes' opinion 'contrary to our engagements and an act of international immorality' and furthermore was 'an exceptionally mean act made worse by hypocritical professions of moral purpose.[11]

Nothing could illustrate better the demoralisation of Allied statesmen than the indictment levelled at the Paris Peace Treaty in Keynes' two books. The leading British economist of the day by no means confined himself to the burning question of reparation, as we have seen, but naturally grappled with that thorny subject with special vigour. From the scanty extracts permitted in these pages it is evident that he placed the emphasis where it belongs, namely, on the immorality and hypocrisy of the Triumvirate.

Chapter Six

MORIBUND EMPIRE

IF WE SEEK to learn the extent of the catastrophe which has be-
fallen our fellow men there are many to enlighten us. General
Smuts, for example, has voiced what millions feel in fitting
terms:

> The most awful calamity in history has overtaken Europe. Do
> not ask me who is the enemy—I do not know. It may be ourselves.
> We do not know what is going to breed out of this war. Forces that
> have been kept under by civilization are now unchained. The world
> will be alive with danger.

And again:

> Europe, a fragmented, broken-up continent filled with people
> glaring at each other in hate is the greatest problem facing man-
> kind.... Who knows what the world of tomorrow will bring in the
> way of new madness?

Such are the fruits of imperialism gathered by the Six Great
Powers in fifty years of *madness*. Is it surprising that *the greatest
problem facing mankind* is, as Smuts suggested, to ascertain *who is
the enemy*? It may appear strange that he professes, like Socrates,
not to know: strange, because every one of our great, wise and
eminent has the answer—the verdict, namely pronounced in the
Versailles Treaty of 1919.

But Jan Smuts thirty years after Versailles answers: 'I do not
know.' Stranger still, he is candid enough to confess: *perhaps the
enemy is ourselves*, sublimely indifferent to the dogma rampant in
the anti-German world. How precisely he came to the conclusion
thus guardedly stated is unimportant. Yet it must be interesting to
admirers of the South African Sage, object in his later years of an
Empire's homage, to reflect that he was no preacher of The Word,
warning his audience against spiritual pride. He was not a deep
thinker like Bernard Bosanquet meditating on the 'ultimate
irrationality' of war; still less was he a disciple of Gandhi who had

111

fought him without violence and vanquished him by *Satyagraha*. Smuts, to be sure, was a thinking man able to father a particular brand of idealism, which he called *Holism*, as well as to command an army against General von Lettow-Vorbeck in German East Africa and participate in the shaping of the Versailles Treaty. As a statesman, a soldier and a widely read politician he knew enough to protest against much that offended him in the Dictate, without attempting anything tangible to redeem it. He was crippled, as an accessory, in his reactions to the new *history*, of which he had learned a good deal. But a recantation was unthinkable, and there is no sign that he had mastered the definitive message of the Documents between 1924 and World War II. To tell the truth he was hampered by his past and by his ambitions for the future.

His manoeuvres to seize Delagoa Bay, exemplified by his delaying tactics during the long chase after von Lettow in Tanganyika, were baulked, but there was German South West Africa, rich in diamonds and indispensable as completing the De Beers colossus; and only through the Dictate could he secure the German possession for South Africa. For him, therefore, the terms of the Dictate were sacrosanct, as to many others who profited in the handout. After all he was the Father, almost the Patron Saint, of a goodly Empire, menaced within by dissensions and without by pressure from the Allies, pressure which culminated in his stand-up fight at UNO. Too much accordingly to expect straight-thinking or straight-talking from the Autocrat, as he appeared, of the Afrikaner Empire, bolstered up, as it was by the Versailles Dictate. Hence his *perhaps* when he virtually admits that *Germany, the sole wicked nation* is a canard.

Just as much as Dr Malan, who wrested the helm from the hands of the Field Marshal, Smuts was the spokesman of an Afrikaner Empire of imposing dimensions. In 1953 the total population was estimated at roughly 13 million of whom 2,750,000 were Whites and 10,399,000 Non-Whites. In principle the conflict between Smuts and UNO was the same as that which flared up between Malan and UNO and still persists. How can it be otherwise when, if UNO has any moral, legal or political basis at all, it is a denial of imperialism? Explicit and implicit in the Charter is the assertion of human freedom and the repudiation of every form of subjection. From this challenge no imperial authority can escape. And the reason is obvious.

The word *imperium* means plenary authority, and the classic pattern was fixed once and for all by Roman jurisprudence. No matter who or what was the organ or source of that plenary authority, all *imperium*, especially the *maius imperium*, rested on the power to coerce, and this power of coercion, symbolised by the *fasces*, invested the authority with unlimited force. This power of life and death embodied in Roman *imperium* is the essence of the imperial concept wherever it rears its head. For that reason, in seeking to account for 'the most awful calamity in history' a British subject will get nowhere unless he is guided by a vivid realism which accepts the view of Europe's Civil Wars as starkly imperialist. And since for a Britisher the Boer War, the First and Second World Wars and the Cold War are links in a chain of similar wars reaching back to Tudor times it behoves him to search diligently among the records, for light on their causes.

He will not search far before he is compelled to admit that all wars of aggression are *au fond* imperialist. In international relations imperialism and aggressive war are convertible terms. Every accession of territory is gained by superior force, backed by imperial sentiment, and held by force, patent or latent. Where native occupiers are few and territory is extensive, force is minimised and it is generally assumed that expansionism achieved in the main by migration should escape criticism. But European expansion overseas particularly in Asia and Africa, which is the most dominant issue in our Civil Wars, has the inevitable taint of violence and war, war against the indigenous population and war between the competing Powers. So long as these wars were waged against distant and weak races and the nations who waged them could indulge in them with a spice of relish, much as Roman Society and the Plebs could enjoy a gladiatorial show, loose thinking about the connection between imperialism and warfare passed muster. Modern Liberals, however, and Pacificists have never been content to hide from their merciless scrutiny the root mischief that for twenty generations has rendered the national annals so gory. Henceforth it will be less easy to shout them down. The woolly thinking that served even the Churchmen so well, when condoning and exalting the crucifixion of the weaker brethren by the stronger is at least confounded by the apotheosis of the terrorist, who is now revealed in his true character as the Lord of the H-Bomb. War in a good cause—such is every war to every belligerent—begins to look less Christian. When the

113

tiny minority of Churchmen, who denounce war as nothing but the frenzy of Moloch-worship, become a majority, the outlook for warmongering will be truly bleak.

To achieve such a degree of intelligence should not overtax even a mediocre Christian brain. There is nothing new about pacificism. Nineteen hundred years ago the matter was plainer to a benighted Pagan in the Imperial City than to any modern Archbishop. The Pagan who is cited here was tutor to the very Emperor who slaughtered Christians without mercy and executed perhaps St Paul himself. In due course Seneca fell a victim to his pupil's bloodlust and thus ended the courtier's career. But in A.D. 63 he was bequeathing to posterity his reflections on war from which we take leave to reprint a passage:

> We are mad, not only individually but nationally. We check manslaughter and isolated murders, but what of wars and the much vaunted crime of murdering a whole people? . . . Deeds that would be punished by us with death when committed in secret, are praised by us because uniformed generals have carried them out. Man, naturally the gentlest of beings, is not ashamed to revel in the blood of others, to wage war, and to entrust the waging of war to his sons, when even dumb beasts and wild beasts keep the peace with one another. Against this over-mastering and widespread madness philosophy has become a greater effort, and has taken on strength in proportion to the strength which is gained by the opposition forces.

If this pagan protest does not put to shame our prelates and parsons the reason is clear. They have become part and parcel of the imperial machinery. The business of Ministers of Religion is to provide the apologetic. There is always a minority who, like Seneca, deplore 'the much vaunted crime of murdering a whole people,' but against our 'overmastering and widespread madness' they have been powerless. They have failed, moreover, to retard the barbarising of warfare which is such a blot on the age we live in.

In the twentieth century the Christian Powers have shamed humanity as never before. 'Forces that have been kept under by civilization are now unchained.' Able writers have done justice to phenomena like concentration camps, mass bombing, planned famine, Hiroshima and Nuremburg. The whole world has beheld the new barbarism in action on a gigantic scale. But perhaps too much stress has been laid on the by-products of the madness and too little heed taken of the stern necessity devolving on the white peoples to diagnose what is eminently *their* disease by probing into its cause with the resolve to effect a radical cure.

Owing to the vast mystification created by mechanised propaganda, which has steeped whole populations in falsified history, it requires preternatural insight and sincerity to determine national rights and national wrongs, to distinguish sharply aggressors and aggressed, and in general, to satisfy the conscience that in any given conflict the better cause has triumphed. Only an optimist could argue that any single citizen of a modern belligerent nation is fit to render judgment in his own cause. There is today in the entire Anglo-American group no individual possessed absolutely of the single eye, no one who could honestly accept a commission to judge with disinterest any major political dispute, 'with malice towards none and charity to all'.

But the man in the street may readily profit by recorded experience in a field in which any sensible person can be detached and fair. That field, of course, is the epoch in which our earliest European history ran its course, and, although on a modest scale, developed all the features of moral and political experience that are recognised as important in the latest sweep of the spiral. We can, if we so desire, actually learn from history and for centuries we have learned *something* from the great repository contained in the historiography and speculation of the immensely significant epoch known as the Age of Pericles. That it has counted so little in our time is a scandal. It is, further, nothing less than disastrous that the lesson deliberately set down to be 'an everlasting possession' by the Father of Scientific History, Thucydides, and interpreted in plain terms by the speculative genius of his younger contemporary, Plato, have been ignored in the rough-and-tumble dogfights of the 'sophisters and economists' of these fifty years.

Only pacificists in our day have focused attention on the sin that breeds warfare, and in the heat and dust of the controversy it is easy to overlook the light thrown on the perennial paradox of the *good war* by the greatest and most original of thinkers, who lived through the genuinely first World War, faced its implications with unclouded vision, and condemned it root and branch. Though less extensive and less horrible by far, the World War of Plato's generation revealed to him more clearly than our World Wars can to a contemporary, the quintessence of all war. As an eye witness

115

of the most catastrophic war of classical antiquity, gifted with superlative insight, he laid bare the sin that bred it and every other outbreak of mass destruction. 'The body and its desires are the main cause of wars and factions and battles,' wrote Plato, 'for all wars arise from the desire of gaining money, and we are compelled to gain money for the sake of the body. We are slaves to its service. And so, because of these things we have no leisure for philosophy.' This observation clearly anticipates Seneca, reminding us that, a whole century previous to Nero, the illustrious humanist Cicero had stamped Platonism indelibly on Roman culture, thus leaving his mark not merely on the best thought of the Empire but on its derivative, medieval culture, which was permeated with Ciceronian philosophy. For although not technically a philosopher, Cicero was sufficiently endowed on the speculative side to absorb, largely through Posidonius, much of what the Greeks had to teach, and on the basis of his study to conclude that of them all Plato was supreme—*raca opinione instar omnium Plato.*

Through Cicero, the adapter rather than the interpreter of Plato or in modern parlance the amplifier, came the leaven of Roman Hellenism which impregnated the early phase of the civilisation referred to by Smuts. And the very core of that Platonism is the exalting of the claims of the soul over the body, mind over matter, which carries with it the renunciation of war.

The modern argument that war is a normal characteristic of civilised communities, is, in fact, valid only if it be granted that war-breeding passions, summed up in *pleonexia*, have corrupted the soul of the ruling class beyond redemption. Perpetual discord is a sign of ingrained greed and spiritual degeneracy, but the natural disposition of civilised humanity is tolerant and kindly. Only a perverted mentality envisages mutual hate as the normal attitude in a society of nations. 'For war,' as Plato showed, 'is not of the essence of states, but has its causes in their internal disease and distraction, leading to policies of expansionism.' So argued Bosanquet during World War I, explaining further that 'all conflicts of pride and interest are capable of solution in harmony with the claims of both parties, if patience, sagacity and goodwill are brought to bear.' In a word, diseased minds are the cause of chronic warfare. As Smuts observed, the enemy is ourselves or in ourselves. Plato, Seneca, Bosanquet agree that the ultimate irrationality, the supreme stupidity, arises from the pull of material interests, the defeat of the higher impulses by the lower, the supremacy of carnal desire in the eternal battle between agape and remorseless greed.

Lloyd George himself admitted that a conference round a table in 1914 might have averted the War, as though in this case, too, 'conflicts of pride and interest' are capable of solution peacefully. But the necessary 'patience, sagacity and goodwill' were lacking. In other words the leaders had no concern with the philosophy championed by Plato, Seneca and Bosanquet. The notable exception should have been Haldane, but he was in the grip of the apostate Grey. His speculative gift was remarkable, and he has been credited with not merely a European outlook but with a veneration for his German 'spiritual home'. And yet in his ostensibly profound exposition of Hegel he betrays a failure to grapple with the *Larger Logic*, the work that is indispensable. He was more defective still in the practical business of applying idealism to our affairs. After his famous visit to Berlin in 1912 he did nothing to check the baiting of the 'big men', as he dubbed them, who had conferred with him, but played the game of the jingoes and afterwards boasted of planning the B.E.F. Is it surprising that such an exhibition of doublethink and twospeak earned him the odium that drove him from office as a Germanophil, doomed to suffer the last indignity of being guyed by H. G. Wells? The ludicrous portrait in *Bealby* may not have been undeserved.

Plato's thoroughgoing repudiation of war, however, rests on a position still broader and more fundamental. It rests on the basic principle of ethical idealism itself, expounded for modern thinkers by Bernard Bosanquet in his masterly treatises on *Value*.

What, then was the theory of values, which figures so prominently in the speculation of the 'twenties, expressed in Platonic terms?

It was Plato who for all time, according to Bosanquet, firstly, laid it down that in the quest for the good, for that, namely, which can satisfy to the full the intelligence and the desire of man—*that which is filled with the more real is more really filled*; and secondly, that the higher the satisfactions the more are our *experiences permanent and substantial*. It is the sensual gratifications that are fleeting and impure, whereas the spiritualised pleasures are relatively lasting and concrete. The higher experiences, moreover, are less egoistic, less selfish, and have the incalculable advantage that they are not diminished by sharing. Hence the insistence of the

School of Green on the stern need, in an age of mechanisation and potential superabundance, to foster in the actual world of half-famished millions, altruism, self-sacrifice, benevolence in the use of wealth. In practice, external goods are not merely a source of gratification to the owner or consumer, but for the good life are a necessary apparatus. They are *choregia*, supplies, and relatively a means, not an end in themselves; but, being consumed in the act of enjoyment and restricted in quantity, they are diminished by sharing and become objects of cupidity, greed, rivalry, thus breeding envy and dissension inside and between states. This inveterate greed may, in fact, be regarded as the besetting sin of homo sapiens. It was the curse of the Hellenic city state, the *stasis* that Aristotle tried to banish, all in vain. Just as the idealists in Britain joined with certain Churchmen in urging genuine philanthropy as an ingredient in national policy and utterly failed to arrest the drift to selfish materialism during the past hundred years.

It is in this field of statesmanship that Plato brings us down to bedrock. There has been a plethora of moralising on the contrast between the rapidity with which wealth is produced and the sluggish growth of the capacity to use it rationally. It is a commonplace that technology has far outstripped the science of living and humanism. The higher culture has done nothing to temper the rapacity of individuals or groups or nations. The urge to get-rich-quick has been enormously intensified as world industry and commerce forged ahead. The opportunities have been multiplied. Never before in the leading nations have so many families possessed so much. In one year in the U.S.A. 30,000 families were reported to have incomes of a million dollars and upwards. The United States sets the pace but in the race Britain has been no laggard. A hundred years ago James Martineau protested that in no other land were there so many people 'crawling round a heap of gold'. As to that, can anyone detect any progress over the last century?

Surely the prestige enjoyed by Cecil Rhodes is a sign of the times. We have seen what his aims were both for himself and his country. Was he not the veritable incarnation of *pleonexia*, a word that connotes not merely greed and grab, but the technique, the getting the better of rivals, the having too much and the notion of over-reaching and fraud? If anyone doubts this judgment after what has already been recorded, shall we not find ample grounds for it in his own last message to the British people?

The world is nearly all parcelled out and what there is left of it is being divided up, conquered and colonised. To think of these stars that you see overhead nights, these vast worlds which we can never reach. I would annex the planets if I could. I often think of that. It makes me sad to see them so clear and yet so far.

Here in five short sentences we have the quintessence of modern English imperialism. For without question Rhodes spoke for his generation. In form his utterance is such as few would have chosen, but in substance it voiced the mind and heart of the ruling classes. Not all our rulers of course. Such *pleonexia in excelsis* did not quite possess a Rosebery, as it animated the Tory stalwarts, and for many the swirling words conveyed a suggestion of *rhodomontade*. Yet few of our rulers escaped the contagion, and when called upon to pronounce on the empire-builder's record they condoned his offences. The white-washing process meant connivance by all parties, and started that collaboration between prominent Liberals and their Tory opponents which heralded the disintegration of British liberalism.

Even the University of Oxford, then dominated by the School of Green, capitulated and bestowed on Rhodes its highest honorary degree. Thus in the home of idealism the apostle of aggression received an almost unanimous vote of confidence. Out of all the College Heads only one opposed the grant and had it not been that the protest came from the illustrious and revered Master of Balliol, Edward Caird, the black mark would have passed unnoticed. All the more significant is the incident; nor is it ever likely to lose its fascination for those who in years to come seek to understand why the seat of learning which, according to Jowett, moulded the thinking of ten per cent of the best brains of England, failed so grievously in 1900 to influence the policy of its rulers.

To many of the rising generation such an utterance as we have quoted may seem hardly sane. Yes, Imperialism rampant, as it was fifty years ago, must seem ludicrous to those who see it in retreat. If Cecil Rhodes could have foreseen that in 1954 the Labour Party Conference at Scarborough would repudiate Imperialism and its offshoot Colonialism *in toto* and renounce in principle all exploitations overseas he would never have penned such arrant nonsense. He did a service, nevertheless, to posterity by putting on record the besetting sin of his era, the unlimited *pleonexia* which corrupted British policy and led to near-perdition in 1914–15.

In so doing he exhibited in its true colours, as sheer aggression, the Cape to Cairo plan, to carry out which he fomented strife with the Boer republics, while Zulus and Matabele were mowed down by machine-guns and scores of native tribes were robbed of their land and virtually enslaved. Stripped of all thin pretences, missionary and philanthropic, the work of the leading Empire-builder has within half a century disclosed its real character, sordid in motive, greedy and cruel in execution—and short-lived.

Apart from any question of over-population and living-space, aggravated in a score of countries by the land monopolies enjoyed by the favoured few, the flag-waving arrogance of the master races inevitably exasperates a world of onlookers and embitters what should be friendly intercourse. Add to the jealousy excited by the euphoria of the wealthy nations the cramping of commercial enterprise by endless tariff restrictions and preferences and you have the raw materials of constant quarrels. Bosanquet summed it up in his blunt contention:

> I feel certain that hostile tariffs are the main cause of war, and I fear there are many evil interests in England lying in wait to exploit any necessary precaution. These barriers to human intercourse are loathsome to me.[1]

As a Liberal, or rather a Radical, Bosanquet was in fundamentals the antithesis of the Rhodes type, as we perceive.

But it was not only tariff barriers that were loathsome to Bosanquet and his fellow-Liberals. As a consistent Liberal he advocated a thoroughgoing idealism, carrying his principles into practice in the Charity Organization movement. In the foreign field he was equally uncompromising, and it is here that he set an example of the higher way of living, as contrasted with the lower, the underworld life of international finance, armament rings, market-rigging in which Rhodes and his kind luxuriated. Like Seneca he lamented the eclipse of philosophy and regretted that the English race was mentally torpid and that the middle class had never really cared for education. In the twentieth century this Philistinism was destined to work untold harm, because for the Great Powers foreign politics dominated the scene even more than the internal class war. Instead of concentrating on the proper task of promoting harmony at home and the abolition of privilege, our rulers led the maritime states of Europe in the scramble for oil, tin, rubber, gold and world markets, setting the stage for every conceivable villainy.

The reason for the debauch has been made crystal clear by the testimony of those best qualified to judge. That testimony has been sifted and published in the new history, so assiduously shunned by those who dread it and have the ear of the multitude. The blessings of civilisation—so we have learned—had been forced on browns, blacks, yellows and reds on a variety of pretexts, satisfying to the white masters, odious to their subjects. The civilising mission, however, did not make sense where the aggressed had, as in India and China, evolved cultures riper in vital respects than that of their conquerors. 'Asia,' wrote Kipling, 'is not going to be civilised after the methods of the West. There is too much Asia and she is too old.' Yet Kipling was, as Charles Kingsley put it, 'as thorough an Englishman as ever coveted his neighbour's goods'. Indeed, if the intruders were prompted by zeal for uplift it is hard to understand why they not merely slew native resisters but fought one another for the futile privilege of bestowing unwanted *Kultur* on the recalcitrants.

Certainly Asians and Africans, as we have noted, repudiate the apologetic of Empire in all its shapes and guises, and at last, since their fetters have fallen away, are freely contributing an invaluable quota to the historiography of the mighty West-East episode and its—for the West—tragic conclusion. We invite an illustrious Chinese observer and an Indian sage to speak for Asia so that some white inquirers may learn what the non-white world thinks of their imperial adventure.

Ten years before Sir Winston announced in the House the bogus nature of his triumph, the celebrated humorist Lin-Yutang published a book[2] to explain the catastrophe as the Chinese people saw it. The book was written shortly before Hiroshima and is less savage than it might have been: but it is pungent enough. We select firstly a short passage to clear the decks. 'Of all the five continents of the earth,' he avers 'only Europe has not yet learned to live at peace. Europe is the focus of infection of this earth, and imperialism is the toxin by which it spreads until the whole world is so sick, so sick.' Unpalatable certainly for our bellicose Crusaders, but hard to refute. Sir Winston's confession, at any rate, that the two wars to end war, in which he takes such pride, left us all roaming around and peering on the rim of Hell, seems to endorse the Asian's charges. Here is another pronouncement from the Orient:

So Europe is upsetting the peace of the five continents. Because of Europe and the European current of ideas and Europe's example of imperialism and materialism to other continents, women in Singapore have to die, Burmese villagers' houses have to burn. . . But being itself a slaughter-house, Europe is now planning to transform Asia and Africa into a gigantic slaughter-house. It still thinks that the world owes Europe a debt, and that the world has to come up to European standards of living. Europe, I know still intends to appropriate the world. There are the British Empire, the French Empire and the Dutch Empire. Even Portugal has got a concession, Macao, in China! . . .

Today Asia and Africa must still be the cows that produce the milk for Europeans. Why? Because Europe wants to raise their standards of living and educate them towards self-government! Who in the first place robbed them of their liberty and their self-government? Who says that the standards of living in India have improved and not deteriorated after two centuries of English rule? Sir Norman Angell does not contradict the fact that the abject poverty of the Indian peasants is worse than even that of seventy years ago, owing to English exploitation and the killing of native industries.

Not a pretty picture of White dominance! But worse is to come.

The democratic leaders of the world are transferring to Asia their sin-smelling and strife-breeding power politics, with the sure result that Asia, by means of a prepared and planned balance of power, will be kept in continual bloodshed and strife and mutual slaughter for the next three centuries, after Europe's noble example.

Not the dictators, not the Fascists nor the Communists are the secular oppressors but the democratic leaders of the world! Further, Lin-Yutang asks the awkward question:

What are you going to Europeanize the world with? The European standards of living, of course. Curious that one does not say the standards of morals . . . suppose material standards of living are not worth raising at all—at the price of increasing class hatred, increasing collectivism, loss of individual freedom, and periodic conscripting of boys of eighteen for war?

Then contemptuously:

We don't need the Four Freedoms, but only one Freedom—Freedom from Humbug.

Next:

Only one thing we know definitely: the greatest force produces the greatest hatred.

122

A distinct score against the champions of the burned earth strategy and unconditional surrender! And further:

> In a truly civilized peace treaty, the 'guilt clause' will be abolished... Only at a peace conference where both opponents insist on fixing the guilt on oneself will there be permanent peace.

If memory serves, we appear to recognize here a touch of real Christianity, the teaching of Jesus, Gandhi and the Friends! What accordingly can be said of the Christian Powers that twice unashamedly imposed on the vanquished a Carthaginian Peace and, before the fighting was done, planned to enlist the decimated German army in defence of Allied hearths and homes?

> If I do not misinterpret Winston Churchill, he is fighting a twentieth-century war in order to take off his boots after the war and climb back in to a nineteenth-century bed, comfortably mattressed in India, Singapore, and Hong Kong.

Had Lin-Yutang been a European, of course, he would have envisaged Sir Winston as planning rather to help John Bull to 'jump into Germany's place' as a supplier of goods to Europe. It would be so easy to point as proof to the savaging of German economy, the Allied ethics of starvation and the reduction of Central Europe to a wild beasts' den.

The mockery of UNO Lin naturally gives no quarter:

> I know eventually it is white insolence that will ruin any world co-operation. . . . And while the conception of power politics remains what it is and the statesmen of the leading powers still sit in their moronic complacency, with no mental comprehension of how the war arose and what it is being fought for, except for certain colonial possessions and the status quo, peace will forever remain an elusive hope. . . . There will be peace in the world only when the English, French, and Dutch Empires collapse. I know this war is not big enough to reverse the process and wipe out the Empires, and I hope World War III will do it. . . . Of all the fifty or sixty nations in the world, only three or four big powers are upsetting the peace of the world. These powers have run over this earth, kicking down people's fences in bad temper and worse manners, robbing them of their liberty and independence, and taking possession of their goods—and have then fought wars among themselves for these goods. First they fought among themselves, and then called upon the entire world to fight for them to keep what they have.

123

In this view, oddly enough, President Wilson would concur, nor would the sentiment native to President Franklin Roosevelt be widely different.

In another sweeping critique Lin-Yutang anticipates the development of UNO high policy:

> The one great fact in this world war is the emergence of Russia and of Asia, but we prefer to ignore it. I have made a passing reference to Sir Norman Angell. As a European Liberal, he is probably as good as any. But as a European Liberal, his liberal concepts of the necessity of world co-operation and standing and falling together are strictly 'white' and limited to West of the Suez Canal, and specifically to a refurbished form of 'Union Now' with England. His notion of Russia and of Asia stands intellectually on a par with the Tory Lady Astor, who says: 'I would like China and Russia to be in the framework of a society formed by America and the British Commonwealth, but they would have to get into the British way of thinking.' Such superb gems can only be cut in London.

Likewise he reflects:

> It is my belief that even if we wanted a modified survival of the nineteenth century fabric in the form of a fairly white domination of the world, it is now a little too late. Asia is too aroused to submit and too big to spank. The West must either plan for co-operation with Asia or plan without it and make ready for a bigger and better war. . . . The emergence of Asia simply means this: *The end of the era of imperialism.* Nothing is going to stop it. To keep up the nineteenth century system, the white man would have to strangle Russia and China. Now it is a little too late. . . . The fact is, that, granted a little common intelligence in the racial make-up, any nation will come up in time. How did nineteenth century imperialism begin, and how did the white man go about conquering the world, and what made him think he was superior to the other peoples? Because the white man had guns, and the Asiatics had none.

He notes, in passing, that:

> Must one really decide now whether Britain is to keep India, Burma, Malay, Hong Kong?
> The problem of the colonies is extremely complex—either 'yes' or 'no' to this question is very awkward. And if the British must keep their colonies, how are we to force the Dutch to give up theirs?

124

As a matter of fact, China and England are already heading for conflict. Churchill has made it amply clear and definite that he is not 'grovelling', and that the 'administration of British colonies' will be the 'sole responsibility' of Britain, which is to tell America to keep her hands off. . . . I have no doubt that if Britain does not return Hong Kong to China, this problem of Hong Kong alone will burst the Peace Conference. I know that the Chinese people are willing to go to war with England over Hong Kong . . . five millions of our soldiers have not died to keep the British in Hong Kong, the booty of the Opium War, and possibly the second brightest jewel in the English Crown. . . . Besides, there is the possibility that Russia may combine with China and India and control the geopolitician's Eurasian 'Heartland' and half of the world's population. That will be the geopolitician's nightmare come true!

Finally, to do justice to Lin-Yutang's survey, mark his appeal to the United States:

There is China, a great pacific power, indoctrinated with principles of human, democratic, peaceful living that are very close to the American temperament. . . . China and India have lived as neighbours without one war in the past four thousand years. . . . Russia will not fight China, nor will China fight Russia. To the Chinese and to the Americans, the future of Asia is simple. There is no problem for the United States, because the United States will let the Philippines go. Other people's jewels don't keep you awake if you have no greed in your heart. No insoluble problems exist if the Christian powers will let Malaya, the Dutch Indies, Siam, Indo-China, Burma, and India go. All of them aspire to self-government, and all of them will give trouble to Europe not when they are masters, but only when they are to be exploited as slaves.

If these sentiments savour of Western truculence need we be offended? In the use of menaces and the big stick our rulers have given a strong lead for ten years: and even in the act of setting up UNO took care to allot supreme authority to the Powers that possess overwhelming capacity to kill. Thus the Victors planted deep the seeds of violence in their model world order, so that it was imperative to be *united* on one thing, namely the division of the spoils—or fight. Power politics took on a new lease of life and new wars were staged to crush opposition on the old assumption that justice is really the interest of the stronger, the defeat of the losers proving them to be the sole sinners. The evil tradition established since 1900 that to them who possess unlimited power to kill belong the glory and the spoils—this is the tradition that Lin-YuTang challenges *à l'outrance*. No amount of placatory assurances of altruistic motives will convince the world of Western goodwill and disinterest.

Unless Asia perceives a genuine reversal of policy, a true change of heart, the plausible schemes of sops and bribes, designed to hinder disgruntled Asians from joining the Communists, must be suspect. The threat of an H bomb blitz can decide no vital issue. To deter is merely to defer. But since the statesmanship of the West is bankrupt what has the Free East to offer?

Does not the statecraft of the Indian Government since Liberation open up a more cheerful prospect? A neutral state pledged to pacification certainly disappoints the western politicians, who are bent on ententes and alliances such as cooked the First World War. Nehru's pacific, middle-of-the-road strategy, however has not only worked well; it is eminently right and proper to a Hindu Nation, which can look back across 2180 years to the noblest kingly name in history, Asoka, the Tolerant and the Peacemaker, and acknowledge him as its inspiration. Surely it is comforting to observe that the countrymen of Gandhi have not only adopted the tradition of Asoka but have engraved his emblem on the Great Seal of the Republic. Contrast the lions, leopards, eagles flaunted by peoples of the West!

Remembering also what the Mahatma and Pandit Nehru have taught the world regarding the methods and ethics of the British Raj, little elaboration is required in this synopsis. But something would be lacking if we omitted altogether the Indian rejoinder to the fundamental blunder of *principle*, committed by Western invaders. An Asian has small patience with the fashionable jeremiads anent the hideous epoch in which we have to dwell. If the leading exponent is silent about the criminal blundering which conducted us to the 'rim of Hell', and declines to inquire remorselessly into the causes that make war inevitable, that only prompts the reflective Oriental to probe the wound and find what the mischief may be.

In Asian eyes the sufferings and humiliation resulting from the barbarous civil war in Europe represent the price their masters were willing to pay for the coveted and elusive monopoly of Asian and African exploitation. To this, Western spokesmen, are, or pretend to be, blind. In the Commons on March 1, 1955 no effective voice was raised in protest when Sir Winston issued his defiance to his Communist Allies. *Thus far and no farther! Annihilation rather than enslavement!* A hopeless impasse, 'laden with doom', meaning *what we have we hold.*

The reaction to this confession, as it really was, we all remember. Our legislators returned to their dogmatic murmurs: nothing but *crambe repetita*, in substance nothing fresh: just a revamping of the outworn creed of peace through strength, peace by deterrents, deterrents so formidable as to attain the degree of absolute power that ensures absolute corruption, self-interest disguised in the hideous shape of self-righteousness. Could anything be more dismal?

As an antidote, then, we hazard the judgment of a famous Indian thinker, Krishnamurti:

> If all of you thought profoundly about the whole question of war, this murder on a grand scale, this murder in uniform, with decorations, shouts of joy and praise, with trumpets and banners, with blessings from priests, if you thought and felt deeply about this and perceived its cruelty and infantile absurdities, its appalling maltreatment of man, forcing him to become a military machine through the many exploiting means of nationalism and so on—if you, as individuals, really perceived this horror, surely you would refuse to be used for furthering war and exploitation.

This confirmation, by a Hindu philosopher, of the idealism sponsored by Buddha and Plato, Jesus and Gandhi, Seneca and Bosanquet, marks the end of the era of white competitive and military expansionism and thus far means a long step towards the Pacificist goal. Krishnamurti, however, in reaching his sweeping conclusion probed many a paradox that still commands popular support, the most plausible perhaps being the argument for war in a good cause by which is really intended war in self-defence. To this plea, we find, Krishnamurti gives no quarter:

> To consider war as defensive and offensive will lead us only to further confusion and misery. What we should question is killing, whether in war or through exploitation. What after all is defensive war? Why does one nation attack another? Probably the nation that is attacked has provoked that attack through economic exploitation and greed. . . . There is such a thing as voluntarily dying for a cause; but that a group of people should send out other human

beings to be trained to kill and be killed, is most barbarous and inhuman. . . . From my point of view, to kill is fundamentally evil, as it is evil to exploit another. . . . Most of you are horrified at the idea of killing; but when there is provocation you are all up in arms. This provocation comes through propaganda, through the appeal to your false emotions of nationalism, family, honour and prestige, which are words without deep significance. . . . One is so proud of being an American or belonging to some particular race, the class and racial distinction is so falsely stimulated in each one of us, that one despises foreigners, Jews, Negroes, or Asiatics.

In these passages, evidently, we have a determined conviction that the rising tide of colour brooks no denial. White dominance indeed rests on no superiority of intellect, morality or culture. A hundred years ago when the mild Chinese struggled to fend off the curse of opium, forced on their country at the cannon's mouth, their name for the English thrusters was 'the laboriously vile', with emphasis on the bad manners, alleged so often subsequently to have 'lost us India'. The differences which distinguish colour groupings are as nothing to the profound identity of nature that proclaims the *unity of men*. Here, anthropology and biology are in agreement with the presupposition of philosophy. Equally peremptory is the verdict of comparative psychology. As Dr Raynard West asserted during World War II: 'Nowhere in a generation of psychoanalytical literature has it appeared that any findings of psychoanalysis are essentially peculiar to any country or race.'[3] So that the racial conceit that brands whole populations as natives, colonials, foreigners, dagoes, wops, niggers is not merely insulting, it is unutterably ignorant. Not without reason, therefore did Dr West add:

Mankind needs to become clear about two truths here. One is that the characters of most men are very similar. The other is that those very similar characters are very mixed and can show very good or very bad qualities *according to circumstances*.[4]

The bearing of this assemblage of views on the question of questions should be obvious. There is no room in a civilised world for imperialism and war. The efficient cause has been notorious since Plato. Only propaganda has veiled the true reason, exposed for our generation in books like *Why War?* and in *Satyagraha* literature as *pleonexia* in all cases. Thanks to virulent propaganda millions of dupes have fanatically marched forth to kill their fellow men for reasons stigmatized by all the best thinkers from Plato to Krishnamurti.

The motives suggested and the passions inflamed by bellicose politicians are illusory; never what Bosanquet would admit to be 'really real'. In action, limited or all-out, they have proved to be a snare and delusion. The ideological trappings still mesmerise multitudes, and are a source of infinite heroism, culminating in Japanese self-immolation comparable with the *devotiones* of the Decii. But the taint of murder and cruelty is inevitable whenever a shot is fired in anger or from greed of gain, in the control or in the man who pulls the trigger. Men go to war, as Plato averred, for the sake of money: the pretence that mass murder is redeemed by a longing on the part of the slayer to save the dead man's soul has worn very thin in view of the grim dénouement, the veritable sin against God and man, condoned and sanctified, as Krishnamurti observes, by the clergy of Christian nations. The thesis of war in a good cause has in fact become farcical, if not grotesque and blasphemous.

It is to be hoped that the mordant critiques of Asians and Africans will help to put across the lesson that the saner spirits in the West failed to impart, and actually induce our rulers to *think*. The prospect is none too rosy. Long since, Matthew Arnold 'often wondered whether upon the whole earth there is anything so unintelligent, so unapt to perceive how the world is really going, as an ordinary young Englishman of our upper class.'

For those who have followed the reasoning set forth above and who realise that wars are bred in the minds of men there can be little doubt that in this appraisal of the intelligence of the ordinary upper class we get the key to the contemporary débâcle. Only inveterate, crass stupidity could have dragged us into forty wars since Waterloo. Arnold died in 1888, two years before the dismissal of Bismarck, in whose absence from the helm our insularity of outlook became, as we have seen, a desperate menace. As regards the vice, which he dubbed Philistinism, there was no such expression in England: 'Perhaps we have not the word because there is so much of the thing,' he dryly observed.

The failing, of course, is common in all lands and in all ages. But nowhere has it developed so prodigiously as in these islands. The empire on which the sun never sets has been a dangerous forcing-ground. How could it be otherwise? Is not the racial pride incarnate in Rhodes rooted in his blind worship of successful aggression? And how can a statesman befogged by misty ideas engendered by the superiority complex achieve the ability of seeing both sides of an international question?

Is not then Matthew Arnold vindicated by the course of events since his death? Who in our turbulent island story since 1900 has risen above the common level of the upper class in his statecraft? Brilliant dialectical displays in superabundance and in a Lloyd George spontaneous eloquence; but of wisdom and the goodwill how little!

Thus civilisation is in mortal peril, largely because absolute and irresponsible power has been in the wrong hands, wielded by men of the Rhodes type, men full of dynamic and general capacity in many instances and in that sense *extra-ordinary*, supermen. But always in calibre *ordinary* both in ethical quality and in intellectual stature.

Surely it is infinitely sad that in a futile effort to arrest the inevitable march of humanity towards liberation and the full life, a few handfuls of arrogant and incompetent rulers endowed with vast, if brief, authority should have been able to touch off in 1914 the train of atrocious disasters which threatens to bury the civilisation of 1900 in a dishonoured radio-active grave.

Chapter Seven

SOPHISTS AND WARMONGERS

THE EVIL WROUGHT by the oligarchies of the Great Powers was rendered possible by the predominance of their pseudo-philosophy in an era of rapidly increasing affluence. The Rhodes type operating in the Kaffir Circus, hand in glove with copper kings, international finance, company promoters, press barons and bureaucrats, exalted big business and the apolaustic way of life inculcated by materialism. The good for man was frankly identified with sensual satisfactions whose content diminishes by sharing, thus substituting egoism for altruism, self-regarding competition for co-operation and strife for mutual goodwill. And yet, as the movement inspired by the School of Green demonstrated, the claims of the higher values were being urged more vigorously than ever before, and even the players in the scoundrels' game whose stronghold was a Foreign Office had to mask their autocratic rule with a show of benevolence. Hence the official stress on the white man's burden and the transcendent merits of law and order, no matter how arbitrary. Hence too the apologies for the bloodstained rearguard actions fought by the Establishments against the forces of self-determination and patriotism, while in every corner of the globe the white man's *mission civilisatrice* was held in derision.

For the system belied, as Caird once for all demonstrated, the very root idea of civilisation. Where in all the story of white domination is there an instance of conquest and alien control which can be reconciled with the brotherhood of man, the good neighbour, the five freedoms, service, equality, liberty? Is not the flouting of these principles the secular sin of wealthy, industrialised and mechanised nations? And is it not inevitable that men who command and perform all the coercive deeds inseparable from invasion and occupation should become brutalised? Moreover, while both the master races and their subjects are demoralised, is not the corruption born of violence more insidious than that born of suffering? Apart from the soul rot, which is cruelty and injustice

131

planted in the wielder of arbitrary power, he cannot escape the associated disease of intellectual dishonesty; he is driven to justify his actions before civilised world opinion by sophistry more or less conscious. Thus we observe in the modern politician who dedicates himself to the scoundrel's game the mentality that was rife in a Cleon or a Thrasymachus; Grey, Rhodes and the jingo school in general are profoundly sophisticated.

A glance at the part played by the Sophists of classical Greece will make this clear. For these men had much to do with the spread of pernicious doctrines. They were the professors of the art of living, the teachers and peripatetic lecturers who undertook the higher education of the time. Their influence, however, tended to undermine morality, public and private, by lowering standards of birth and ideas of justice. Thrasymachus was only one of the school and thanks to Plato became the classic exponent of the heresy *might is right*. As a class, being materialists and individualists, they were hedonists and utilitarians in theory, and in practice addicted to avaricious scales of fees that earned them the reproach of being mercenary. Such in general terms are the grounds on which the disrepute attaching to sophistry has been based for four and twenty centuries.

It is the misfortune of the British as of all other democracies that excessive influence is accorded to the affluent section of the community. Ambitious citizens know that success depends on the ability to outshine their fellows in public speaking. Everywhere in the so-called free world something like the wordy arts that prevailed in small Hellenic city states is rampant today. In the market place of Athens, in the law-courts, the Assembly, the clubs, the gymnasium, the theatre, in philosophical côteries and on 'Change the eternal debate that makes up life in public swayed the minds of young and old and decided their fate. Then, as always, inducements to excel in controversy were strong and, since talent can be developed by practice and instruction, professionals came forward to assist, and soon evolved the art and theory known ever since as rhetoric. Although many of these specialists were charlatans some were highly accomplished and gifted with considerable speculative ability, amounting even to genius.

Gorgias, for example, soon earned fame by his eloquence and turned the prestige won by his brilliant addresses to good account, drawing hosts of pupils who paid handsomely for his services.

Being versed in Ionian philosophy he made a name for himself also in that field. His metaphysical books lacked nothing in subtlety, and propounded an arresting thesis. It was he in fact who first defended the famous paradox: 'Nothing exists; if anything exists it cannot be known; if anything exists and can be known, it cannot be expressed in words.' The challenge to all seekers after knowledge certainly lacked nothing in precision!

The scepticism fathered by Gorgias was reinforced by other sophists. Protagoras was much admired for his sweeping nihilism, conveyed in the aphorism, 'man is the measure of all things', a pronouncement that saps the foundations of science, philosophy and theology, as meaning that what appears to each individual to be true is true for him and that there is no objective truth by which a statement can be tested. The climax of his scepticism was reached in the dictum: 'Concerning the gods, whether they exist or not I am unable to say, owing to the obscurity of the subject and the shortness of human life.' Yet in spite of his seeming agnosticism or atheism Protagoras may not have been a revolutionary; but the disintegrating influence of all such scepticism on traditional morality, especially in public life, was formidable. It was inevitable therefore, that Socrates, Plato and Aristotle, who were bent on the creation of a positive, authentic idealism dedicated to goodness and truth, should in their turn restate, in order to refute, these half-baked sophistical theories. To that extent their labours were critical and devastating and they have been charged with unfairness by Grote and others of utilitarian tendencies; but, even though the imputation of avarice and dishonesty was undeserved by some, the movement led by Protagoras and Gorgias wrought much mischief. It needs no great insight to comprehend the disastrous consequences that flew from the demoralisation of a ruling class whether in a tiny Greek republic or in a colossal modern democracy. Illustrations of such contamination crowd recent history, as should be evident to all.

If it be self-evident to civilised and semi-civilised men and women that justice, goodness and truth form an impregnable basis for the good life, and that they make up an indivisible whole, it is no less evident that justice and truth are so inextricably blended that in the story of human affairs great and small *justice is truth in action* and conversely that *injustice is falsehood in action*. Perhaps that aphorism helps to make it clear that the entire tale of inglorious wrong contrived by the ministers of our age is the translation of foul lies into horrifying action, and that however facile such propositions may sound—even otherworldly ones like the commonplace *God is love*—yet taken seriously they are the only practical principles. When we reach the realities of experience and life, political and moral, these abstract formulae go into action and form the stuff that makes history. In the age of super-violence, an age pullulating with atrocities, it is vital to realise that every injustice is falsehood in the act, *the lie* manifest in crime. We cannot be too exacting, therefore, in our demand that the nation's affairs be conducted with relentless veracity, and in appraising the record of the leaders this aspect of their statecraft must rank high in the final reckoning. How then do our leaders answer to this acid test? Their attitude to justice and truth is of transcendent import, and cannot be too scrupulously examined. If some are the liars that many believe them to be, the unjust acts authorised by them should be treated as the work of dishonourable politicians, not of licensed prevaricators whose integrity must never be called in question.

After all it is not larceny or bribery or physical violence that has polluted the conduct of politicians in modern times; the pollution comes from mendacity. On this sin reticence on the part of a historian is inexcusable. The lies that did most damage were those sponsored by Balfour and his jingo alarmists, regarding the German menace, the bogy of invasion. It was against those that Morel prophetically warned the nation. Stop trusting these men's *veracity*, he urged when they sought support, for 'if we do, we murder truth and in murdering truth we encompass our own destruction. May the Lord deliver us from a pharisaism which in its ultimate consequences must be fatal to us and to every liberal influence in the world.'

In so writing Morel laid bare the root of the Upas tree whose sap poisons the relations between the nations of the earth, which then had become a prey to the habit of falsehood among our rulers. Thus arose the cult of the lie which counts its victims by scores of millions dead and has not after forty years slaked its thirst for blood, sweat, toil and tears.

The new history has elaborated Morel's contention in hundreds of treatises and the important facts are too solidly established to be shaken. Not so familiar, however, are the implications of the moral débâcle which attended the political convulsions. How is the ethos displayed by these propagators of falsehood to be judged? That they were guilty of the most dishonourable conduct brooks no denial, and in their official capacity they were shameless.

Of course it is chiefly in the case of Grey that the habit of falsehood was so sinister that some explanation is called for.

The fatal dualism ascribed to Grey in Dean Inge's *Fall of the Idols* is a polite description of the habit of falsehood which was his chronic disease in guiding England towards the abyss. There were others, less polite, like Morel and Francis Neilson, who treated it as a lurid example of the mendacity which became endemic among the men who held the reins of power from 1900 onwards.

But the enlightenment in England reached a small minority. For the bulk of the nation the only channel through which the academic history could percolate was the Popular Press. Whereas Cecil Rhodes commanded the services of numberless supporters in the press and among the politicians the following of the thinkers, of the School of Green and the revisionists, was small. In Oxford, the home of idealism in 1900, there were many academic groups in which the School of Green was little understood. R. G. Collingwood, Professor of Metaphysics, is instructive on that point. Not many dons had the speculative capacity to grasp the teaching of T. H. Green, Edward Caird, F. H. Bradley and Bernard Bosanquet, to name a few of the School. In any event, when the acid test arrived with the intrusion of Cecil Rhodes and his millions, the home of lost causes lived down to its reputation. By conferring on the most flamboyant exponent of militarist money power in British history the benediction of an academic élite, Oxford endorsed the civilising mission propagated by bribes and trickery, backed by bullets, for which Rhodes had been censured by a Royal Commission, and accepted the tainted millions without compunction.

To appreciate the meaning of this capitulation one must realise what Caird and his supporters stood for, and how natural it was that they tried to stem the ultra-imperialist tide. The nation was agog with the All-Red-Route expansionism of Rhodes and Joseph Chamberlain and looked on with bated breath while annexations and tariffs added fuel to the flames of party strife. Not many onlookers then could perceive the bearing of Oxford idealism on foreign policy or the connection between the annexation of the Transvaal and the drift to war in Europe. Still less did the politician or the man in the street comprehend the driving force of the conviction shared by all civilised men and voiced by philosophers and scientists as the society of man. They doubtless sensed the threat to imperial ascendancy from the reinforced philanthropy inculcated by the Churches and in practice relegated to the heavenly kingdom; but neither then nor fifty years later did they suspect that almost unconsciously the bulk of the human race was thinking along the line of revolutionary ethics, and that the theory of power politics had no rational basis.

There has been so much talk of impersonal forces, the spirit of the age, social pressures, economic laws, as the governing agencies in shaping human affairs that the personal equation often drops out of sight. Yet the story hammered out of the state papers demonstrates beyond question the enormous power exercised by a few individuals in crisis after crisis where the psychological moment arrived to strengthen a tendency or take a vital decision. The last word rests with sometimes a single functionary, sometimes an inner ring, but never with the sovereign people. Fateful actions determining war or peace have not once in a century been submitted to or ratified by more than a small group of autocrats, and the bigger the democracy the more does the iron law of oligarchy prevail. Thus the intensely personal and individual character of the oligarchs counts for everything once the huge assemblage of interests opposed to peace is about evenly balanced against the vast array of pacific forces; hence the furious battles that rage round the character and capacity of Wilhelm II, Nicholas II and his Ministers, Poincaré, Grey, Presidents Wilson and Roosevelt, not to mention the Dictators. More relevant to the present diagnosis of the moral degradation which made a hell of Europe is a study of the typical peacemaker and his counterpart in the camp of the makers of war.

Because the myriads of degraders have monopolised the organs of publicity for so many years it has been easy to disparage, ignore or smear the idealists who in the Victorian era strove to halt the onward march of materialism. The spate of new books—30,000 per annum—washes over, and tends to wash out, the works of the masters. Bosanquet's classic, *The History of Aesthetic*, is *terra incognita* to the hosts of muddle-headed critics of the fine arts, Caird's *Evolution of Religion* has been swamped by floods of ingenious scepticism, dogmatism, theosophy, supernaturalism, rationalism, existentialism, fundamentalism, agnosticism, atheism, materialism, monotheism, polytheism, anthropomorphism, spiritualism, all inviting earnest attention and explanation as examples of the search for the Infinite in which every religion participates. By tracking down this unity of aim and principle through centuries of growth and by exhibiting all varieties of cult and theology as the outcome of development Caird was able to depict the whole process as a gradual progress from lower and cruder conceptions of the Infinite to the higher and more refined. Inevitably too, as an idealist, he found the highest in the conception of self-sacrificing love, dying to live, the Cross, of which the familiar exposition resides in The Sermon on the Mount, whose content makes an end of hate, envy and all uncharitableness for those who accept it.

In the rough and tumble of everyday life this lofty creed suffers the fate which all deplore, but at the worst within a modern nation there are powerful agencies that keep the creed alive as an element in popular thought, tending in that way to point the way to happier things. It is common experience, however, that Christianity has never been tried, and the golden rule is far more honoured in the breach than in the observance. In private life and in business, if at times a smattering of Christian altruism survives, the occasion is marked with a white stone, although innate kindliness plays a large part in social relations and real deference is paid to conventions that generally presuppose an awakened moral sense. Precepts that exalt self-sacrifice, however, commonly enshrined in the current religions, suffer from the imputation of other-worldliness, and as Peter Howard, a favourite columnist of the Beaverbrook Press, asserted, met with nothing but contempt from editors and colleagues when alluded to in Fleet Street. In this episode evidently we encounter in a glaring form the same revolt against the restraints of New Testament ethic that led Grey to his fatal dualism and inspired Cecil Rhodes to swindle Lobengula out of his heritage or an investor in Chartereds out of his good money. The matter was considerably altered, however, when Rhodes, Chamberlain, Lansdowne or Grey was confronted with a code that had not merely pulpit and other worldly sanction but was powerfully reinforced by modern speculation and the most advanced science. So hard is it to understand the blindness of these men and millions of their followers that one can hardly credit that they had any share of the modern enlightenment or that they ever heard of the conviction of civilised human beings which was destined to sweep away their most cherished illusions.

It is not too much to say that two malignant diseases have brought the leading nations to the brink—mendacity and cruelty. With their associated vices of *pleonexia* and hatred they accounted for the major disasters of the age and have been faithfully recorded in diplomatic history by the leading scholars of the Powers. The actors in the drama who concern us most nearly are principally the five. They had their way and set the stage for fleets and armies and financiers and are, so to speak, known to the police. Yet the enigma remains—how did Lansdowne and Grey, in tune with Rhodes and Chamberlain, embrace a line of conduct which clashed with the well-known philosophy of Caird and Bosanquet and the rest of the Resistance?

If we stop for a moment to observe the mentality of Edward Caird, we note first of all an Olympian air natural to a 'master of those who know'. A glance at the author of the *Critical Philosophy of Kant* lecturing to a crowded Balliol Hall on the 'Moral Philosophy of Aristotle' was enough to convince an undergraduate that his disapproval of Cecil Rhodes and the Boer War had no touch of insincerity in it. The reverence to which William Temple testified accompanied him from Glasgow to Oxford and had more in it than admiration evoked by a magnificent intellect. Like Bosanquet who, when he came under the tutorship of T. H. Green was regarded as the best equipped undergraduate of his time, Caird had an enormous store of the *humaniora* which so largely make up genuine culture. If it was impossible for either Caird or Bosanquet to rival Hegel who had read 'all the best', there were few provinces of consequence in which they were entire strangers. Both had drunk and drunk deep of the Pierian spring. On every vacation for many years Caird read alternately the Iliad and the Odyssey; while Bosanquet has acknowledged his debt to Plato and Hellenism in no uncertain terms. What it meant to be steeped in Homer, whose chief distinction, as Matthew Arnold pointed out, was to be always *noble*, should be self-evident. There was nothing inspiring in the achievement of the Greeks and Romans that was inaccessible to Caird or Bosanquet. In philosophy the modern world could show nothing to rival the *Metaphysics* of Aristotle but the *Logic* of Hegel. Nothing in all prose literature to equal the *Apology, Crito*, and *Phaedo*, written to commemorate the martyr Socrates—'of all the men of his day whom we have known the best and wisest and most just'. No other school to match Plato's—'the olive groves

of Academe'—that lasted 900 years and came to life with the
Renaissance, never again to be submerged. Equally at home with
Sophocles, Dante, Goethe, Milton and Shakespeare and with
Europeans (scholars and gentlemen), their whole energies dedi-
cated to the promotion of justice, goodness and truth. Worlds
apart from the insularity and scraggy mental ideology of a Cecil
Rhodes or an Edward Grey.

It is in this, the flagrant, appalling contrast between this mental
idealism equipment and the mind of the men who held the reins
of power among us in the critical decade before 1914 that the key
must be sought to the enigma of the Bonne Entente. There is a
taint in all its words and deeds.

From the outset the Alliance was steeped in sophistry. The
document in which it was supposed to be published to the world
was a deliberate fabrication intended to deceive and converted into
a shameless lie by the secret articles which formed the real contract.
The mendacity of Lansdowne and Delcassé became the basis of
the Alliance under Grey, and set the problem for students of
the period—how to assess the degree of dishonour involved in the
deception and in the contemplated aggressions. Intellectually the
vice of the statesmen who forged the Declaration can be nothing
less than that of Protagoras who denied that the conception of a
common objective truth should control men's thinking. Lansdowne and Delcassé definitely perceived that the secret articles
transformed the Declaration into a lie; Lansdowne confessed that
the project was dishonourable and if made public would brand its
authors as treaty-breakers[1]; but committed the nation to the crime.
In so doing they virtually excluded from international diplomacy
the obligation to respect veracity. Next, seeing that the conception
of a common objective truth is not to control our thinking, there is
no reason why the conception of a good common to all men should
control inter-state relations. Here the thesis of Thrasymachus
received its sanction, and there was no impediment in theory or
practice to hinder a Foreign Secretary from adopting sophistry in
its extreme form. The theory that, because Britain and France had
abundant power to coerce Egypt and Morocco, British and French
statesmen were free to consider nothing but their national interests,
if disgraceful in a Greek sophist under parallel circumstances, had
really become more flagitious thanks to the spread of modern
cosmopolitanism through the society of man.

Grey's joyful complicity *ex post facto* is an added offence, whether he had seen the Lansdowne-Cromer correspondence or not. The plea of ignorance, which so often was his excuse, might have been difficult in that case to refute, but it was otherwise with the Five Secret Articles. His entire policy for nine years—persisted in by his successors for another forty years—pivoted on those same five articles; so that actually he not merely sanctioned the lie but accepted it as his directive. Any pretence that he had not studied their contents was, moreover, negatived by the naïve dismissal of the Articles that held him a willing slave to French Chauvinism as a few clauses of no importance. After all much shrewdness and a tenacious memory are needed to make a success in equivocation at the highest level. Grey's pretence too, that it was not a Triple Entente was merely a blind to lull the suspicions of the Liberal mass who detested the corrupt and dangerous Russian autocracy. Lansdowne's hole-and-corner pact with Delcassé was concealed from the nation and Europe for seven years and to this day has been understood by a mere handful of specialists only. Dissimulation, equivocation, evasions, denials and flat-footed lying by ministers were needed to deceive the people. None of that was imaginable in diplomacy conducted by men of the Caird-Bosanquet stamp.

How would they have characterised the lying and the cruelty implicit in the famous Entente? It is pitiful to think that like Bernard Shaw and millions more, Bosanquet believed it was the Kaiser who struck the first blow, that he never heard Grey admit that the Kaiser did not want war. He actually was taken in by Grey's affectation of regret that he had not pursued a more positive policy of conciliation. That Lansdowne or Grey could stoop to lying he could not suspect, and the evidence never reached him. And there precisely lies the stumbling-block. No ingenuous Britisher could dream that a Minister of State would lie and deceive him. Indeed such is the legend of Ministerial integrity, that, in the teeth of a mass of incriminating evidence adduced by specialists, the official historian Dr Gooch pronounced Grey to be the *noblest* of the statesmen who went to war in 1914.

The eccentricities of war hysteria are scandalous, but some are understandable; hero-worship for instance is inevitable during the fever, but as a rule it is short-lived. Lloyd George was acclaimed in the House as the man who won the war. Yet the cheers that greeted Field Marshal Sir Henry Wilson's eulogy, culminating in 'You, you alone, won the war' had not long died away before Bonar Law derided him as the drummer-boy and dealt him the knock-out at the Carlton Club. Similarly Presidents Wilson, Franklin Roosevelt, Truman enjoyed brief moments of worship as saviours of the world, soon to be eclipsed by new idols. All the more surprising is the persistence of adulation wasted on the author of *Twenty-five Years*.

Assuming that Dr Gooch meant seriously, despite the habit of falsehood cultivated by Grey from his apprenticeship to Foreign Affairs under Lords Kimberley and Rosebery up to the composition of his autobiography, that he was in retrospect the noblest Roman of them all, the inference must be that the disease of insincerity did actually infect the whole of semi-official as well as official historiography after 1906. It was not only that the acts and professions of Cabinet Ministers violated the conviction of all civilised men by the systematic persecution of a sister nation, but that, after their crime was exposed through the pulverising of the Versailles Dictate, with rare exceptions British scholars put up a smoke-screen of shoddy sophistry to obscure the reality.

The contamination of official and semi-official history, resulting from the fixed idea that in external affairs a Foreign Secretary of the Lansdowne and Grey class does not lie, explains the refusal of British scholars to state plainly the virus in the soul-rot that drew down on Europe what the Pope on Easter Sunday, 1957, called this night of the world. 'A night full of groaning and hope, but night.' Since 1938 most of these critics have toiled to discredit Hitler as 'an utter liar'; and since 1947 Stalin's diplomacy has enjoyed an even more sinister celebrity, as it did for twenty years preceding 1940. But when it comes to a probe of the false policy of the Entente the slur on Grey is seldom accepted as a stigma to be eradicated by a scientific examination of his record, but is met by a counterblast intended to present him as a saint. For that is what Dr Gooch implied when he pinned the label of *noblest* on his hero. Gilbert Murray was another of the claque. Yet both of these partisans had before them definite proof that Grey's Continental repute as a prevaricator was thoroughly justified. Morel had drawn their attention to bare-faced lies uttered by Grey before and early in the war, comparable with the false charges which the Allies relied upon to make good their case at Versailles.

141

That for a decade after 1906 Grey was the power behind the denigration of Germany is beyond dispute. The jingo Opposition supplied the frenzied propaganda and Grey, whose duty it was to blast its authors, connived. Even in the House he treated them as fellow-travellers, affecting a studied moderation, yet in each crisis emerging to play the part of supreme official incendiary. Such a crisis arrived in March 1915, six months after he dragged England into the conflict.

This was the momentous crisis when Nicholas II made his Allies toe the line. And thus Poincaré and Grey, in secret, signed away Stamboul and much else of Turkey to the Tsar. This tremendous capitulation, nevertheless, although given to the world by Lenin's orders in 1917 has been for practical purposes buried in oblivion. In England only the *Manchester Guardian* published the text—since when silence! Yet its terms are unequivocal and scholars like Gooch are fully aware of their commanding importance.

Not merely did Grey abandon the century-old British maxim 'the Russians shall not have Constantinople' but he executed a flight from the unyielding position occupied by himself seven short years earlier. In 1908 when Austria altered the status of Bosnia-Herzegovina, by previous agreement with Isvolski, Grey had blocked the path to an Austro-Russian understanding through a denial to Isvolski of the control of the Straits which Aehrenthal had conceded to him at Buchlau in September.

To square the judgment passed by the Editor of the British Documents with the facts of Grey's twenty-five years is a plain impossibility. Apart from everything else he was open to the damning charge of insincerity. If he was not a wolf in sheep's clothing he was at heart on the one issue that counted insincere. He was a Tory jingo posing as a Liberal. As such he was compelled to act a part. But the intriguing problem of his ethical quality remains, to baffle others besides a Gooch or a Gilbert Murray. For it is a question of degrees and grades of vice and virtue.

How far was Grey untruthful, false, insincere, how far dull and stupid? To what extent was he the victim of the code which spawned the Five Secret Articles? How far was his opportunism individual and temperamental? Was he really, as Foreign Secretary, ignoble, *pace* Dr Gooch and the rest? In his private life he was voted charming and correct, but there was nothing to mark him out from other north country squires; and it is his conduct of the

Foreign Office that matters. His *Twenty-five Years* is his apologia, every page of it composed to defend a thesis, the contention, namely, that not he but the Kaiser was the architect of the war.

As to that, seeing that Gooch, with his comprehensive knowledge of the Documents, pronounced the *Kaiser's War* thesis of Versailles to be a *legend*, it will always remain a flat contradiction that he also pronounced Grey to be the noblest of the statesmen who sponsored the war. The paradox, however, is rendered less violent when the assumption with which an English historian approaches the record of a British Foreign Secretary whose honour is impugned is kept in view. The first maxim of British diplomatic *history* is that all Foreign Secretaries are honourable men.

Bernard Shaw's gibe: 'An Englishman is never in the wrong applies without reserve to Downing Street,' the self-righteousness which he pillories counts for a great deal in private life and in public affairs generally, but in foreign relations it is crucial. Yet nothing can produce national soul-rot more infallibly than an overdose of conscious rectitude. In every dispute with the foreigner it at once passes over to bias, lop-sidedness, slander and false-witness-bearing. And organised slander makes hatred and eventually massacre.

In the business of slandering a sister-nation no other Foreign Secretary has been so successful as Grey. His *Twenty-five Years* reeks of this vicious habit, and examples have been detected in every chapter. Many historians have castigated the vice, notably the highly competent scholar Hermann Lutz, in *Lord Grey and the War*. There, in relation to the malignant charge that Germany's Turkish policy had helped to breed the Armenian atrocities of 1895 and 1896, Lutz convicts Grey of having deliberately circulated *a total untruth* prompted by *an excess of moral indignation*.[2] And this excess receives a cool appraisal which most foreigners and many British must endorse. To avoid unfairness Lutz allows Grey to speak for himself, selecting as essential the lengthy disquisition printed on pages 131–134 of his first volume. One of these paragraphs strikes the keynote, and this is how it runs:

> German policy seems to have been based upon a deliberate belief that moral scruples and altruistic motives do not count in international affairs. Germany did not believe that they existed in other nations, and she did not assume them for herself. The highest morality for a German Government was the national interest.

143

Such was the Grey case in a nutshell. What has historical criticism to say in reply?

In the same volume, observed Lutz, Grey had asserted that British Foreign Ministers had been guided, not simply by national interest, but by Britain's *immediate interest*.[3] Accordingly it leaps to the eye that Grey accepted national interest as the legitimate principle of British policy, coolly admitting that British Ministers were opportunists and assuming that their hand-to-mouth opportunism, having promoted British supremacy, was not merely rewarding but right. But what was right in Downing Street was wrong in the Wilhelmstrasse.

Not that he condescends to explain his double standard. All he does is to jump with agility from the position that British policy based on short term calculations of self-interest is laudable, to the position that any calculation of national self-interest in Berlin is wicked. More than that, Germany did not even profess, or as he expresses it, *assume* moral scruples and altruistic motives for herself, whereas, after disclaiming these in a candid moment, he assumes them as a matter of course for England. Such is the clowning that passed for his exposition of statecraft in London and Berlin. No wonder that Dr Lutz resented such a 'sound scourging'.[4]

What every non-British scholar is bound to dispute is Grey's postulate of the moral superiority of English foreign policy over that of any other Great Powers. Modern historians who share the convictions of all civilised men must especially deny the right of any Foreign Secretary to exaggerate the vices of a rival nation by underrating the faults of his own if nothing else. The dogma of society forbids a display of self-righteous detraction by the spokesman of any people. As the successor of a long line of ministers and monarchs who have determined English foreign policy for centuries each must expect to be judged by the tradition which he inherits as well as by the course taken by himself. Which being self-evident, Grey was extremely rash to embark upon a comparison between the ethic of Downing Street and that of the Wilhelmstrasse. Had he been truly civilised in his conduct of Anglo-German affairs the last thing he would have suggested was that his own moral scruples and altruistic motives surpassed those of the Kaiser and his ministers, not to mention the German people, whom he included in his vilification.

To begin with he was the representative for eleven tragic years of an establishment which had a militant past, and a present which had evolved consistently out of that past. It was his fate to preside over its conduct during the decade which was to crown its achievement with success or disaster; and having precipitated the catastrophe which millions feared he resorted to the barbarous device of denigrating the enemy whose noble policy he had largely helped to ruin. Having viewed from a safe distance the quagmire to which the Allies had reduced the Central Empire he thought fit to embitter their defeat by robbing them, the Germans, of their good name. Before provoking reprisals by odious comparisons he should have bethought himself of the record.

In the record of English foreign policy even Grey must have been alive to grievous defects and sins. Dr Lutz recalls[5] some modern instances which indicate that 'perfidious Albion' is no capricious verdict of one envious foe. First on his list comes Ireland 'with its sanguinary story . . . which lasted for centuries and will be remembered for centuries to come'. Next he recalls 'the infamous concentration camps of the South African War and the burnings of farms and homesteads in order more rapidly to break the brave resistance of a small nation of Whites'; Denshawai follows and lastly 'Russia's doings in Persia, which Grey endeavoured to shield as far as possible in face of the indignation in his own country and to defend; these evil deeds of Tsarist Russia, to whom Grey accorded his aid and friendship, and who had the Jews, who dragged out a difficult existence in her confines, killed in their thousands in loathsome pogroms'. Certainly these examples of atrocities perpetrated in Grey's twenty-five years with his approval or by his authority stamp him as a jingo of the Rhodes school for all his moral scruples and raise the question of his title to pose as the European censor of international ethics.

For the legacy of violent deeds inherited from the past he was not responsible except in so far as he imbibed the spirit of them and infused it into his own words and deeds. He could have given, however, a bent to policy in harmony with the Liberal impetus fostered by Bright, Cobden and Gladstone. He had his choice under Campbell-Bannerman, and reverted to methods of barbarism. In his case they were directed not against a 'small nation of Whites' but against a vigorous commercial rival which could conceivably sap the economic foundations of the top-heavy empire

145

bequeathed to his generation by our ancestors. As the minister in charge of that enormous heritage he undertook to ward off possible threats and, since Germany could not be openly assailed for the reasons advanced by Bonar Law, Birkenhead, Carson *et hoc genus omne*, it was necessary to mask the eventual aggression with a show of moral scruples and altruistic motives. Moreover since no real grounds for an attack on the Central Empires existed it was prudent to hasten slowly and nine years of shifty diplomacy were needed to work on the Anglo-German lunacy. To whip up British resentment roused by the 'million pinpricks' of German competition in world markets to a degree of hatred necessary to sanction an ultimatum required the intervention of just such a politician and just such a propaganda as was portrayed here in his memoirs. The British public had to be bluffed into believing that Germany was the sole wicked nation in Europe and the three pages in question are particularly illuminating since with raw, crude pharisaism they concentrate on the most sensational horror of the two pre-war decades, and affect to explain the massacres executed by Abdul Hamid under the aegis of his friend the Kaiser. Thus the nation was to be weaned away from its old Anglo-German amity.

Grey's lame excuses for his appalling prejudice merely rivet the guilt more tightly round his neck and it is only because the crime against humanity implied in his misconduct is so terrible and the proof is so complete that the controversy was shifted by the defence to other ground. Baffled in the attempt to sustain his complete untruth—elaborated but unaltered in the Versailles Dictate—his defenders fell back on the flimsy argument that although the evidence disproves his thesis of 'Germany the sole wicked nation', Grey believed it and, because he was Grey of Falloden, when he opened his lips no dog should bark. Was he not the noblest of the ministers in the greatest crisis of our history?

In fact the clash between appearances and reality was so crashing that the only explanation advanced by scientific historians came to be that Grey was a sort of Jekyll and Hyde personality or a hypocrite. From the outset of his political career, indeed, the frightful imputation of hypocrisy and perfidy tenaciously clung to his statecraft, rendering it inevitable that his character should be a leading theme in all serious discussion of war guilt, as being ultimately the determining factor in shaping the world order of the most catastrophic of the centuries.

The enigma lies in the enormity of the sin diagnosed by Dean Inge in *The Fall of the Idols*. In foreign policy Grey had renounced the christian code and substituted for the principles of justice, goodness and truth the pursuit of the nation's immediate interests. In practice, for generations that has resolved itself into the ancient heresy, justice in the interest of the stronger, with its glorification of violence and aggression. Such was the tradition inherited by British ministers and it is only in the context of that long tradition that non-British observers can accept Grey's sincerity as credible. To evolve the mentality of the minister who cherished an 'appalling prejudice' against Germany and yet denied that he was moved by it to an anti-German policy, while nevertheless he firmly believed himself to be just, good and truthful, nothing less than generations of successful self-seeking could suffice. The self-deception which no individual could encompass in a lifetime was made more comprehensible when viewed as achieved by an endless chain of practising predecessors, that train of potentates, those functionaries, counsellors, ministers and monarchs stretching back to the Plantagenet dynasty who had built up Great and Greater Britain. Unconsciously and consciously it was that ancestral chain of ministers whose precepts and example Grey followed, and by scanning the doings of some outstanding members of the line, it is possible to grasp the essence of their policy and its ethos. Seen as a continuous stream broadening down from precedent to precedent its character of aggressive expansionism dedicated to unlimited *pleonexia* becomes transparent. Its unity of aim and purpose is unmistakable. With the expulsion from Normandy died serious expansionism on the Continent, but the spirit of the movement persisted into the Twentieth Century; so that the Joan of Arc episode is illuminating and paves the way for an assessment, by modern standards, of the English achievement. But if the historian is to do full justice to 'the unshakable conviction of superiority over other folk and of destination by Providence to act, from generations ago, as administrator of morality and progress for the good of backward peoples',[6] he must bear in mind the moral qualifications of the islanders at the outset. Only thus can he compare the moral assets then existing with those discernible at the close of the era of conquest. To trace the working of the dogma of a divine commission (to rule beyond the seas) from the débâcle in Normandy to the débâcle of World War II is to follow the development of British Sea Power from small beginnings to world supremacy, accomplished, if Churchill is to be believed, after 1815 and about a century later with incalculable consequences.

In tracking down the origin and essence of 'the conviction of superiority over other folk' which Dr Lutz relies upon in his amiable desire to acquit English policy of chronic hypocrisy it is instructive to observe how Shakespeare renders the complex. 'I thought upon one pair of English legs did march three Frenchmen' (III *Henry V*, II, vi, 116) connotes superior power and in the use of it the direction is ruthless. 'When the blast of war blows in our ears, then imitate the action of the tiger.' Such is the military attitude from first to last both in the fifteenth and in the twentieth century. There is just a hint in Shakespeare, as there was in Virgil, that warfare was not all glory and gain. 'I am afeered there are few die well in battle; for how can they charitably dispose of anything when blood is their argument?' But far more significant than the slaughter of Frenchmen at Agincourt and Crecy was the burning at the stake of Jeanne d'Arc.

Anatole France leaves us in no doubt regarding the French (and world) view of that atrocity. From the moment she was surrendered to the English, he wrote, the Maid was doomed. Thereafter came the martyrdom and to cap the grisly proceedings 'The Lord Chancellor of England sent to the Emperor, to the Kings and to the Princes of Christendom letters in Latin; to the prelates, dukes, counts, lords and to all the towns in France letters in French. Herein he made known to them that King Henry and his Counsellors had had sore pity on the Maid, and that if they had caused her death it was through their zeal for the faith and their solicitude for Christian folk.'

The affinity between the minds of King Henry and his Counsellors on the one hand and on the other the Allied leaders at Versailles, Nuremburg and UNO emerges most forcibly in the letters protesting the purity of their motives and their concern for morals or religion, exactly as their modern imitators find a mantle of holiness in Wars for Righteousness for the security of their way of life and the Free World. Already in 1431 the technique and style of imperialist aggression which was to prevail for five centuries was defined, circumstances altered—a White Diaspora in which England played the leading part, in rivalry with Portugal, Spain, Holland and France, brought the five continents into the European orbit, and repeated on a global scale the cycles of history traversed by many peoples, including the Greeks and the Romans—but the lesson which the forerunners might have taught our ancestors went unheeded, and not even Christian teaching, much less the enlightenment of the eighteenth and nineteenth centuries in Europe changed the foreign policies of the maritime states. *Tu regere imperi populos Britanne memento, (parcere subjectis et debellare superbos)* was good enough for kings, chancellors and foreign secretaries; and in practice was the maxim that led Europe to the brink in the nuclear age. From first to last there was in action no genuine observance of Christian principle in the masters of foreign policy; nor did the group who ran the Foreign Office at the crisis of 1900 exhibit a trace of the humane doctrine common to all civilised men, when the issue of war or peace hung in the balance.

The quintessence of the tradition deriving from the Plantagenet era having been clarified by Anatole France it follows that sundry examples of the same should be glanced at to bring out the fundamental wickedness of it.

After the Plantagenets the Tudors. From 1485 to 1603 the international scene offers fewer object lessons than it did under the Plantagenets. Yet in one respect it was instructive. The drain on the thinly populated African tropics—millions transported to the plantations and millions killed in slave raids—has been already mentioned and it remains merely to stress the astounding capacity of Europeans to reconcile with their consciences the most loathsome exploitation of their fellow-beings so long as it is profitable. The pre-eminence of England in the slave trade, however, is less significant than the wars waged against the competitive slavers, who scoured the same waters. When, by the decision of the Pope, the riches of the East were assigned to the Portuguese, the West to Spain, to be disputed later by the English, the French and the Dutch, the stage was set for the international wars beyond the seas that generated the devastating conflicts which culminated in the present century. When the mentality of the Ministers of our age is examined it is obvious that in England the unbroken though fluctuating tradition derived from the Plantagenets and the Tudors must not be ignored, and the attitude of the Pitts, Burke, Fox, Canning, Palmerston, Gladstone, enriching that tradition, has to be taken into account when examining the records of Salisbury,

Balfour, Lansdowne, Campbell-Bannerman, Chamberlain, Grey, Churchill and others who moulded British policy in the past hundred years. In this sketch of the catastrophe which overtook Britain since Grey went to Downing Street it is enough to indicate the prevailing temper of the oligarchy which steered the ship of state by recalling a few of the episodes that marked its course. An inspection of the forty-three Premiers who directed British policy since 1721 reveals one name that deviated from the line followed by the other forty, the name of Mr. Gladstone. The deviations in theory are considerable in the case of Palmerston, but in practice even the Socialists in general conformed to the rules of the game in foreign affairs throughout the World Wars which shook the Empire and started the disintegration of the mid-century period. While the civilised sections of many nations were imbibing the humanism which will eventually sweep away racialism, colour bars, hostile tariffs and power politics, no change of heart was visible in Downing Street. Under compulsion concessions were made overseas but the Ministers who rendered both World Wars inevitable remained impenetrable, fortified by the superiority complex, and throughout the fifty years of the anti-German crusade never dreamed of granting to their Teutonic cousins the elementary rights conferred on the humblest nation by the enlightened opinions of the modern world.

If the dominant sentiment of the judges was hate it is equally clear that the enterprise which they were serving was inspired by greed, *pleonexia*. The prize was *aurum et opes*, plunder, French territory and its revenues and so it was to be until the war to end war had achieved its purpose—'perpetual war for perpetual peace'. World War I was for the Allies the repetition on a vast scale of the greed, hate and injustice manifest in the Plantagenet invasions of Normandy.

The Frenchman (Anatole France) relates the bald facts, in all their pitiless, impious cruelty, in order to convict the slayers of the Maid not merely of ruthless cruelty and treachery but of shameless hypocrisy. More lenient than Anatole France, Dr Lutz is disposed to credit the modern Englishman with a sluggishness of conscience inconceivable to the Frenchman, yet explicable to the German, through the deadening influence of centuries of successful egoism. There is good sense in this explanation, no doubt, but what applied in 1900 hardly applied in 1400, since the conditioning process counted for less in 1431 than congenital egoism in spurring on an insular race, led by arbitrary rulers, to the direst of crimes.

It seems fitting finally to allow another Frenchman to state his view of the eternal dispute. The most useful appears to be General Huguet who, after Paul Cambon, was more closely identified with the development of the Anglo-French entente than any other French official. He wrote his book in 1922 and delayed publication (till 1928) 'until the time when the principal English actors would have left the stage'—six years later.[7]

After observing gratefully that the 'powers that be' in London definitely and strongly proclaimed the will to defeat Germany he noted that they were not precluded from seeking 'more immediate and more profitable ends. The security of Egypt and of India were numbered amongst them and nobody could deny their legitimacy; but the extension of British power in the East was also one, the possession of Mesopotamia, the mastery of the Bosphorus and of the Dardanelles were three more, and they had for their sole object the guaranteeing of fruitful exploitation of oil-bearing countries, not only to the profit of the British Admiralty, but also of the powerful English oil syndicates, with more personal and less patriotic interests.'[8]

From the moment of the Armistice 'the self-interest of England showed itself without reserve'. So wrote General Huguet.[9] Furthermore: 'Every immediate object had been attained. Germany's Navy existed no longer, her mercantile marine had been shared between the victors, Constantinople was hers, the Turkish Empire appeared to have ceased to exist, the security of Egypt and India was better assured than ever, a few military expeditions seemed all that was necessary to secure complete mastery of the East. The ambitious designs of her financiers and business men were on the point of being realised. She went as far even—to give effect to the long-desired wishes of her Jewish subjects—as to re-establish for their benefit and under her aegis, the ancient Kingdom of Judea.'[10] More disconcerting, if possible, is his firm conviction that the English character is 'summed up in a strong animality, deeply selfish and egoistic like all animal natures, and, like them, ready to sacrifice all for its needs and instincts, without ever being turned aside by any intellectual or moral scruple. Honest and simple in its daily life, it becomes harsh, vindictive and pitiless once its general and particular interests are at stake or its security appears to be

151

menaced; every other consideration is then subordinated to its own preservation or that of its privileges.'

'Emerson', writes Huguet, 'was equally struck with this obvious contradiction, and could not prevent himself from saying with astonishment that " . . . private life is its place of honour. Truth in private life, untruth in public, marks these home-loving men"'. And he goes on: 'Their political conduct is not decided by general views but by internal intrigues and personal and family interests.

'And thus we are witness to a strange dualism in the English character, considered either from the point of view of the individual or of the mass.

'Personally, and in his private life, the individual is without doubt an egoist, but endowed at the same time with the best qualities of simplicity, honesty and loyalty.

'In his public life it is the reverse. The mass, guided solely by the power of money and the search for material gain, becomes harsh, implacable, scarcely scrupulous, sometimes false, and forms today the uncongenial race, whose overthrow would be generally welcomed throughout the world with a sigh of relief and deliverance.'[11]

Most British subjects flatter themselves that they are renowned for 'the best qualities of simplicity, honesty and loyalty'—personally and in their private lives, but they rarely exhibit these qualities in their dealings with the foreigner. Naturally, therefore, there is a large cosmopolitan literature published by foreigners who scent the dualism discussed by Dean Inge, Dr Lutz and General Huguet. The dualism, however, is not so much manifest in the cleavage between the standard in private life and the standard observable in public life. The mass in every nation can be credited with much the same degree of natural simplicity, honesty and loyalty, qualities that show themselves in an infinite variety of forms, according to circumstances. Such differences as exist are due to differing stages of development. Actually, however, every community has its special experience and that constitutes a factor in the mental make-up of its members, so that a Russian, a German, a Spaniard, an Italian, a Dutchman, a Swede, an American, an Englishman betray indiosyncrasies which to a close observer belong to a national type. *Au fond*, however, there is an identity of culture and political experience which renders all Europeans and their New World offshoots, in spite of their late arrival among the progressive nations, relatively competent in the arts of life, pioneers in science, commerce and industry and full of energy in manipulating world affairs. There is little point, therefore, in drawing marked distinctions between Demos in England and Demos in any other Western country, so far as their attitudes to the outside world are concerned. 'Guided solely by the power of money and the search for material gain' the mass rallies to the oligarchy in each act of aggression, so long as it appears to pay, and often when it has become a liability. The mass takes its cue from the few and it is the oligarchy always who determine foreign policy. Inside the frontier, in domestic affairs the oligarchs in modern Europe are often selfish but, since the industrial revolution, have generally reduced privilege to a minimum so that all citizens are equal in the eye of the law. To that extent the ruling class is civilised in its conduct of domestic business. It is in handling external business that barbarism has triumphed in the twentieth century. The ruling classes have submitted to Demos at home and the class war has ceased to breed civil war in several countries, although, as we have seen, the oligarchy which controls foreign policy came after 1914 to rely more and more on killing-power in gaining its ends. The assumption that, because a nation is semi-civilised at home, its rulers may lawfully and morally behave as barbarians abroad, produced the mentality stigmatised by Dean Inge and General Huguet as dualism. Inside the frontier, behind the moat, the principles of Christianity and Civilisation entrenched themselves, so that a Cabinet Minister became, at least nominally, the servant of the public and even a notorious murderer could claim the protection of the law; whereas beyond the seas the custom and the conventions which passed for international law offered no protection whatever to the weak against the strong. In practice accordingly, as General Huguet discovered, we were witness to the 'strange dualism in the English character' which, deeply planted in the few, infected the mass.

It is by no means irrelevant to adduce from comments on the characters of leading men; they are all legitimate targets, besides being as well tribal gods plastered with officially inspired eulogies and honours. If the propaganda takes up a mediocrity and by puffing inflates him to heroic dimensions, the public is deluded and debauched. And the consequences are utterly disastrous. For the net result is the perpetuation of oligarchy and a rule of bad men.

Chapter Eight

THE MORAL ISSUE: FROM SARAJEVO TO SUEZ

MORAL CORRUPTION IS a theme alien to practical politics, whose protagonists seldom rise above the demagogic level. When, however, Churchill declared that Communism rots the soul of a nation, he glimpsed for a moment a great moral issue, namely that debated by political schools of the nineteenth century when fighting the battles for and against Free Trade and Protection, Jingoism and Pacificism, Civilisation and Barbarism.

At that time Liberalism was opposed to the use of force, coercion and war in dealing with the foreigner, and for half a century after Waterloo imperialism was under a cloud. The élite of British thinkers created an atmosphere in which humanism permeated foreign policy. The impact of the Liberal élite, however, was too slight to influence the political Establishment after 1900, and the fatal dualism espoused by Grey became normal in Downing Street henceforth.

True, in dealing with external affairs they found it embarrassing to flout the code adopted by scientists and illuminati of many lands. To revert to the predatory expansionism of the Elizabethans in an era of enlightenment was difficult, and the only feasible line was to take refuge in organised sophistry. 'Back to Thrasymachus' became the order of the day. Hence the quibbling and the apologetic, resting on the false assumption that superior killing-power was an infallible sign of superior virtue. The formula varied, but it was taken for granted that conquest conferred a right to annex, occupy and rule backward and weak countries; and that resistance to the invader was contumacy, to be quelled by scientific killing. *Debellare superbos* was exalted into a duty imposed by the very conviction, the unity of man, which forbade it. It was actually argued that by slaying the rebellious victims of aggression, dubbed mutineers, rebels, terrorists, the invaders could not merely ensure the happiness of their surviving kith and kin but could even save the souls of the slain, the doctrine which, when the aggressors were Russian

Reds and the aggressed were Finns, corrupted—so they alleged—the very souls of the aggressors and ennobled the Resistance.

Such an abuse of power, in Churchill's words, rots the soul, and, as he saw it, betrayed the nature of Communism in Russia, where the dictatorship of the proletariat had from the first reposed on unlimited force employed in the interest of a Party, whose leaders formed an absolutist group. Their rule was in fact recognised as a dictatorship over the proletariat, by whose agency the bourgeoisie was liquidated or enslaved. So ran the tale.

The remarkable failure of Churchill to acknowledge, in the policy of the Allies since 1914, the rot which set in among his own group of leaders accounts for his war record, and the blindness with which he had clung to the belief that justice is the interest of the stronger. No other politician in Britain has so persistently striven to foster the belief that the paramount duty of the nation is to preserve *at all costs* its imperial heritage.

There was a brief interlude in his worship of the Jingo god; after 1904 when he deserted the Tories, whom at the time he denounced as *not a party but a conspiracy*. Then, for about seven years, he affected to espouse Liberalism and a peace policy. But, having been captivated by the ravings of the fire-eating Sir John Fisher, in 1911 he was placed in charge of the Fleet, with the specific duty of preparing it for war with Germany.

Confining our scrutiny to the moral conflict interwoven with the military and diplomatic struggle, the rights and wrongs present themselves as a theme appropriate to the student of ethics, whose prime concern must be justice. No more relevant approach, moreover, can be conceived than that supplied by the leading moralists, especially Caird and Bosanquet; whereas the case for the immoralists needs no fresh treatment, having been dinned into the ears of young and old by Kipling, Rhodes and their myriad collaborators for generations. Nothing is easier than to identify in the forty years' war waged by these materialists the *pleonexia* which had led firstly to the conquest of a quarter of the globe and secondly to the furious struggles for the lion's share of the spoils.

The conflict between Cecil Rhodes and Edward Caird, accordingly, is to be interpreted as one in which the higher values discussed above were sacrificed to the lower, meaning that the triumph of those who chose war in 1914 over those who championed the dogma of the unity of man and strove to avert a resort to arms

155

constituted a terrific defeat for the just cause. That the Allied victory in 1918 confirmed the triumph of the unjust reason excites the most profound interest. What has been the moral effect on the warring peoples?

If we follow Plato in his contention that it is better for the soul of a man to suffer than to inflict injustice, we can have no hesitation in ascribing to the victors the major share of that rot of which Churchill spoke. For in his view it was the injustice inherent in Communism and specifically wreaked upon the Finns that rotted the Bolshevik soul and made it so odious in victory and abject in defeat.

On his side Stalin was satisfied that both World Wars were in origin imperialist. In that conviction the Kremlin has never wavered, as Krushchev and Bulganin testified. When Stalin and Churchill met at Moscow, Teheran, and Yalta each side knew what the other wanted. Dissemble as they might, the plane on which they conferred was barbarous and base judged by the civilised code. To renounce national egoism, to cast aside all weapons as useless, to foster goodwill instead of hate, to practise self-sacrifice, to postpone claims of right to claims of duty were inconceivable absurdities in these conferences. Yet no less was demanded by the higher ethic based on modern speculation and modern science.

For Churchill, drenched with the 'doctrines of supermanity' rampant in the ruling class, especially the Tory society to which he clung, the dogma of the unity of man was unthinkable. For it was a dogma inherent in the ethic of idealism and, as he boasted after Harrow and Sandhurst, he did not know even what ethics meant. Accordingly since this dogma remained in his political career an unknown quantity he was well qualified fundamentally to play the game with Comrade Stalin. Born and bred in the milieu depicted by Wilfrid Scawen Blunt, Lady Oxford and others, he shared to the full in the superiority complex which prompted even the mild Gerald Balfour and kindly George Wyndham to pervert Darwin's evolution to serve jingo propaganda. Obsessed with the 'Rule Britannia!' delusion they stood the Darwinian hypothesis on its head and argued that to ensure the survival of the fittest (themselves) the unnatural elimination of the unwanted (by them) was a patriotic duty. A glance at the everyday discussions, permitted by Blunt, is all that is needed to recall the atmosphere.

In the nineties the recoil from Liberalism was in full swing. Ten years after the invasion of Egypt Cromer kept the pledge to evacuate by creating a 'veiled Protectorate' thus squelching the Nationalist movement and paving the way allegedly for the inter-nationalising of the country, for the profit of Europe. Sir William Harcourt explained that 'It is not Egypt only they want us to swallow, but the whole of East Africa'; and complained 'of the brutality of the British public, which insisted upon the slaughter of the Matabeles to procure itself markets for its goods. "It used," he said, "to be slaughter for the glory of the thing, but they have given that up now. Now it is slaughter for trade".'[1]

More remarkable still was the jingo attitude to recalcitrant whites, even those in the British Isles. On August 7, 1892, Blunt recorded how he 'drove with the Balfours . . . had a grand dis-cussion about patriotism, Gerald maintaining that patriotism was the Imperial instinct in Englishmen, who should support their country's quarrels even when in the wrong. . . Gerald has all his brother's scientific inhumanity in politics, and it is a school of thought decidedly on the increase, for it flatters the selfish instincts of the strong by proving to them that their selfishness is right. . . On our way home we renewed our argument as applied especially to the Irish. "They ought to have been exterminated long ago," said Gerald, "but it is too late now".'[2]

From the Irish Nationalists to the Germans was but a step and in 1897 not Irlandia but Germania became *delenda*. To that gospel by 1911 Churchill's thinking became attuned; and at his first conference with Stalin at Moscow, in September 1942, the harmony was confirmed. A few years of intimacy followed and on February 27, 1945, he rose to the occasion. 'The impression I brought back from the Crimea and from all my other contacts is that Marshal Stalin and the Soviet Union wish to live in honourable friendship and equality with the Western Democracies. I feel also that their word is their bond. I know of no other Government which stands to its obligations, even in its own despite, more solidly than the Russian Soviet Government.'

In this and other utterances equally sagacious the Prime Minister strove to placate the Ogre whom he had for many years plastered with insults. At length he was at home, seated with the Marshal on his throne of skulls, conferring and carousing, filled with respect for 'this great rugged war chief', 'a man direct and even blunt in speech', and yet 'with that saving sense of humour which is of high importance to all men and all nations'. From Stalin in return compliments were scarce but Beaverbrook was able, after pumping the Marshal, to report a flattering reference to Churchill as 'the old war-horse . . . our symbol of victory'. Likewise the infallible Press Lord paid due homage to Stalin's wonderful sense of humour, an assurance greedily swallowed by multitudes who had been disturbed by pictures of convivial conferences where the Marshal's bursts of laughter suggested not so much humour as derisive shouts directed at his guests. Many had been puzzled by the sudden glory radiating from that 'callous, crafty and ill-informed giant' who figures in Churchill's mature judgment less appealingly than he did after his transfiguration in June 1941. The Churchill-Roosevelt cult of Stalin may be said to have lasted barely five years, from 1941 to 1946, but in that brief space of time how much was accomplished!

Verily the Triumvirate did a mighty work, destructive work; and the mainspring was the contempt for ethics shared by all three. No matter how they varied in their private codes they were united in that worship of power which brooks no opposition. Killing-power was theirs, irresistible and limitless, and the will to use it. In that vital respect the three were soulmates, and had they been less egoistic the union of hearts would have evolved into the world-mastery which each Triumvir sought for himself.

Beneath the temporary unity, however, there were strains and stresses which disrupted the combine. Three imperialisms were two too many, and to make a straight fight two had to merge. Yet the preliminary merger was far from easy. Anglo-American imperialisms collided in fact as soon as victory was achieved in 1918. There were many bones of contention but in 1919 as in 1956 the most spectacular was Middle East oil. The contestants clashed at once in Mosul, where America demanded from Britain—who had claimed a half share as against a quarter each to Turkey and France—half of the British share. The eventual compromise may be regarded as the first long step towards the partnership cele-brated by Eisenhower and his Ambassador in London in 1957.

On this early phase of Anglo-American competition a dash of pungent comment was supplied by Isaac Marcosson in *The Saturday Evening Post* where he revealed to the American public that the scramble for oil in Mespot was no new thing then, and illustrated the bitterness of the struggle by quoting from the biography of Sir Percy Cox. From this biography Marcosson had learned that 'this eminent public servant' with strong backing from Sir Edward Grey spent his life in Bagdad and Arabia securing oil concessions, frustrating the 'knavish tricks' of awkward competitors, especially Germans. The proudest boast, indeed, of the biographer, was that Sir Percy was astute enough to convert the Persian Gulf into an English lake, 'though why', remarked Marcosson, 'London should suck the riches out of all that arena predominantly or exclusively was not explained'. The answer to his concluding question, it may be added, is of extreme interest to many peoples besides the American.

Unfortunately for the Anglo-American merger, there was the Russian claim to a share; and, although in abeyance for nearly forty years from 1917, Stalin was free to register it openly, thanks to the vacuum in Central Europe, which guarded his Western flank. In this way the Arab States, exposed to intensified cultivation by Russia, became no longer the pawns in 'the scoundrels' game', but principals ready to play power politics like the rest.

In this connection a glance at the Operation Suez, which rendered 1956 memorable in British annals, should be instructive. Already the Abadan imbroglio had elicited the charge that in thirty years Persia had received a beggarly £100,000,000, a figure which, exact or not, points to a rankling grievance. In the end Persia submitted to *force majeure* and the question of fair shares ceased to embarrass the contenders for oil. American companies got a new deal, as well as Persia, and peace descended; or would have descended overall had not the Russians begun to convince the Moslem world that Codlin was their friend, not Short. In that crusade, in spite of numerous handicaps, the Soviets possessed initial advantages in Asia and Africa which rendered them formidable, chief of these being the racial memory of white aggressions. As Russian strength, depleted by the war, recovered under the vigorous régime of the Politburo, the perennial latent threat to the *beati possidentes* rapidly ripened; and the heavy post-war sacrifices became more urgent than ever and more oppressive. Ideologically too the Russian bid for oil grew menacing as the Arab States became accustomed to proletarian ways of thinking. They began to draw comparisons; if anti-God Communism offended the worshippers of Allah, the Christian was still the Infidel, the Giaour;

and it was the 'Christian' Powers, Britain and America, that had foisted Israel on to the body of Islam.

The battle, moreover, was largely a financial contest, dollars and sterling versus roubles. In that contest the advantage was all with the West, but militarily and strategically the Kremlin was dangerous, and the Western Front demanded a vast deployment of striking power that taxed the resources even of America almost to breaking point. In that case one might have looked for a stocktaking of the profits and losses incidental to crusading, to ascertain whether exclusive, competitive exploitation was really a paying game. Long ago experts like Professor Parker Moon and J. A. Hobson exposed the delusive blessings of empire, and should have dispelled the fog. Since they wrote, statisticians have not been idle, and economists have no difficulty in proving that by plain commercial standards the whole business is insane and doomed to end in universal ruin if persisted in much longer. If we take the United States alone it transpires that the tax-payer suffers a staggering overall loss.

Confining ourselves to the 'defence' budget of the United States for 1957, it was reported to envisage a total expenditure of $72,000,000,000 for July 1956 to June 1957. Next, it was calculated that out of this total 78 cents of every dollar were allotted to military services: and of those 78 cents, 8 were needed to meet the cost of past wars. Of that sum again in the new appropriations, amounting to $59,800,000,000, a round $40,000,000,000 were earmarked for simple killing-power.

On the other hand Eisenhower with difficulty obtained from Congress authority to spend $200,000,000 for Arab countries partly on arms, partly on economic aid, representing together one half of one per cent of the expenditure on armaments. How much of that beggarly fraction was to go on arms and how much on butter was apparently left to Eisenhower's discretion. Thereafter on March 23, 1957, it only remained to round off the plan of campaign by stiffening the Anti-Communist Oil Front by a military gesture, and so the press announced in triumph IKE PUTS TEETH IN THE BAGHDAD PACT. It was also explained that, as soon as the United States was voted into the Military Committee of the Pact, the Sixth Fleet and other forces would co-operate with the military planners and thus defend the Middle East against Russia. Thus once more the plan, the purpose, the intention of the 'Free West' was openly confessed. Just as in the earlier stage of the World

Wars the oil of the Middle East was to be denied to Germany *at all costs*, so at astronomical expense Russia too was to be excluded.

At bottom the fight for the spoils was one and the same from 1900 to the Cold War, and first and foremost came the root cause specified by Marcosson and implied in the whole diplomacy and press propaganda of the Western Powers. Britain and France having extracted from Arab Sheikhs and the Shah concessions in the poverty-stricken Moslem states proposed, with the aid of the United States, Holland and Belgium to hold them against all comers, regardless of the scores of thirsty countries that coveted a portion. After Russia in 1945 and 1956 showed a desire to revive her old claims, exclusion became more risky and far more expensive; militarily for obvious reasons and morally because the title of the wealthiest nations by sheer killing-power to shut out poor countries grew more universally offensive as the world grew smaller. Next to the Germans, the Russians had the most powerful reasons to challenge the Western monopoly, since in two wars Russian sacrifices had enabled the West to achieve it. When arguing the case for a liberal proportion as compared with the United States, London relied on the sacrifices made by Britain, and so the Kremlin are merely copying their Ally in stating their case. There are eminent historians who contend, moreover, that the 'historic sin' of modern Europe was the closing of the Straits against the great Russian nation.

This much cannot be gainsaid. If sacrifices in the Allied cause and the signatures of Grey and Poincaré on the Treaty of March 1915 count, in weighing the relative claims to the stranglehold on oil and commerce at Suez, the Anglo-American *partnership* designed to exclude Russia is an outrage, comparable with the Anglo-Russian pact of 1907 to exclude Germany.

Of all the Allied Ministers who controlled European affairs during that period, the British offer the most intriguing objects of study. It has been recalled that when Grey pledged his word to Cambon and sowed the seed which sprouted in 1914 he abandoned the splendid isolation which kept Europe on an even keel since 1871. He also made himself liable to the reproach foreshadowed by Sir Thomas Sanderson,[3] then the Nestor of the Foreign Office. For Sanderson warned the novice explicitly that a Cabinet which by foreign entanglements unauthorised by Parliament dragged England into war would be exposed to impeachment; and in so doing, by some instinct, he seemed to indicate, quite vainly, the very pitfall into which Grey would stumble. Six years later, in 1912, he, Grey, exchanged the letters with Cambon which convinced Cambon and the Quai d'Orsay that they had him trapped.

To appreciate the Frenchman's coup the obvious course is to place the Cambon correspondence side by side with the letter Palmerston wrote to Clarendon in 1857, explaining his rejection of a nearly identical proposal made by Napoleon III fifty-two years earlier:

> We want to trade with Egypt and to travel through Egypt, but we do not want the burden of governing Egypt... Let us try to improve those countries by the general influence of our Commerce, but let us abstain from a crusade of conquest.[4]

Both schemes amounted to a conspiracy against the integrity and independence of Egypt and Morocco and aimed at an Anglo-French monopoly of the North African coast of the Mediterranean.

Within fifty years from 1857 Egypt had become more important than ever, after the old trade-route overland was replaced by de Lesseps' waterway. The Canal was opened in 1869, a monument to French engineering, Egyptian labour—125,000 natives were said to have perished—and partly Egyptian, partly borrowed capital; and soon, although the Company was Egyptian, it became the chief bone of contention between France and Britain. In 1875 Disraeli profited by the Khedive's financial straits to purchase his shares for a mere £4 million, thus gaining a footing in the directorate, but the French control exercised through Paris survived, until in 1882 England invaded Egypt. Then followed the Anglo-French fight for the country and the Canal. For, with the rapid growth of world-trade the temptation to control the Canal grew ever stronger, and Egypt herself was an alluring field for Western Finance. When finally the strife ended in 1904 and the Lansdowne-Delcassé deal went through, it became clear that the victimisation of the luckless Egyptians and Moroccans was to be permanent. Thus the proceedings of 1956 and 1957 exhibited to a roused world opinion the real nature of the Anglo-French Mission and the intensity of the uncivilised spirit that pervaded it. The parallel between the shady diplomacy of Lansdowne-Delcassé and the sinister plan of Eden-Mollet-Ben Gurion will remain one of the most fascinating and instructive themes for all who seek to understand how the white man came to grief in what should have been the golden age.

Had there been in the power politics of the Western governments even a tinge of the civilised mentality which accepted the dogma of the unity of man there need have been no halt in the upward march of homo sapiens. Observers like Wilfrid Scawen Blunt, in the spirit of Caird and Bosanquet, detested the barbarism which missionaries of empire like Cromer and Rhodes exuded in their All Red schemes. Cromer personally disliked Egyptians and considered that their proper fate was to be Anglicised, to pay the exorbitant interest on British and French loans, to support a Civil Service on the Indian Civil model, staffed, says Blunt, with English officials of quite moderate quality. Above all native Ministers were directed by British advisers whose advice was law; and education of the natives was scandalously restricted. The strongest conviction of all was the belief that natives were incapable of administering their own affairs and were 'better off' under the paternal despotism of a Cromer than as free men.

As to that whole question the *Times* Correspondent in Cairo, January 1876 commented: 'Egypt is a marvellous instance of progress. She has advanced as much in seventy years as many other countries have done in five hundred.' At that point the Canal had been opened not more than seven years, and yet advance was rapid both before and after. Between 1863 and 1879 the population increased from 4,833,000 to 5,518,000; exports increased from £4,454,000 to £13,810,000 and imports from £1,991,000 to £5,410,000 in 1875; and the government was run by the 'spend-thrift Khedive' Ismail.

From this startling disclosure the natural inference could only be that, given a capable native ruler unfettered by an alien overlord, Egypt can take her place alongside other free countries in the modern world of science and industry. What Turkey accomplished under Mustapha Kemal almost overnight should be an inspiration to any backward people. To be genuine, reform and progress in the arts of life must come from within a community, and the acid test of that progress is supplied by the advance of education, from the elementary stage to the highest levels. It has been pointed out[5] that, as in India, and every other quarter of the Empire, Cromer's Egypt was crippled by the starving of the schools, while the incubus of theocratic suspicion was allowed to weigh heavily on the liberal-ising elements. This connivance at obscurantism was always a temptation to a foreign overlord. It was easy for an English proconsul and his subordinates in the Civil and other Services, drawn from the class described by Matthew Arnold, and later by men like Sir Ronald Storrs, as being lukewarm about education for the masses at home, to wink at the smothering of native aspirations in this vital matter. They had only to follow a policy of drift, agreeable to native reactionaries, to hinder young Egyptians from qualifying for the leading positions in administration, finance and industry, as well as in the professions. In the primary schools English, not Arabic, was used for important subjects, and the practice of subsidising poor scholars, to enable them to pass through the primary schools and then to study at a French university, was dropped, ostensibly to curb expense; so that, when Cromer resigned at last, only one eightieth part of the national expenditure was allotted to education. In an epoch when the first concern of a liberated Turkish province was a national school and university system, Egypt under the Occupation was condemned to chronic illiteracy and an exclusiveness that shut out natives even from key positions in Egyptian cotton factories. In Germany, where private initiative and popular resources counted for so much in promoting Culture, the proportion of the national expenditure devoted to education was fully ten times that granted to the mentally starved Egyptians, a sinful perversion of authority that gives the measure of Cromer's enlightened régime. Moreover, instead of encouraging Egyptians to staff the schools, relays of English teachers were hired, at needless expense, to impart instruction in the English language and in scientific commonplaces, instead of aiming at a training in the humaniora which could have placed the educated native on a level of culture comparable with that of an educated European. In that way the peasantry remained sunk in illiteracy, and the few instructed Egyptians were incapable of competing on equal terms with their alien masters in the professions and other skilled occupations.

Thus it became fashionable in Britain to belittle the enthusiasm of a far-seeing friend of the Arabs, such as Wilfred Scawen Blunt or Dr Brailsford, who urged the claims of the natives to fair play in their own land. It was no mere whim that prompted Brailsford to write:

> The result of all these causes, the neglect of the mother tongue, the defects of the education itself, the absence of a University and the appointment of foreigners to every post the holding of which

might encourage a capable man to study or write, may be traced in the utter death of all intellectual life in Egypt, and in the crudity of mind which prevails among the small 'educated' class. The level of culture is incomparably lower and the educated class incomparably smaller than in any other country of the Near East with which I am acquainted. For that the responsibility rests with us. The Nationalists have agitated fiercely for better education and more of it.[6]

Such was the light thrown on the Egyptian scene early in 1914. Nine years Grey had wasted in helping France to dig in along North Africa from Tunis through Algeria to Morocco, as well as in Syria. England's reward was to be a tighter grip on Egypt and the oil-bearing sheikhdoms around the Persian Gulf. In these Arab states the problem was how to make a rational use of the promised oil revenues, rendering inevitable a period of trial and error, with results to be verified in the near future. Unfortunately co-operation on the side of the oil companies and the foreign control was hampered by the Cadillac complex of the chiefs and the profiteering of the intruders; and so it had to be until Arab sultans and sheikhs imitated the example of Persia whose Shah and Parliament, after bitter experience, took a new partner, Italy, into a genuine partnership in 1957. Fifty years too late a major step was taken towards the liberation of the Moslem states, a step on the rough road to economic freedom which lies before them. In this fashion must come the end of the bogus 'peaceful penetration', associated with imperialism and colonialism, which disgorged two world wars and continues to breed disaster simply because sundry Great Powers in their dealings with one another reverted to the barbarous sophistry 'justice is the interest of the stronger,' a heresy masked by ceaseless chatter about the five freedoms and the rights of man.

The classic instance of rank injustice inflicted by Christian nations on a weak Moslem people occurred in 1911 when, in desperation and beset by Anglo-Russian exploiters, the Persian National Assembly appealed to the United States for the loan of a financial adviser. In response to this modest request the American Government cautiously replied that a certain Mr Morgan Shuster was qualified for such a post and Mr Shuster was duly appointed Treasurer-General for three years. In the teeth of Anglo-Russian obstruction Shuster, backed by the Majlis, set on foot a plan of sweeping reforms that instantly bade fair to extricate the country from financial slavery, with consequences momentous to Persia.

In his book *The Strangling of Persia* Morgan Shuster told the story. It is a chapter in the tale of the Free West at large in the Middle East, already summarised in this essay—the tale of a National Assembly at grips with not only foreign intruders but with a corrupt palace gang in league with the alien, the Majlis forced to dismiss Shuster and, prior to its final dissolution, an undertaking extorted from the government never again to import a foreign adviser unless with the express approval of Russia and England.

The same procedure was followed, with modifications caused by the active intervention of America, in the Abadan affair forty years afterwards. The settlement was a hole-and-corner affair and once more right was decided by might. As a result of the Free West's loss of face and the stirring of conscience through endless tribulation the old brutality has become less brazen. But more significant still, admissions are forthcoming that no alien dominance can be healthy or beneficent. In 1957 a Lord Chancellor not merely stressed the fact but put the reason for it pithily and simply from the juridical point of view: 'What we are seeing now in some parts of the world where it was least expected is, I am convinced, a spontaneous expression of that timeless longing inseparable from the human being, for justice. . . That the young in these countries, blinkered and intellectually constricted from birth, should nevertheless express their needs is, in my belief, yet another manifestation of the law of nature, or as it became known in mediaeval times, the law of God.' Had Professor Arnold Toynbee in his wide survey of imperialism through the ages concerned himself more with the elucidation of this idea, long since expounded by Plato in his search for justice, and by Oxford idealism, as the unity of mankind, he would have clarified the main thesis of his noble work—the intrinsic vanity of the imperial idea. For is not the stagnation of civilisation and the decay of culture in the universal empire precisely what Brailsford and Blunt exposed to view in Egypt under the Occupation? Intellectual death for the masses and half-baked literacy for the few—what can better serve the purpose of a ruthless foreign autocracy? No amount of palliatives, no recitals of good intentions, can impress peoples animated with the sentiments voiced by the Lord Chancellor, Viscount Kilmuir, at the American Lawyers' Convention in London July 24, 1957. The pity is that the

revolution which has converted—so we are told—threequarters of
the world to a rejection of colonialism in every form had to be
precipitated by the crimes and follies of a small minority of violent
autocrats, masquerading as friends of peace through strength,
strength meaning nothing but killing-power, and money and the
skill to use it destructively.

As for the sanction provided in the scheme of things for the law
of nature or of God, proclaimed by Viscount Kilmuir, that is
visible in the corruption which ensues on its violation. It turns on
the axiom that it is worse for the soul of a man to inflict than to
suffer injustice, to which appeal is made elsewhere. If we seek a
contemporary example nothing could be more instructive than the
plight of French imperialists in Algeria. There a hundred and
twenty years of repression have come to a head and France has
been warned that the cancer of Algeria is destined to destroy her.
In Cyprus the moral corruption attending the violation of the law
of God and nature was thrown violently into relief when Lord
Strabolgi deplored the degradation of Field Marshal Harding into
a hangman, and again was hinted at by Sir Harold Nicolson in a
review of a timely book on Cyprus by an Englishman familiar with
and close to the life of the island. Speaking of Harding's relentless
methods the author writes: 'The last link in the fierce chain of
circumstances was our execution of your Karaolis.' When Durrell
paid his last visit to the village where he had once been so happy
and beloved, his Cypriot friends averted their eyes: 'The sight of an
Englishman had become an obscenity in that clear honey-gold air.'[7]

The moral of this revulsion of feeling in the Cypriot village is
too obvious for words. The day has passed when a Protecting
Power can without discredit hang a youthful patriot who risks all
to shake off the foreign yoke. What made the hanging obscene was
the hypocrisy of which it was a glaring example. While London was
hanging heroes of the *Enosis* crusade in Cyprus, it was proclaimed
over the London radio that 'an unfree society is an intolerable
society; and even if some sort of security could be bought at the
cost of freedom or any other fundamental human right, that security
would be simply not worth having.'

Yet the decision of the Cypriots to exercise their fundamental
human right of free self-determination was treated as a crime; its
supporters branded as rebels and terrorists, to be extirpated, if
need be, without mercy. Such was the policy decreed by a Cabinet

whose Lord High Chancellor, addressing the American Bar Association, confessed that every infringement of a human being's freedom was an offence against the law of Nature or rather of God. Little wonder that the simple villagers, who had shared with their kinsmen in Metropolitan Greece the memory of Byron and Gladstone, awoke with a shudder to the real character of English protection in Churchill's grim and ferocious epoch.

The Terror decreed by London to bolster up the preferred position enjoyed by British oil companies in the Middle East was for them and most civilised men an unclean thing. In the eyes of Viscount Kilmuir himself, the legal luminary of the Cabinet, it was mortal sin, and yet no protest came from him or his colleagues. He was evidently ready, like the rest, to eat his own words.

It is no part of a commentator's function to explore the mind of his Chancellor and psychoanalyse his motives and impulses, but it would be foolish to forget that international politics is a scoundrels' game, and absurd to accept at face-value the praises of British justice with its double standard.

When one reflects that such self-contradiction, or hypocrisy, at top levels implicates the nation as a whole, one can hardly complain if the victims of such doublespeak and doublethink, and world opinion at large, find the insincerity obscene, and include the habit in their assessment of the English ruling class and all who have caught the infection. In the struggle for predominance it was bound to be a grave handicap that innumerable sufferers throughout the five continents have reason to resent this ingrained vice. Nothing else explains the astounding consensus of opinion at UNO when for the first time, and perhaps the last, on a burning question members were unanimous, really united in checking Anglo-French *pleonexia* and rebuking its lawlessness. Amid the bickerings and stresses, the slogans and the propaganda of the seventy nations, the principle of the unity of man was at work, fermenting even in the minds of the politicians, and qualifying them to distinguish between good and evil in international relations, and incidentally to cherish a healthy scepticism towards any Power that advertises itself as the moral leader of the world.

The secret diplomacy which cursed Europe and America since 1904 was but the culmination of the foetid and septic process which week by week for the health of its soul the world is still called upon to inspect at close range and comprehend. Incredible to relate, as the world nears the 1964 milestone, that duty becomes more imperative than ever, as eighty nations behold the two power blocs armed with the H-bomb sparring for position in the foolish death-grapple. For such has been the corruption at the highest levels that the select individuals who staged the ceaseless horrors of the age never for a moment for the health of their souls got to grips with the moral leprosy that polluted all their secret diplomacy. So penetrating, indeed, is the pollution that the very conception of moral health long ago ceased to count in the calculations of our masters. In a word, the indispensable condition of a better world order is a strenuous battle for *justice* blended with goodness and truth, and that has never in fifty years been the dominant inspiration of the great powers. At the same time the grim fact remains that just as the Divine Ruler of the Universe has endowed every human creature with freedom to make what he will of his life, yet ensures that none of His purposes shall be impaired thereby, so peoples and rulers may make a hell upon earth for themselves and one another but the Divine Justice shall be undiminished. For, as Plato taught, God is the beginning, the middle and the end, and eternal justice is his minister.

If the rulers of this century had glimpsed the lesson of the philosophers and scientific humanists of today—plainly laid down for all time in the Sermon on the Mount—they could not have abandoned themselves to devil-worship. Above all they might have profited by the superabundant evidence, pressed on their attention by historians from Thucydides and Tacitus onwards, that war, the scourge of Europe, has its root in *pleonexia* and can be averted by timely adjustment of conflicting claims.

The Macmillan declaration on his elevation—'England was great, England is great, England will be great'—meant and was intended to mean that he bound himself to carry on the policy pursued by a legendary Churchill, saviour of England, saviour of Europe and saviour of the world, in spite of the dire consequences past, present and future of the said policy.

It is as such crowning effort that the Suez fiasco must be assessed. The obloquy fell on Eden but his action was taken with the full concurrence of his friends. The blitz on Egypt, moreover, was foreshadowed by Churchill's declaration of cold war at Fulton, Missouri and but for the prompt suppression of the war by the United States and UNO, would have launched the third World

War under the worst possible auspices. Power politics, in that event, would have reached its full stature, its climax, and would have revealed in action its capacity for evil. Two world wars, followed by Korea and Vietnam, having apparently taught the responsible British ministers nothing, and the sputniks not having as yet opened their dim eyes, they were all set to detonate the vast orgy of murder by a second conquest of Egypt.

From this review of certain features of the past forty years it should be clear that the convulsions which have shaken Europe to its foundations are due to the madness generated by moral corruption. The soul-rot ascribed to Communism differs but little from that of Western ruling groups. From July 30, 1914, up to the lightning attack on Port Said has been pursued a selfish, blood-dripping, policy of *pleonexia*, of greed, in defiance of the dogma of all civilised men, namely the unity of mankind, laid down by a Master of Balliol and described as the law of Nature and indeed of God by a Lord High Chancellor, himself an hon. Fellow of Balliol. Characteristic of the mentality which has so outraged the law of Nature and of God is the basic thesis that German competition in the world market is a provocation to be checked by violence. Every German success is a *pinprick* and ' a million of these pinpricks constitute the greatest *casus belli* the world has ever seen'. Such was the doctrine that pervaded the Grey diplomacy—so flagrantly that even President Wilson had eventually to confess that the struggle lately concluded had been a commercial and industrial war.

In similar vein forty years later Eisenhower virtually clinched this indictment, when his spokesman boasted that the Sixth Fleet was scouring the Mediterranean to prevent Russia from gaining a stranglehold on Middle Eastern oil, though why the Anglo-American stranglehold, which excluded fifty nations from the area, was sacrosanct remained a mystery. For the subterfuge by which Allied spokesmen tried to cover up the infamy of the Suez blitz— by dragging the herring of Hungary across the trail—could deceive nobody who remembered that it was the Allies who opened the gates of Hungary to Stalin's armies. It was to the credit of the Opposition in the House that the flimsy equivocations in the House offered by Eden to prove that a full-scale, high-powered war against a weak nation is no war, provided that the onslaught is sudden and paralysing, but must be defined as police action, were greeted with storms of Homeric laughter.

To round off this appreciation of the moral corruption which has polluted our century we take next the latest of the three aggressions —Egypt, Cyprus, Oman—which were designed to tighten the stranglehold on Middle Eastern oil. Of these Oman seemed to be the least wicked because the tribal rising was spontaneous and extreme care was taken by the Foreign Office to appear disinterested. The killing of the Imam's followers was to be done by the Sultan's levies, only the efficiency of the Sultan's killing-power was to be Britain's responsibility. Partly, as the Government press explained, this was done to avoid shocking observers at UNO and partly to lull Islamc suspicions of the Infidel who shows his friendship by killing Moslems. The problem was, therefore, how to assist in slaying Arabs without being detected by their kinsfolk. The leading jingo journals, accordingly, realising that the government were in 'a bit of a mess', were eager to discuss the situation and asked 'what the Foreign Office was playing at in Oman? . . . Why were they resorting to such shabby tricks' to prevent newspaper correspondents from telling the truth? There was no doubt, averred the journal, (*Daily Mail*, August 3, 1957), that the Foreign Office officials on the spot had resorted to a deliberate policy of lying; not just small terminological inexactitudes but outright barefaced lies. *The Times* likewise complained of these lies as 'serious cases of misinformation'. Correspondents were told officially that the Cameronians had arrived in Bahrein. In fact they had gone straight to the seat of war at Sharjah. Lie number one. They were told next that all further military operations were suspended because the Sultan was victorious—his flag flying over Iski. That was lie number two.

Another 'government' journal (*Daily Telegraph*, August 5, 1957) two days later assured its readers that the Foreign Office was directing operations down to the minutest detail, as at Suez, and that London had its eye on repercussions at UNO as much as on Arab racial sentiment. Accordingly the *little men* who might have been scapegoats were exonerated and the charges of lying were firmly pinned on Downing Street. This is the revolting picture painted by the press as *a bit of a mess*.

The ugly feature of the mess is of course the bare-faced lying designed to hide up facts. That is the defect which was disclosed and appraised above and yet demands further notice from the standpoint of ethics. What has the virus of lying to do with the

171

soul rot ascribed by Churchill to Communism?

The answer is not difficult to find. Those who during their study of ethics have written essays on *the unity of virtue* are aware of the interdependence of the separate virtues, notably justice, goodness and truth, which may be named the cardinal virtues. They merge into one another, though different, and each in turn is prominent in any moral situation, according as the faculties of will, intellect and feeling are present in every moral (or immoral) act. There is moreover such an intimate nexus binding all three that there can be no justice where there is no goodwill, no goodwill where there is no truth or justice.

Conversely injustice, badness and untruth are correlates. They form a whole of evil constituted by the essential unity of vice. Consequently, while in the field of international relations the primary virtue is justice, the cardinal virtues of goodness and truth rank equally with justice in the scale of values; they are really aspects of the divine excellence that in germ exists in all human beings. There can be no justice where there is no goodness and no truth, and in every successful attempt to promote human happiness the three virtues are indispensable, their activity regulated as we have seen by the law of Nature and the will of God. In the conflict with the trinity of evil, composed of injustice, hatred and lying, they have suffered a smashing defeat thanks to the enormous power of organised mendacity. But in the long run international affairs will be settled in accordance with the law of Nature and of God; and the soul-rot which has corrupted the white man's world through its disastrous leadership will be checked.

The application of the moral calculus evolved by philosophy and religion to the power politics of the Big Six is bound to be a major task for future historians. The question before them, if historiography is to be critical and educative, will be: how did the groups of statesmen who controlled the vast resources of North America as well as those of the Russian, French and British Empires, shape the world-order of the century? The essential blunders and crimes which explain the resulting catastrophe, having been verified by international scholarship, are the theme of the foregoing pages. Already, it has been demonstrated that the moralists have the last word, and that the great edifice of world power in the hands of the Big Six rests on a foundation of injustice, hatred and lies, and is therefore morally rotten and intolerable.

NOTES

PROLOGUE

1. *Social and International Ideals* (London, 1917)
2. See p. 24 ff.

CHAPTER 1

1. J. A. Hobson, *Imperialism: A Study* (3rd edition, London, 1938)
2. *Imperialism* (New York, 1926)
3. Ibid, pp. 564–6
4. 'Patriotism in the Perfect State', in *The International Crisis* (London, 1915), p. 152
5. Quoted by Hobson, *op. cit.* pp. 129–30
6. Hobson, *op. cit.* p. 130
7. Hobson's book was first published in 1902

CHAPTER 2

1. M. B. Reckitt, *Maurice to Temple: A Century of the Social Movement in the Church of England* (London, 1947)
2. Reckitt, *op. cit.* pp. 157–8
3. *Acts of the General Assembly of the Church of Scotland, 1638–1842* (Edinburgh, 1843), pp. 724–6 and 755
4. Reckitt, *op. cit.* p. 20
5. Reckitt, *op. cit.* p. 20
6. See below, p. 48–9
7. Reckitt, *op. cit.* p. 147
8. Reckitt, *op. cit.* p. 55
9. Reckitt, *op. cit.* p. 151
10. Reckitt, *op. cit.* p. 152
11. Reckitt, *op. cit.* p. 25
12. Reckitt, *op. cit.* pp. 21–2
13. Reckitt, *op. cit.* pp. 24 and 27
14. E. R. Stettinius, *Roosevelt and the Russians* (London, 1950), p. 212
15. K. M. Panikkar, *Asia and Western Dominion: A Survey of the Vasco da Gama Epoch of Asian History, 1498–1948* (London, 1953), pp. 149–50
16. Panikkar, *op. cit.* p. 487
17. Panikkar, *op. cit.* p. 265
18. Panikkar, *op. cit.* p. 265
19. D. Varé, *The Two Impostors* (London, 1949), p. 116
20. W. S. Blunt, *My Diaries* (London, 1919–20), I. 262
21. J. S. Ewart, *The Roots and Causes of Wars* (London, 1925), I. 17

CHAPTER 3

1. W. Lippmann, *United States Foreign Policy: Shield of the Republic* (Boston, 1943), pp. 140–1
2. H. Butterfield, *History and Human Relations* (London, 1951), pp. 182–224 : ' Official History: its Pitfalls and Criteria '
3. H. Butterfield, *op. cit.*, p. 217
4. G. P. Gooch, *Studies in Diplomacy and Satecraft* (London, 1942), pp. 104–7
5. H. Lutz, *Lord Grey and the World War* (London, 1928), p. 62
6. Gooch, *op. cit.* pp. 164–5
7. Oxford and Asquith, *Memories and Reflections*. (London, 1928), II.8
8. P. Noel-Baker, *The Arms Race* (London, 1958), p. 41
9. *Le Gaulois*, 12 July 1905
10. J. Fisher, *Memories* (London, 1919), pp. 203 and 207
11. Fisher, *op. cit.* p. 182
12. D. Lloyd George, *War Memoirs*, I. 9
13. *Speeches on Foreign Affairs, 1904–1914 by Sir Edward Grey* edited by P. Knaplund (London, 1931), p. 232
14. Fisher, *op. cit.* p. 15
15. Fisher, *op. cit.* p. 18
16. *British Documents on the Origins of the War*, X. pt. II. pp.787–8

17. *British Documents*, XI. 52–3
18. *British Documents*, IV. 617
19. *British Documents*, V. 239
20. Gooch, *op. cit.* p. 107
21. Grey of Fallodon, *Twenty-Five Years* (London, 1925), II. 43
22. Gooch, *op. cit.* p. 104
23. Gooch, *op. cit.* p. 107

CHAPTER 4

1. Keynes, *Economic Consequences of the Peace* (London, 1920), p. 55
2. Keynes, *op. cit.* p. 51
3. Keynes, *op. cit.* p. 55
4. Keynes, *op. cit.* p. 47
5. H. W. V. Temperley, *History of the Peace Conference of Paris* (London, 1920–4), I. 458
6. Temperley, *op. cit.* II. 73
7. Temperley, *op. cit.* II. 90
8. Keynes, *op. cit. pp.* 278 and 2
9. Keynes, *op. cit.* p. 47
10. *Memoirs*, I. 1
11. *International Affairs*, XVII, no. 3, p. 130
12. Sidney Fay, *The Origins of the World War*, p. 558
13. G. P. Gooch, *Recent Revelations of European Diplomacy* (London, 1940), p. 3
14. *Studies in Diplomacy*, p. 107
15. Fay, *op. cit.* p. 558
16. G. P. Gooeh, *op. cit.* p. 3
17. M. Voigt, *The Nineteenth Century and After*. CXXXVIII (Sept. 1945), p. 101
18. Voigt, *op. cit.* p. 103
19. Lin Yutang, *Between Tears and Laughter* (London, 1945), p. 126

CHAPTER 5

1. *The Second World War* (London, 1948–1954), I. 8
2. Quoted by F. O. Miksche, *The Danubian Confederation*, (Camberley, 1953), p. 30
3. Quoted by Miksche, *op. cit.* p. 31
4. Miksche, *op. cit.* pp. 12–13
5. Miksche, *op. cit.* p. 24
6. Quoted by Miksche, *op. cit.* p. 1
7. *The Diary of Lord Bertie* (London, 1924), I. 1
8. R. N. Current, *Secretary Stimson* (N. Brunswick, N.J., 1954), p. 26
9. *New Statesman*, 14 Nov. 1914
10. Temperley, *op. cit.* II. 73
11. Keynes, *A Revision of the Treaty*, pp. 134 and 136

CHAPTER 6

1. J. H. Muirhead, ed., *Bernard Bosanquet and his Friends* (London, 1935), p. 311
2. Lin Yutang, *Between Tears and Laughter* (London, 1945); quo-
tations are from pp. 20–3
3. Raynard West, *Psychology and World Order* (London, 1945), p. 26
4. West, *op. cit.* p. 36

CHAPTER 7

1. *British Documents*, II. 355–6
2. Lutz, *op. cit.* p. 48
3. Lutz, *op. cit.* p. 66, note 70
4. Lutz, *op. cit.* p. 44
5. Lutz, *op. cit.* p. 48
6. Lutz, *op. cit.* p. 49
7. V. J. M. Huguet, *Britain and the War: a French Indictment* (London, 1928), p. vii
8. Huguet, *op. cit.* p. 208
9. Huguet, *op. cit.* p. 209
10. Huguet, *op. cit.* pp. 209–10
11. Huguet, *op. cit.* pp. 219–20

CHAPTER 8

1. W. S. Blunt, *My Diaries* (London, 1919–20), I. 100 and 142
2. Blunt, *op. cit.* I. 85
3. *British Documents*, III. 184-5
4. T. Rothstein, *Egypt's Ruin.* (London, 1910), p. 6 n.l
5. Rothstein, *op. cit.* pp. 315
6. *The War of Steel and Gold* (London, 1914), p. 118
7. L. Durrell, *Bitter Lemons* (London, 1956), p. 249

INDEX

Abyssinia, 46
Abadan, 166
Acropolis, 10
Acton, Lord, 19
Afganistan, 76
Africa, 41, 44, 50, 64-65, 68, 93, 100, 121-122, 124
African Journey by Mrs Paul Robeson, 44
Aegean, 6
Aegina, 6, 8, 15
Aeginetans, The, 6
Aegina aggression, 8
Aegospotami, 7
Algeria, 44, 65, 167
Alsace-Lorraine, 75
Armenia, 76
Angell, Sir Norman, 122
Anglophile, 46
Anglo-Russian Pact, (1907) 161
Arabia, 159
Archidamus, 10
Aristides, 6
Aristotle, 10, 118, 133
Arnold, Matthew, 129-130
Ashanti, 48
Asia, 43-44, 50, 64-65, 93
Athens, 1, 6ff., 132
Asquith, Lord, 29-30, 54, 56, 65, 68, 76, 101, 103, 105
Austria, 55, 73-74, 88, 95-99, 108
Austro-Hungarian Empire, 95-96, 101

Bagdad, 159
Bahrein, 171
Balfour, Lord, 68-71, 101, 150
Balkans, The, 76
Bandung Conference (1955), 100
Beaverbrook, Lord, 60
Belgium, 48, 57

Belgrade, 96
Benes, Dr, 99-100, 102
Ben Gurion, David, 162
Berlin, 94-95, 105
Bertie, Sir Francis; (Ambassador in Paris), 104
Bismark, 93, 129
Birkenhead, Lord, 146
Boer War, 25, 29
Bonar Law, Andrew, 65, 71, 141, 146
Bosanquet, Bernard, 1, 2, 5, 23, 30, 117, 120, 127, 135-136, 140, 155
Bosphorus, The, 91
Bosnia-Herzegovina, 142
British Empire; Population Figures, 27, 29
British Evacuation of India: (1947), 43
Budapest, 104
Buddha, 127
Bulganin, Marshal, 156
Burma, 45, 122
Butterfield, Prof Herbert; (Cambridge Professor of Modern History), 52, 56, 61, 77, 101

Caird, Edward (Master of Balliol), 119, 136-138, 155
Cambon, Paul, 65, 151
Campbell-Bannerman, Sir Henry, 51, 56, 150
Carson, Sir Edward, 146
Carthaginian Peace (1919), 101
Casualties of World War II, 106
Caucassus, 76
Ceylon, 45
Cicero, 116
Cimon, 7, 9, 12
China, 42, 48, 76, 93-94, 124-125
Church Assembly of 1940, 35
Church of England, 34-35
Church of Scotland, 34-35

Church of Scotland; General Assembly (May, 1756), 34

Church of Scotland; General Assembly (May, 1940), 35

Churchill, Sir Winston, 10, 41, 44-45, 51, 53, 59, 65, 92, 95-97, 101-102, 105, 107, 121-123, 127, 148, 150, 154-156, 158, 171

Church Times; August, 1908, 38

Christian Socialists, 38-39

Clare Luce, 90

Clemenceau, President, 84

Cleon, 18, 132

Cobden, John, 58

Cold war age, 40

Communism, 109, 170-171

Conant, Dr, American High Commissioner for Germany, 89-90

Confederacy of Delos, 7, 10, 14

Constantinople, 53, 73, 93, 142, 151

Corinth, 6

Cox, Sir Percy, 159

Crowe, Sir Eyre, 51

Cyprus, 167-168

Daily Mail, 171

Daily News, 57

Daily Telegraph, 171

Death duties, 58

Delos, Confederacy of, 7, 10, 14

Demos, 14

Dorian States, 11

Eden, Sir Anthony, 59, 96-97, 101-102, 162, 169

Egypt, 44-45, 91, 94, 151, 157, 162-166, 169-170

Eisenhower, President, 158, 160, 170

Elihu Root, 69

Emerson, Thomas, 1

Enosis, 167

Entente Cordiale: 46, 65, 67, 75-76, 79, 101, 141, 150

Esher, Lord, Member of Committee for Imperial Defence, 68

Fascism, 100

Fay, Sidney Bradshaw of Harvard, 61, 87, 89-90

Fisher, Sir John, 66-72, 135, 155

Food Famine attributed to World War II, 106

France, 48, 55, 60, 62, 65-67, 72, 74, 76, 93, 102, 107

France, Anatole, 148-150

Francis Joseph, Emperor, 96-97, 104

Franco-Russian Alliance, 51

Free Churches, 39

Free Trade doctrines, 29

Gandhi, Mahatma, 37, 42, 126-127

Geneva, 109

German East Africa, 44

Germany, 48, 53, 55, 57, 59-61, 63, 65-72, 74, 79-94, 101, 107, 109, 146-147, 155

Gladstone, William Ewart, 58, 76

Gold Coast, 44

Gold of the Rand, 9

Gooch, Dr, G. P., 61, 63-64, 66, 71-75, 88-89, 140-143

Gore, Bishop, 38

Gorgias, 132-133

Greeks, Ionian, 7

Grey, Sir Edward, 29, 50-59, 61-78, 91, 96-97, 101, 103-104, 117, 132, 135, 136-141, 154, 161

Habsburg Empire, 96-98, 102, 104

Haldane, Lord, 54, 56, 65, 103, 117

Harcourt, Sir William, 54, 56, 58

Harding, Field Marshal, 167

Hellas, 3, 6

Hellenic Empire, 6

Herrenvolk thesis, 44

Hitler, Adolph, 91-92, 95, 109

Hitler Crisis (March 1938), 86

Hitler-Molotov Meeting; (November, 1940), 91

Hiroshima, 34, 114, 121

Hobson, J. A., 28, 21-32, 44

Homer, 13

Hong Kong, 31, 94, 123-125

Horace, 107

Hungary, 170

Ionian Greeks, 7

Imperial Christianity, 32

Imperial Conference (1926), 24

India, 42-45, 93-94, 122-125, 151
India; British Evacuation (1947), 43
Inge, Dean, 133, 152-153
Ionian Greeks, 7
Ireland, 9
Irish Nationalists, 157
Italo-Austro-German Alliance, 51
Italy, 46, 56, 79, 93, 109, 165

Japan, 50, 109

Kaiser Wilhelm II, 67-71, 73-74, 78, 82, 89, 136, 140, 144
Kenya, 44
Keynes, Maynard, 107-110
Kilmour, Viscount, 167
Kimberley, Lord, 141
Kingsley, Charles, 121
Kipling, Rudyard, 21, 25-26, 31, 42, 63, 121
Kitchener, Lord, 42, 105
Koh-i-nor, 31
Krishnamurti; Hindu Philosopher, 127, 129
Krushchev, 156

Lacedaemonians, 6, 16
Lansdowne, Lord, 51, 54, 75-76, 137-141
Lang, Archbishop, 32
League of Nations, 109
Lenin, 100
Leonidas (at Thermopylae), 15
Lettow-Vorbeck, General Von, 112
Lippmann, Walter, 50
Lloyd George, David, 65, 68-69, 86-87, 99, 101, 130, 140
Lobengula, 137
Lin-Yutang: (Chinese Philosopher), 42, 94, 122-126
Lobengula, 137
Lothian, Lord, 86-87
Lutz, Herman, 143-145, 148, 152
Luxemburg, 55

Macdonald, Ramsay, 104
McKenna, Hon Stephen, 65
Mahan, 21
Mahatma Gandhi, 37, 42, 126
Malan, Dr, 112
Manchester Guardian, 55-58, 60, 66, 75, 94, 101
Marathon, 6, 9, 15

Masaryk, Jan, 98-102
Masaryk, Thomas, 98
Maynard Keynes (at Versailles), 48
Megarian aggression, 8, 10, 15
Megarian decree, 6
Mesopotamia, 26, 91
Militades, 6
Militarism of Sparta, 10
Miksche, Col F. O., 97-99, 100-102
Milner, Lord, 29
Molotov, 91, 93, 101
Molotov-Hitler Meeting (November, 1940), 91
Mond, Sir Alfred, 64, 102
Morel, E. D., 101, 104, 134, 141
Morocco, 44, 165
Mosul, 158
Mussolini, 109
Mustapha Kemal, 163

Napoleon III, 162
Napoleon Bonaparte, 95-96, 100, 104
Naval expenditure (1900—1913), 66-67
Navalism; Athenian, 10, 19
Nazism, 109
Nehru, Jawaharlal, 42-43, 126
Negro slavery, 44
Nicolas II of Russia, 72, 78, 91, 94, 96-97, 104, 136, 142
Nicolson, Sir Arthur, 52
Nigeria, 44
Noncomformist Churches, 34
Northcliffe, Lord, 53, 60, 71, 105
Northcliffe Press, 59, 69
Nuremberg, 114

Oman, 170-171

Palacky; Czech Historian, 96-97, 100
Palmerston, Lord, 10, 76
Pan-Anglican Conference (1908), 38-39
Panikkar, K. M. (Ambassador to China and Egypt), 42-43, 45
Parker Moon, Prof (of Columbia), 30, 41, 47
Pausanias (at Plataea), 15
Peace Treaty (1919), 102
Peloponnesian Confederacy, 10
Peloponnesians, 17

Pericles, 1, 3, 6-11, 13-22, 115
Persia, 7, 76, 91, 94, 145, 165-166
Phoros, The, 6
Plato, 1-5, 12-13, 16, 18, 55, 81, 115-118, 127, 129, 132-133, 138, 156
Pleonexia, 5
Poincaré, President, 72-73, 85-86, 136, 142, 161
Poland, 92
Polidaea, 8, 15
Population of British Empire, 27, 29
Polynesia, 93
Port Arthur, 73
Potidaea Aggression, 8
Prague, 99, 104
Prussians at Waterloo, 9

Quakers, 35, 37

Robeson, Mrs Paul, 44
Rhodes, Cecil, 20-21, 25-26, 28-29, 40-41, 44, 63, 118-120, 130-131, 135-139, 145, 155
Roosevelt, President Franklin, 41, 136, 141
Rosebery, Lord, 8, 23-33, 50, 54, 59, 63, 119, 141
Ruskin, John, 25-26, 28, 63
Russia, 52-53, 55-56, 60, 62, 65-67, 72, 74-76, 78, 91-96, 100, 102, 108-109, 124-125, 142, 159, 161
Russia—Tsarist, 50, 76, 93-94, 101
Russian Revolution (October, 1917), 98

Salamis, 6, 9, 15
Salisbury, Lord, 76, 149
Sarajevo, 94, 96, 106
Seneca, 114, 116-117, 120
Serbia, 73, 78
Shakespeare, William, 148
Shaw, George Bernard, 106
Sims, Admiral, 42
Singapore, 122
Slave holding, 10
Smuts, Jan, 111
Soudan, 44
South African War, 52, 145
Spain, 93
Sparta, 6, 10, 14, 16, 47
Socrates, 2, 4, 11, 22, 133
Spartan Confederacy, 6

Stalin, Josef, 41, 45, 53, 93, 95, 100, 109, 141, 156, 159
Stamboul, 76, 142
Stettinius, U.S. Secretary of State, 41
Stimson, U.S. Secretary, 105
Subhas Chandra Bose, 45
Suez, 91, 159, 161-163, 169-171
Sun-yat-sen. 42

Tacitus, 169
Tagore, Rabindranath, 42
Talleyrand, 95-98, 100-101
Tanganyika, 112
Teheran, 156
Temperley, Prof Harold, 56-57, 72, 77, 88
Temple, Archbishop, 38, 109
Tennyson, Lord, 25
Themistocles, 6
Thermopylae, Leonidas at, 15
Thrasymachus, 3, 20, 22, 81, 132, 154
Thucydides, 3, 6-7, 11, 16-19, 115, 169
Tibet, 76
Tirpitz, Admiral Von, 67-68
Truman, President, 141
Tsarist Russia, 50, 76, 93-94, 101
Tshushima, 73
Tunis, 48, 53, 76, 142, 165
Tunisia, 44
Turkey, 158, 163-164
Tweedsmouth, Lord, 67

United States of America, 41-42, 46, 48, 50, 62, 89-90, 99, 108, 118, 124-125, 168-170

Vasco de Gama (1498), 43
Venezuela, 48
Versailles, 48, 51, 79, 87-89, 98, 103, 107-109, 111-112
Vienna, 95, 97-100, 104-105
Vienna Parliament; Composition of Parties, 98
Vietnam, 169
Vitteti, Leonardo; Councillor, Italian Embassy, 46

Waterloo, 129
Webster, Daniel, U.S. Senate, 41
Welfare State, 58
Wells, H. G., 117
West, Dr Raynard, 128

West Africa, 44

White, Ambassador, Emissary of Elihu Root (1907), 69

Wilson, President Woodrow, 49, 86, 90, 104, 136, 141

Wilson, Field Marshal Sir Henry, 141

World Markets, Priorities in, 9

World War—First, 10, 14, 16, 51, 81-83, 87-89, 97, 113, 161

World War—Second, 23, 30, 51, 55, 79-80, 89, 97, 106-108, 113, 128, 161

World War—Third (Cold), 51, 89, 97, 113, 161

Yalta, 156

49382

Central Lending Library
Brunswick Road
Tel. 20020, 20684

Hours of Opening.
  Adult 9—8.
  Wednesdays 9—1.
  Saturdays 9—5.
  Junior 9.30—7.
  Saturdays 9.30—5.

Closed on Sundays and public
holidays.

Copies of byelaws may be seen
at the Library.

This book may be renewed
(unless required by another
reader) by returning it for
reissue or (once only) by post
**or phone by quoting the
book and transaction card
numbers and date due back
before it becomes overdue.**